Advance praise for

Journeys of Social Justice

"Despite the many cracks in the glass ceiling of leadership in politics, culture, and higher education, the prevailing and stereotypical image of a leader is that of a white male. If someone were asked to pick a leader out of a lineup, a white male would likely be first chosen, with a woman of color likely chosen last. This is why this volume is so important. It dares discuss higher education leadership by weaving together the narratives of women who have led, and who have studied leadership. The volume addresses the ways that women of color leaders must both be present in their cultures and be fluid enough to use (and transcend) culture to strengthen their leadership. This book offers personal stories and policy prescriptives. And, most importantly, it inspires aspirational women of color, and those who must work with them, to transform the culture of higher education so that diverse leadership is far more enthusiastically welcomed."

—Julianne Malveaux, President Emerita, Bennett College for Women,
Greensboro, North Carolina

"Through personal example and the public platform provided by their office, college presidents can be powerful change agents on their campuses as well as in their local communities and the society at large. In particular, women college presidents of color have a unique opportunity to use their positions to advance the causes of gender equity, educational access, and social justice. Through the clear, resonate voices of six outstanding women presidents and related reflections, Menah Pratt-Clarke and Johanna B. Maes provide a scholarly and compelling perspective on how women of color can lead their campuses forward while effecting change on campus and throughout our society."

—Elsa M. Núñez, President, Eastern Connecticut State University

"*Journeys of Social Justice* is a highly commendable contribution to scholarship that examines role of leadership in the academy. The authors present invaluable lessons of struggle, persistence, and success when navigating academic terrains that are not always hospitable. The editors, Menah Pratt-Clarke and Johanna B. Maes, masterfully weave the narratives from women of color presidents, supported with empirical scholarship to uncover complex intersections of gender, race, class, leadership, and cultures(s) within the academy. This book is especially timely at this poignant juncture when higher education landscape is experiencing significant changes."

—Reitumetse Obakeng Mabokela, Vice-Provost for International Affairs
and Global Strategies & Professor of Higher Education,
University of Illinois at Urbana-Champaign

Journeys of Social Justice

BLACK STUDIES
& critical thinking

Rochelle Brock and Cynthia Dillard
Executive Editors

Vol. 88

The Black Studies and Critical Thinking series
is part of the Peter Lang Education list.
Every volume is peer reviewed and meets
the highest quality standards for content and production.

PETER LANG
New York • Bern • Frankfurt • Berlin
Brussels • Vienna • Oxford • Warsaw

Journeys of Social Justice

Women of Color Presidents in the Academy

Edited by Menah Pratt-Clarke and Johanna B. Maes

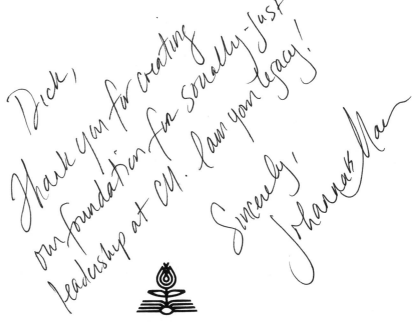

Dick,
Thank you for creating
our foundation for socially-just
leadership at CU. I am your legacy!
Sincerely,
Johanna Maes

PETER LANG
New York • Bern • Frankfurt • Berlin
Brussels • Vienna • Oxford • Warsaw

Library of Congress Cataloging-in-Publication Data

Names: Pratt-Clarke, Menah A. E., editor. | Maes, Johanna B., editor.
Title: Journeys of social justice: women of color presidents in the academy /
edited by Menah Pratt-Clarke, Johanna B. Maes.
Description: New York: Peter Lang, 2017.
Series: Black studies and critical thinking; vol. 88 | ISSN 1947-5985
Includes bibliographical references.
Identifiers: LCCN 2016034693 | ISBN 978-1-4331-3183-7 (hardcover: alk. paper)
ISBN 978-1-4331-3182-0 (paperback: alk. paper) | ISBN 978-1-4331-4072-3 (ebook pdf)
ISBN 978-1-4331-3737-2 (epub) | ISBN 978-1-4331-3738-9 (mobi)
Subjects: LCSH: Minority women college administrators—United States.
Educational leadership—Social aspects—United States.
Classification: LCC LB2341 .J595 2017 | DDC 378.1/11—dc23
LC record available at https://lccn.loc.gov/2016034693
DOI 10.3726/b10802

Bibliographic information published by **Die Deutsche Nationalbibliothek**.
Die Deutsche Nationalbibliothek lists this publication in the "Deutsche
Nationalbibliografie"; detailed bibliographic data are available
on the Internet at http://dnb.d-nb.de/.

The paper in this book meets the guidelines for permanence and durability
of the Committee on Production Guidelines for Book Longevity
of the Council of Library Resources.

For women of color in the academy and those
who support their advancement

Contents

Foreword

JULIANNE MALVEAUX

What does a college president look like? For many the answer is White, male, over 55, and perhaps bespectacled. His hair, in the image, might be graying, or it might be a hearty headful of bouncing brown hair. But he'd be White. He'd be male. He'd never have anyone say to him, "You don't look like a college President." Unfortunately, despite the many cracks in the glass ceiling of leadership in politics, culture, and higher education, the prevailing and stereotypical image of a leader remains that of a White male. If someone were asked to pick a leader out of a lineup, a White male would likely be first chosen, with a woman of color likely chosen last.

That reality hit me upside the head on the day I once sat outside a meeting room, appropriately adorned in designer knit, and a colorful kente scarf. I was on my phone, tapping away, when from nowhere a black coat was plopped on a table and I was asked for a coat check tab. I looked up to find a White woman, clad in an almost identical designer knit, glowering down at me, when I realized that I actually was sitting near the unattended coat check area. I was silent for a few seconds, counting long enough to swallow the caustic comment on the tip of my tongue. Saved by a colleague! Another woman, African American, walked up with a big smile, greeted me by my first name, and turned to the coat-toting woman and said, "I guess you haven't met Dr. Malveaux." She went on to say that the meeting was on the first floor, not the lobby, of the hotel and there was a mistake with an earlier communication. The coat-toter did manage to put her hand out as we greeted each other, but she didn't refer to her faux pas, and neither did I. You don't look like a college president.

Stereotypes allow some to define what a college president looks like, what a leader looks like, and what a change agent looks like. Stereotypes need to be shattered, but also examined. What does it cost for a woman to live inside somebody else's stereotype? This important volume, *Journeys of Social Justice:*

Women of Color Presidents in the Academy examines these myriad of questions. It dares discuss higher education leadership by weaving together the narratives of women who have led, and who have studied leadership. The volume addresses the ways that women of color leaders must both be present in their cultures and be fluid enough to use (and transcend) culture to strengthen their leadership. This book offers personal stories and policy prescriptives. And, most importantly, it inspires aspirational women of color, and those who must work with them, to transform the culture of higher education so that diverse leadership is far more enthusiastically welcomed.

For me, reading this was like listening to Roberta Flack's "Killing Me Softly," listening to sisters "strumming my pain with (their) fingers, singing my life with (their) words." These essays, reflective, bounce off each other, and bounce off the experiences that I, and so many women of color in higher education leadership, have had in the academy. An excerpt from Paula Allen Meares in chapter five reveals this reality:

> During my chancellorship, some were surprised when they met me. Some thought I would be taller. Others were surprised that *I* was the chancellor: I just didn't look like what they had envisioned. Once, someone asked if I were the secretary, and another asked, "Where is the Chancellor?" The so-called typical profile of a chancellor/president/vice president is still majority male, at least six feet tall, and graying or balding. The typical chancellor possesses a disciplinary background—medicine, bench science, business, law, or engineering.

In chapter four, Irma McLaurin writes of the "constant scrutiny" that women of color president's experience. Those who scrutinize really ought to be singing praises of awe. Every President has to do her job well, and that alone requires juggling. There is pressure to raise money, and a multitude of constituencies—board, faculty, staff, community, alumni, and others—to satisfy. Women of color have to juggle more than demanding constituencies. We must also juggle our intersectional identities and community responsibilities that others may not have. We have all been taught, "those to whom much is given much is required" (Luke 12:48). On one hand, we embrace some stereotypes, and on another hand we are required to transcend them. We are leaders on our campuses and in our communities, role models to our students, but also to others. We walk on a tightrope of expectations and scrutiny understanding that a false step, a stumble, can be fatal to our careers and to our communities. We, in the words of Paul Lawrence Dunbar, "wear the mask" that disguises our vulnerability and our humanity.

The women who have contributed to this volume are women of courage. They have transcended the racist, classist, hierarchical demands that they both assimilate and acculturate, at least as they share in these pages. They have dropped their Dunbar mask and embraced their vulnerability to serve those who will follow them. They have shared their triumphs, and also their frustrations. They have stepped out of the shadows of invisibility, broken the silence that surrounds being "other," and challenged their colleagues to remove the blinders that may have shaped their perceptions and behaviors, however subtle. As I read these essays, I found myself nodding, hollering, and occasionally laughing. They hit home. They are singing the lives that are not always sung, writing lives that are too rarely written, from, as Menah Pratt-Clarke in chapter two writes "beneath the adobe ceilings, the bamboo ceilings, and the plantation roofs."

While these accomplished high achievers have made history, shattered ceilings, and been stellar role models, they have paid a price for their success. In elbowing their way into a space that was less than welcoming, they have experienced loneliness, isolation, burnout, and marginalization. These are fierce and feisty women, reflective and resistant, who have chosen to walk down a road that Gabriella Gutiérrez y Muys describes as "a yellow brick road," and as "treacherous." How can a career path be both the source of the optimism associated with an Oz-ian yellow brick road, and the danger and pessimism associated with treachery? These women's stories explain the duality, the mask wearing, and the double-consciousness WEB DuBois refers to in *The Souls of Black Folks.* On one hand, there is the absolute joy of making a difference, especially when it is a difference in the lives of our students. On the other hand, there is the frustration of feeling as if one is banging her head against the brick wall of resistance.

I recall many joyful days as President of Bennett College, but I also remember extremely frustrating ones. I often despaired, wondering if I really made enough of a difference, and why I had to fight so hard, sometimes to do so. On a particularly despondent evening, having come home alone and a bit unaffirmed after three events, a colleague happened to drop by just in time to put a halt to my pity party. She walked me outside my home and pointed to one of the new well-lit buildings that was constructed during my leadership (exceeding all expectations). "This is what you did," she said. "Don't ever doubt that you made a difference." Of course it is not all about the bricks and mortar. It's about the students who traveled internationally with me, the students who had access to new entrepreneurial studies programs, and the grateful notes I still get from students and parents who remind me that I made a difference in their lives. Still the question remains—why do we have to fight to make a difference?

In chapter six, Menah Pratt-Clarke and Jasmine Parker share this insight from Lee and McKerrow (2005, pp. 1–2):

Social justice leaders strive for critique rather than conformity, compassion rather than competition, democracy rather than bureaucracy, polyphony rather than silencing, inclusion rather than exclusion, liberation rather than domination, action for change rather than inaction that preserves inequity.

The women who have contributed to this volume, social justice leaders all, have provided us with an opportunity to think about the real meaning of the term "diversity and inclusion," to think about the meaning of leadership, and to augment leadership stories with leadership lessons from those who are "other." Menah Pratt-Clarke's vision in producing this volume is to be commended. She has engaged in revolutionary scholarship, and we are all in her debt.

Reference

Lee, S. S., & McKerrow, K. (2005, Fall). Advancing social justice: Women's work. *Advancing Women in Leadership Online Journal, 19*, 1–2. Retrieved from http://www.advancingwomen.com/awl/

Acknowledgments

Menah Pratt-Clarke

I want to first thank the series editor, Rochelle Brock, for her commitment to this book. I am grateful for the Black Studies and Critical Thinking series and for the vision and commitment of scholars who have created places for work on race and gender in the academy. I am also grateful for the women of color in the academy who continue to inspire me daily by their deep passion, commitment, and desire to transform spaces that were not meant for them. Women of color scholars who are writing about leadership, higher education, and women are so critical for documenting the journeys of women of color leaders that are often absence from books about higher education leadership. Their work was a very important contribution to this book.

This book would not have been possible if the women who ascended to the top—Paula Allen Meares, Phyllis Wise, Rusty Barceló, Cassandra Manuelito-Kerkvliet, and Waded Cruzado—were not willing to take time to share their journeys. My co-editor, Johanna B. Maes, has been a wonderful partner. I am grateful for her willingness to take a chance to work together to move these stories from silence to the pages of this book. I want to also thank Julianne Malveaux, who wrote the foreword, for her willingness to support this project. This project could not have happened without the other contributors, Jasmine Parker, Melissa Leal, Tanaya Winder, Irma McClaurin, Valerie Lee, Gabriella Gutiérrez y Muhs, and Victoria Chou. Thank you.

I want to thank my parents, Dr. Mildred Pratt and Dr. Theodore Pratt, who instilled in me a deep passion for learning and who despite the racism and discrimination they endured as Black scholars, demonstrated to me the capacity of using education for transformation of lives. My children, Emmanuel and Raebekkah, and my husband, Obadiah, have always been my source of strength and support. My brother, Awadagin, remains a constant inspiration to me.

My friends, Mercedes, Alfreda, Watechia, Kevin, Marc, Darlene, Patsy, and Gellert, and many others, give me such joy and laughter—laughter that sustains me and provides an incredible source of motivation. Finally, I want to acknowledge my ancestors, those who were enslaved from Africa in America in Texas and Alabama, and those who returned to Africa, to Freetown, Sierra Leone. You are a constant reminder of the power of the human spirit to overcome, to survive, and to thrive. Thank you.

Johanna B. Maes

My sincere thanks and blessings to Dr. Menah Pratt-Clarke for finding me in this world of higher education, valuing my research, and then inviting me to be a part of this important project. Your grace and patience as a friend and colleague is forever priceless.

I'd like to acknowledge those woman warriors who have played a significant role in my personal and professional life. To my late grandmother Dora Pino Baca, who only had an elementary school education and spent her life working hard, manual labor so that I could have power and knowledge as a woman and as an educator. To my best friend and writing partner Dr. Elena Sandoval-Lucero for being my confidant and supporter in all things Chicana and academic. To my coast-to-coast Hermanas from the National Hispana Leadership Institute, and particularly to the Class of 2004, who first embarked on this leadership journey with me as we together created a foundation of Latina Leadership that will last throughout our lifetimes and beyond. To my biological sisters Theresa, Linda, and Paula, and my sisters in spirit—Annette, Celina, Esther, Elizabeth, Helen, Elvira, Laura, Tracey, Sue, Ruby, Christina, Steph, Carol, Elena TF, and Amy—thank you for cheering me on every day and always.

Thank you to Drs. Waded Cruzado, Rusty Barceló and Elsa Nuñez for blessing me with your powerful narratives and trusting that I can effectively share them with the Academy, first in my dissertation research and now within the pages of this book. I continue to learn from your leadership and strength and will model it always.

An extra thanks to the brilliant social justice warrior faculty and staff at University of Colorado Boulder's Leadership Residential Academic Program/Ethnic Living and Living Community and to my extraordinary friends and colleagues at CU, past and present, for your constant encouragement while I taught, advised and counseled students, and juggled consulting projects in addition to completing this book. Thank you for promoting me and recognizing my value as a Chicana in higher education.

To my husband Anthony Gettler who holds my hand and heart through the waves of life while together we tackle the many injustices in our world. Thank you for letting me lean on you not only during this project but every day. I love you.

To my late father, Gilbert L. Maes, who continues to guide me with his spirit and love. I am because of you, Dad.

Finally, to the first generation college scholars that I have the privilege to educate at the University of Colorado Boulder—thank you for allowing me to highlight and honor your brilliance as you at times sit silently as "The Only Ones" within the walls of our emotionally challenging university. I hope you see the possibilities that can happen with your own lives through the beautiful voices in this book. You are my legacy.

Part I

Setting the Stage

1. Introduction to Journeys of Social Justice: Women of Color Presidents in the Academy

MENAH PRATT-CLARKE AND JOHANNA B. MAES

Opening Reflections from Menah Pratt-Clarke

This book represents an act of social justice. It is about creating the space for the voices of women of color leaders in the academy. The inspiration for this book arose from the Faculty Women of Color in the Academy (FWCA) National Conference. The conference was the result of conversations among colleagues at the University of Illinois at Urbana-Champaign (the initial host institution) about how to support faculty women of color in the academy. As we thought about the struggles and challenges, we wanted to create a sacred, comfortable, and safe space for conversation and dialogue. We wanted faculty women of color to have an opportunity to come together to talk, to be empowered, to support each other, and to network. We wanted to create a place in which wisdom could be shared, connections could be made, and role models could be celebrated.

Over the past four years, the Faculty Women of Color in the Academy conference has been this space. FWCA attendees have had the opportunity of listening to and engaging with women of color university presidents, chancellors, and other high-level administrators through keynote addresses and panel sessions. This book embodies the voices of those senior women—rarely heard and little researched. The women's voices contribute to the very small body of research on women of color presidents in higher education (Chen & Hune, 2011; Maes, 2012; Moore, 1982; Turner, 2007; Valverde, 2003). As the vision for this project began to unfold, I realized that there was a talented pool of women of color scholars who had done dissertation work on women of color presidents. I reached out to one of those scholars, Dr. Johanna B. Maes, and asked her if she would be willing to co-edit this volume with me. I was delighted when she agreed.

The significance of this work lies in the reality that women of color remain significantly underrepresented in senior administrative positions within higher education institutions. While women represent 26% of college presidents, only 4% of college presidents are women of color (Reid, 2012). Even then, women presidents (including women of color) are more likely to head community colleges than four-year institutions. In addition, women are least likely to be presidents of prestigious institutions that are doctorate-awarding universities (Lloyd-Jones, 2011; Waring, 2004).

The unique contribution of this book is that it highlights women presidents and chancellors who are or were at four-year institutions, including doctoral-granting institutions. The women represent Asian-Americans, African-Americans, Latinas/Chicanas, and Native Americans. The book is organized into two sections. The first section, "Setting the Stage" provides the context and background for the second section, "On the Stage." "On the Stage" includes the voices of five women of color presidents, as well as scholarly reflections about the leadership experiences of women of color in the academy.

The second chapter in "Setting the Stage" is entitled "Reflections from Below the Plantation Roof." This section includes my reflections as a Black woman scholar and administrator. The plantation roof is analogous to the "glass ceiling" referred to by White women, the "adobe ceiling" for Latinas (Martinez, 2008, p. 31), and the "bamboo ceiling" for Asian-American women (Lloyd-Jones, 2011, p. 10). As an African-American woman, I have chosen to call it a "plantation roof." I jointly report to both the President and the Provost, but I am also a tenured full professor. I sit near the top—in the symbolic "big house" on the university "plantation," but also under the roof as a vice president and vice provost. I serve at the will and dispensation of the president and provost. At the same time, my tenure status as a full professor creates a small window for me to think about and write about issues of race, class, and gender in higher education administration. This chapter includes an overview of existing scholarship on women of color presidents and provides a social justice lens and model through which the experiences of women of color presidents can be analyzed.

Chapter 3 is entitled "The Adobe Ceiling over the Yellow Brick Road" by Dr. Gabriella Gutiérrez y Muhs. As the editor of *Presumed Incompetent: The Intersections of Race and Class for Women in Academia,* Dr. Gutiérrez y

Muhs (Gutiérrez y Muhs, Nieman, Gonzalez, & Harris, 2012) provided the opening keynote for the 2012 FWCA conference. Her chapter explores the complicated journey of women faculty to full professorship, which is often a necessary stepping stone in the journey to a presidency.

Chapter 4 is "The Labyrinth Path of Administration: From Full Professor to Senior Administrator." This chapter is a revised transcript of a panel session at the 2012 conference with three women of color administrators. The panel included Dr. Irma McClaurin, who held several senior administrative positions including President at Shaw University; Dr. Victoria Chou, currently interim dean for the School of Education at Dominican University and Dean Emerita for the College of Education at the University of Illinois at Chicago; and Dr. Valerie Lee, the retired Vice Provost for Diversity and Inclusion, Vice President for Outreach and Engagement, and Chief Diversity Officer at The Ohio State University. These senior scholars and administrators share their wisdom and insights from their journeys.

The second section, "On the Stage," focuses on the voices of five women of color presidents. Most of these chapters were informed by the keynote addresses at the Faculty Women of Color in the Academy Conference. Each presidents' chapter reflects their own story in their own voices. Each chapter is followed by a reflection and analysis of their journey and story in the context of existing scholarship about leadership and issues of race, class, and gender.

Chapter 5 is the voice of Dr. Paula Allen-Meares, former Chancellor of the University of Illinois at Chicago. Her chapter is entitled, "A View from the Helm: A Black Woman's Reflection on Her Chancellorship." Chapter 6, "Reflections about African American Female Leadership in the Academy," provides a reflection and analysis of her narrative, including contextualizing her experiences in light of existing scholarship on Black women in the academy. Chapter 7 profiles Dr. Phyllis Wise, an Asian American woman of Chinese descent. Dr. Wise is the former Chancellor for the University of Illinois at Urbana-Champaign. Her chapter is entitled, "Re-envisioning the Academy for Women of Color." Chapter 8, "Reflections about Asian-American Female Leadership in the Academy," contextualizes her experiences within scholarship about Asian-American women. It also includes my personal thoughts and reflections based on serving as a member of her leadership team.

President Emerita Cassandra Manuelito-Kerkvliet, a member of the Navajo (Diné) Tribe, is profiled in Chapter 9. Her chapter, "My Climb to the Highest Rung," represents her journey to presidencies at Dine College and Antioch University Seattle. The reflection, "Reflections about Native American Female Leadership in the Academy" in Chapter 10 examines the experiences of Native American women leaders. In Chapter 11, Dr. Rusty Barceló speaks about her experience rising into the presidency of Northern New Mexico University. As a Chicana, she shares her story through her chapter, "Journeys into Leadership: A View from the President's Chair." Chapter 12 is entitled "Thriving as Administrators at America's Land Grant Universities" by President Waded Cruzado. President Cruzado, a Latina from Puerto Rico, is currently president of Montana State University. Chapter 13, "Reflections about Latina/Chicana Leadership in the Academy," provides an analysis of the experiences of Drs. Barceló and Cruzado as Latina leaders. The work ends with "Closing Reflections" and final thoughts in Chapter 14.

Through these book chapters, a rich landscape is painted of the experiences of women of color in ascending to and leading higher education institutions. These women have varied academic backgrounds, cultural perspectives, and life experiences. Yet, their narratives have some common themes. The stories reflect (1) the importance of their cultural heritage; (2) the role of family values; (3) the necessity of professional mentorship and support; (4) the presence of personal resiliency; and (5) the need to lift others while climbing and thriving.

This work, then, as inspired by the Faculty Women of Color in the Academy conference, recognizes and affirms that the academy cannot survive and thrive without women of color in the academy—without their scholarship, without their voices, their perspectives, their viewpoints, and their leadership. This book affirms the importance of our place in the academy. Through this scholarship, we clearly see that women of color can climb to the highest rung; can penetrate the abode ceiling, the bamboo ceiling, and the plantation roofs; can sit in the president's chair; and can thrive as leaders in the academy.

Opening Reflections from Johanna B. Maes

This book is about power and resilience and spirit.

I had the fortune of being on Menah Pratt-Clarke's radar soon after I published my doctoral dissertation, *The Socio-cultural and Leadership Experiences of Latina Four-Year College and University Presidents: A Través de sus Voces (Through their Voices), (2012)*, which is still one of very few pieces of academic research that focuses on the personal, professional and leadership experiences of Latinas presidents of four-year institutions. Menah and I toyed with a number of ways in which we could combine our research interests and finally we decided that we should provide a platform for the narratives, the *testimonios* of these women *through their voices* in a comprehensive book. These voices speak of women who are trailblazers and powerhouses within their institutions. Yet many members of the larger Academy have not been afforded the opportunity to learn of their accomplishments, their struggles, and their unique and transformational visions for themselves, their respective colleges and universities. Even the women who come after them, who are indeed their legacy, are not aware of their accomplishments in higher education.

I am one of the women who is a part of the legacy of the amazing women featured in this book. As a faculty member who teaches multicultural leadership at the University of Colorado Boulder, a tier one research institution, ironically I have experienced many of the personal, academic, and emotional mishaps that many of our women presidents have faced. Together we have battled racial microaggressions in the academy (Perez & Cuerva, 2012), whether they appeared as biases because of our race, class, gender, or sexual orientation. We have been considered "invisible labor" or "cultural taxation" (Williams June, 2015) where we as faculty of color or administrators act as a "one-person minority affairs office" who are called upon to mentor, parent, and advise the students of color at our respective institutions while we receive little to no additional compensation or recognition. It can be a miraculous feat that a woman of color in higher education travels from student affairs to professor to dean to provost to the presidency while experiencing the extraordinary personal and professional situations that few White men in higher education face. The women featured in this book are indeed a phenomenon in the Academy and sharing their stories in this format is long overdue.

Finally, as it rings true for many women of color in the Academy, many of us create our own *counterspaces* (Williams June, 2015) which sometimes are our classrooms, informal groups and organizations or literal corners of our world. These are spaces where we can retreat, develop strategies to battle the various microaggressions and misfortunes we experience on a day-to-day basis on our campuses, and also where we can sit and heal so we can further our mission as "The Only One" at our institutions. The Faculty Women of Color in the Academy conference and other shared spaces are counterspaces to laugh and cry with one another while also building collective power to change the fabric of higher education—one woman of color at a time. This book is a counternarrative and a counterspace for women of color and others who support their journeys. It is our hope that others in the Academy can reflect on the wisdom, experiences, and knowledge in these chapters and use them to expand the trajectory of all women of color who teach and lead in our nation's colleges and universities.

Editors' Note:

Dr. Menah Pratt-Clarke has more than 20 years of administrative, academic, and legal experience in higher education, with a focus on large-scale institutional transformation. She is the Vice President for Strategic Affairs and Vice Provost for Inclusion and Diversity at Virginia Polytechnic Institute and State University (Virginia Tech). She is also Professor of Education in the School of Education in the College of Liberal Arts and Human Sciences.

She has a bachelor's degree from the University of Iowa with a major in English and minors in Philosophy and African-American Studies. She received her master's degree in Literary Studies from the University of Iowa and a master's degree in Sociology from Vanderbilt University. In addition, she earned her PhD and JD from Vanderbilt University. She is licensed to practice law in Illinois and Tennessee.

Her research interests include critical race studies, Black feminism, and critical race feminism, with a particular focus on issues of transdisciplinary analysis of diversity issues in higher education. In addition to publishing several articles and book chapters, *Critical Race, Feminism, and Education: A Social Justice Model*, was published in 2010 (Palgrave Macmillan). Forthcoming projects include a book on the journey of Black women from sharecropping to the academy and reflections of chief diversity officers on race, class, and gender issues in Cuba.

Dr. Johanna B. Maes has nearly twenty-five years of experience in K–12, higher education and in the nonprofit sector. She has developed, implemented, and evaluated innovative curricula, experiential educational initiatives and trainings that focus on multiculturalism, inclusivity, gender bias, and culturally competent teaching methods for audiences ranging from K–12 and university students, to nonprofit and business executives, to school administrators.

She is a graduate of two of the nation's leading leadership development/management institutes- Harvard University's Kennedy School of Government Executive Leadership Program and the Center for Creative Leadership Executive Leadership Program. Both institutes focus on leadership development, conflict resolution, interpersonal communication, strategic planning and the importance of collaborative decision-making processes.

In addition to being an Independent Education Consultant, Dr. Maes is also a faculty member at the University of Colorado Boulder's Leadership Residential Academic Program/Ethnic Living and Learning Community. She has developed and implemented curricula on topics including multicultural education, race/ethnicity/privilege, cultural competency, Ethnic Studies, multicultural leadership development, service learning, and social justice.

Dr. Maes has co-authored a number of academic articles relating to issues of education inclusivity, transformational leadership, women in leadership, action research methods, and Latina academic achievement. As a formally trained journalist, who received her Bachelor of Science degree through the University of Colorado School of Journalism and Mass Communication, Dr. Maes has been a guest columnist/journalist for *The Denver Post*, *La Voz*, and *El Semanario* newspapers, respectively. Dr. Maes received her Master's degree in Multicultural Education from Regis University and her Ph.D. in Education Leadership and Human Resource Studies from Colorado State University.

References

Chen, E. & Hune, S. (2011). Asian American Pacific Islander women from Ph.D. to campus president: Gains and leaks in the pipeline. In G. Jean-Marie & B. Lloyd-Jones (Eds.), *Women of color in higher education: Changing directions and new perspective* (Diversity in Higher Education, Vol. 10, pp. 163–190). Bingley: Emerald Group Publishing Limited.

Gutiérrez y Muhs, G., Nieman, Y. F., Gonzalez, C. G., & Harris, A. P. (2012). *Presumed incompetent: The intersections of race and class for women in academia.* Boulder, CO: University of Colorado Press.

Lloyd-Jones, B. (2011). Diversification in higher education administration: Leadership paradigms reconsidered. In G. Jean-Marie & B. Lloyd-Jones (Eds.), *Women of color in higher education: Changing directions and new perspective* (Diversity in Higher Education, Vol. 10, pp. 3–18). Bingley: Emerald Group Publishing Limited.

Maes, J. (2012). *The socio-cultural and leadership experiences of Latina four-year college and university presidents: A través de sus voces (through their voices)* (Doctoral dissertation). Retrieved from Proquest Dissertations and Theses database (UMI No. 3509591).

Martinez, S. R. (2008). *Latina presidents of four-year institutions, penetrating the adobe ceiling: A critical view* (Doctoral Dissertation). Retrieved from Proquest Dissertations and Theses database (UMI No. 3341931).

Moore, K. (1982). *Women and minorities. Leaders in transition: A national study of higher education administrators.* Washington, DC: American Council on Education.

Perez, H., & Cueva, B., (2012). Chicana/Latina testimonios on effects and responses to microaggressions. *Equity and Excellence in Education, 45*(3), 392–410.

Reid, P. T. (2012). Black and female in academia. *Back to the presidency spring supplement 2012, Diversity in leadership.* Retrieved from http://www.acenet.edu/the-presidency/columns-and-features/Pages/Black-and-Female-in-Academia.aspx

Turner, C. (2007). Pathways to the presidency: Biographical sketches of women of color firsts. *Harvard Educational Review, 77*(1), 1–38.

Valverde, L. (2003). *Leaders of color in higher education: Unrecognized triumphs in harsh institutions.* Walnut Creek, CA: Altamira Press.

Waring, A. (2004). Road to the presidency: Women of color assuming leadership roles in the academy. In C. Battle & C. Doswell (Eds.), *Building bridges for women of color in higher education* (pp. 4–17). Lanham, MD: University Press of America.

Williams June, A. (2015). *The invisible labor of minority professors.* Retrieved from http://http://chronicle.com/article/The-Invisible-Labor-of/234098

2. *Reflections from Below the Plantation Roof*

Menah Pratt-Clarke

Introduction

In my role at Virginia Polytechnic Institute and State University, I serve as the Vice President for Strategic Affairs, the Vice Provost for Inclusion and Diversity, and Professor of Education. I have appointments in the School of Education, the Department of Sociology, the Africana Studies Program, and Women's and Gender Studies Program. Prior to coming to Virginia Tech, I was the Associate Chancellor for Strategic Affairs, Associate Provost for Diversity, Title IX Officer, and Associate Professor at the University of Illinois at Urbana-Champaign. I had appointments in the School of Education, the College of Law, the Department of Sociology, Gender and Women Studies, African American Studies, and the Institute for Government and Public Policy. Before joining Illinois, I served as the University Compliance Officer, Assistant Secretary of the University, and University Counsel at Vanderbilt University. While at Vanderbilt, I taught African-American Studies and English at Fisk University, and taught English and Public Speaking through American Baptist College's program in the men's and women's maximum and minimum security prisons. My positionality in higher education is a reflection of my desire to combine administrative and academic work to engage in transformational work around diversity, involving traditionally underrepresented and marginalized groups based on their intersecting identities that have been disempowered by society. For me, it is about being a Black feminist scholar-activist in the academy and challenging borders, boundaries, and barriers.

My journey in higher education has been to validate, legitimize, and empower myself in order to validate, legitimate, and empower others. I have intentionally pursued the study of seven different disciplines and areas of study through five degrees: a bachelor's, two master's, a law degree, and a doctorate. My scholarship encompasses issues related to the law, race, sociology, gender, literature, history, and education. In the process of my journey, I stumbled across Black feminism, Black feminist thought, critical race theory, and critical race feminism. I read bell hooks and I heard her talk about the White supremacist capitalist patriarchy. I learned that there is a hegemonic power and force that creates and maintains oppression. My parents had taught me several key lessons: racism is real; sexism is undeniable; and that as a Black woman, I will need to work twice as hard, be twice as good, and even then, I may not get what I deserve. They told me that there was a "system" that I had to fight. I heard that word all my life ... "the system, the system, the system." It was not, however, until I began to experience the operation of this system in my life that I knew what they were talking about. It was the "no's," the closed doors, the salary disparities, the "you can't," and the "I won't let you." It was the stop signs and red lights. It was the microaggressions in meetings by White men and White women. It was emails of disrespect. It was the advancement of lesser qualified White men and women. It was the exclusion and lack of mentoring. It was my experience of "the ceiling."

As Vice President and Vice Provost, I sit below a "ceiling." It is a metaphor for the barriers that exist for women's professional advancement. The ceiling has often been called a "glass ceiling." For Asian American females, it has been referred to as a "bamboo ceiling" (Lloyd-Jones, 2011, p. 10). Latinas have referred to it as an "adobe ceiling" (Martinez, 2008, p. 31). I like the cultural connection associated with adobe and bamboo ceilings, compared to the glass ceiling which is often associated with White women. In fact, for women of color, it often appears that one cannot even see above or even fathom or imagine what really lies on the other side. Martinez (2008, p. 31) notes the difference between the adobe ceiling and the glass ceiling:

> for White women, the glass ceiling means that they can see what is available in top ranks, although the glass ceiling may preclude them from breaking through to the other side, to the top ranks. However, for Latinas the ceiling is adobe; they cannot see through it, to what is above this ceiling, and it is a thick barrier that does not shatter like glass. Metaphorically, it is much more difficult to break through an adobe ceiling than through a glass ceiling, and thus to make it through to the other side, to the top ranks of leadership.

I have decided to contextualize the "ceiling" from my experiences as an African American woman whose great grandmother was a slave. I have chosen to call the ceiling a "plantation roof."

This analogy squarely situates my experiences within the complex construct of enslavement, in which African American women were subject to experiences of oppression, denigration, dehumanization, marginalization, racism, and sexism from White men, White women, and even Black men. Many of my experiences as a Black woman in the academy involve a similar experience of oppression and marginalization. The academy, is, in many ways, a plantation (Fournillier, 2010, p. 56). Though a plantation can be inherently a place of disempowerment, it can also be a place of empowerment. As Fournillier (2010, p. 60) notes, her position on the academic plantation creates a special responsibility:

> I am an Afro Caribbean scholar, a Trinidadian woman, a researcher/writer and a labourer on the plantation. But I can transcend the isolation and use the networks available on the plantation as resources. I can find venues in which I can resist, write, speak about, and write back. I have a responsibility to share the experiences and to give voice to my deep fears of being punished by the owners of the plantation for daring to speak out and or back.

I, too, realize the power of my positionality, in spite of its inherent powerlessness.

I am sitting on a plantation in the academy, under the roof of the "big house" where I work as a senior administrator. I am also a tenured faculty member. These identities allow me to have a unique vantage point from which to study the experiences of those above me in the roles of presidents and provosts, just as house slaves had the unique opportunity to be present, yet invisible, in the lives of the White plantation owners. My tenure status allows me to continue to use my scholarship to shape my own thinking and engagement with issues of race, class, and gender in the academy. Yet, I too, must fight the fear of being punished for speaking out, writing about, sharing, and reflecting about experiences in a sacred and often hidden space. Very few women of color have occupied the sacred and hidden space of a college presidency. Writing about women of color presidents in the academy is a small act of rebellion. It is about fighting against invisibility. It is about moving women of color presidents from the margins of invisibility to the center and to visibility.

The Invisibility of Women of Color Presidents

Just as house slaves were often invisible in the sight of their masters, women of color presidents are often invisible in the fields of higher education. The press release from the American Council of Education report "The American College President 2012" (2012) reflects the peculiar position of women of color presidents. The press release states:

> The 2012 report provides a sobering look at the continuing challenge of diversifying the ranks of the college presidency. While women have increased their representation (26 percent in 2011, up from 23 percent in 2006), the proportion of presidents who are racial and ethnic minorities declined slightly, from 14 percent in 2006 to 13 percent in 2011. However, when minority-serving institutions are excluded, only 9 percent of presidents belong to racial/ethnic minority groups, unchanged from 2006.

While the press release specifically mentions the representation of women (26%) and presidents of color (13%), it does not mention the percent of representation of women of color. Although the Women in Higher Education's press release (Cook, 2012) on the report concludes that "women of color are sorely underrepresented in higher education top leadership," it also does not specifically mention the percentage of women of color. A careful review of the report itself reveals that there is no statistic about the representation of women of color presidents, except as either part of statistics on women or statistics on minorities.

In many ways, these women are invisible. Women of color, in fact, represent only 4% of university presidents (Reid, 2012). This invisibility is the result of the difficult and complicated history in the United States of people of color, including Asians, Latino, Native Americans, and African Americans. As Wilson (1989) noted,

> It is ironic that the two institutions most identified with preserving the nation's ethical mores and democratic philosophical values—the church and the university—are the two institutions most resistant to diversity and democracy in their practices and in their leadership. Thus it is apparent that the limited presence of women of color in higher education administration has its roots in the history of America and cannot be understood separately from that history. (p. 85)

Access to educational opportunities often occurred as the result of legal cases, legislation, executive orders, student activism, and community engagement.

Early educational efforts for African Americans included the establishment of Black public land grant colleges in 1890. Around that same time, Latinos were beginning to have opportunities at institutions in the southwest. Asians were pursuing education in California and the west (Wilson, 1989, p. 87) and the Haskell Institute was founded for Native Americans (American Indian Higher Education Consortium, 2015). The slow progress towards educational opportunity was accelerated in the 1960s and 1970s.

Executive orders about affirmative action in 1961 and 1967, as well as the Basic Educational Opportunity Grant legislation in 1972, which provided financial aid on the basis of need, helped advance larger groups of minorities (Wilson, 1989, p. 88). These race-based efforts, however, do not reflect the double burden of gender that women of color have faced and continue to face in higher education.

Although women first entered into higher education in 1830s (Nidiffer, 2001, p. 13), and small gains were made through the 1930s, significant growth in women's participation in higher education did not begin until the late 1970s (Nidiffer, 2001, p. 14). In their early experiences, women were often expected to be grateful for crumbs that fell from the boys' table (Nidiffer, 2001, p. 13). Affirmative action programs contributed significantly to the increase in White female participation in the academy (Jones & Komizes, 2001, p. 243). As challenging as the journey has been for White women, as reflected by terms such as the glass ceiling, glass cliff, and labyrinth (Sanchez-Hucles & Davis, 2010, p. 172), the challenges have been magnified and multiplied for women of color.

The journeys of women of color have been described with phrases such as "concrete wall" and "sticky floor" (Sanchez-Hucles & Davis, 2010, p. 172). The role of "old boy networks," combined with the "triple jeopardy" of multiple stereotypes associated with gender, race, and ethnicity, have contributed to the slow advancement of women of color into leadership (Sanchez-Hucles & Davis, pp. 173–174). Latina, African American, Asian American, and Native American women have had unique but related experiences in higher education, including hostile work environments, discrimination, prejudice, salary inequity, stereotyping, and tokenism (Huang, 2012, pp. 55–59; Machado-Casas, Ruiz, & Cantu, 2013). The reality for women of color is that they face multiple challenges, including balancing parenting and family obligations, racism, sexism, and microaggressions.

African American women administrators often experience loneliness, isolation, and burnout (Huang, 2012, pp. 60–62). Black women are often asked to assume greater roles related to service on committees, student support, and mentoring, while often being unsupported in their research, particularly on topics of race and gender. African American women experience the "double whammy" based on their race and gender intersectionality (Edwards-Wilson, 1998, p. 26). While the importance of mentoring is recognized as a strategy for advancement, it is challenging for Black women in the academy to receive the necessary mentoring within an organization. They often must rely on support from informal networks, including church and family (Huang, 2012, pp. 64–65).

For Latinas, potential barriers to advancement include the "triple oppression" of racism, sexism, and classism (Huang, 2012, p. 116). For some, the "fourth oppression" is accent discrimination (Huang, 2012, p. 105). Latinas often have to navigate stereotypes and cultural expectations related to gender roles (Huang, 2012, p. 100). Similar to African American females, they also face greater service obligations, including committee appointments and serving as liaison with external communities and organizations. In addition, their scholarship is also often devalued (Huang, 2012, pp. 104–105).

While there has been less research on Asian American/Pacific Islander female administrators (Chen & Hune, 2011; Lum, 2008), the existing work reflects that they, too, have experienced unique challenges in higher education. Those challenges include the existence of the model minority stereotype, navigating gender roles relating to caring for family and extended family, accent discrimination, experiencing sexualized harassment, and being in spaces that are gendered, sexualized, and racialized (Huang, 2012, pp. 79–83). They also face a lack of mentoring and professional development opportunities (Huang, 2012, p. 92). In addition, they experience isolation and marginalization; lack of support for their scholarship; and an overall "chilly" campus climate (Chen & Hune, 2011, p. 179).

Finally, the experiences of Native Americans in the United States are grounded in a history rooted in boarding schools, forcible removal, and assimilation (Huang, 2012, p. 52). Tribal Colleges and Universities play an important role in creating and sustaining access. As a result, tribal heritage, family, culture, and community play a significant role in leadership styles of American Indian women in higher education (Huang, 2012, p. 53; Manuelito-Kerkvliet, 2005; Turner, 2007).

Although almost 125 years have passed since these early efforts to address educational opportunities, time has not erased the historical legacy of race, gender, and class oppression in higher education, particularly for women of color. Overcoming these obstacles requires a variety of tools, including strong networking skills, access to mentoring, and professional development opportunities. Yet, women of color often have limited access to these resources as administrators because they tend to be in staff rather than line positions. As Reid (2012) noted, "in regularly reviewing announcements of minority administrators, one observes that minorities often receive positions without faculty-line control, such as diversity officer or associate dean. These rarely lead to higher positions." Many women of color are continuously tracked into lower-level administrative positions like serving as registrars, directors of financial aid, and directors of diversity and equity programs (Lloyd-Jones, 2011). As a result, they often do not have the type of experience necessary for career advancement (Sanchez-Hucles & Davis, 2010). These positions also limit their access and exposure to those with power and influence who are essential for career advancement and promotion. Thus, few rise and successfully garner a university president or chancellor position.

The invisibility of women of color is not limited to administration. It is also reflected in the limited amount of scholarship about women of color senior administrators and presidents. Scholarship about race, class, and gender in higher education has often been devalued: "The inability and unwillingness of White committee members to value and understand a different epistemology approach other than dominant Eurocentric epistemology results in the systemic devaluation of important work and contributions of a scholar of color" (Sanchez-Hucles & Davis, 2010, pp. 176–177). Even though the research is limited, there are some key scholarly works on women of color presidents.

The Scholarship on Women of Color Presidents

Turner's (2007) article, *Pathways to the Presidency: Biographical Sketches of Women of Color Firsts*, was one of the first significant articles on women of color presidents of public, baccalaureate degree-granting minority serving colleges. She examined the journeys of three women of color presidents: Juliet Garcia, President of the University of Texas at Brownsville, a Hispanic-serving institution; Karen Swisher, President of Haskell Indian Nations University, a Bureau of Indian Affairs funded campus; and Rose Tseng, President of University of Hawai'i at Hilo. Each woman was the first female president of their institutions. Key findings related to the importance of mentoring; family and interpersonal connections; early educational and career success; and a leadership style focused on facilitation and building community out of difference (Turner, 2007, p. 15). Although the women experienced gender bias, race and ethnic stereotyping, and accent discrimination, they courageously persevered (Turner, 2007, p. 21). Their commitment to core values, including treating others with respect, seeking consensus, and openness with information enabled them to focus on achieving personal and professional goals while being grounded in their own cultural identities (Turner, 2007, pp. 22, 30).

In more recent scholarship, women of color presidents are profiled as either part of scholarship about women presidents or as part of scholarship about minority presidents. For example, *Women at the Top: What Women University and College Presidents Say about Effective Leadership* (Wolverton, Bower, & Hyle, 2008) profiles nine women presidents. Through storytelling, the women share their journeys, beliefs, and engagement strategies. The book reveals that leadership is often an evolving process, focused on a strong sense of self and self-confidence, but also an awareness of organizational and institutional culture. Key themes include work-life balance, a focus on action, and a commitment to achievement. The importance of competence, credibility, and communication is emphasized. The women of color include an African American woman, Mamie Howard-Golladay of Sullivan County Community College; a Native American woman, Karen Swisher of Haskell Indian Nations University; and a Latina, Mildred Garcia of California State University, Dominguez Hills.

In a similar work, *Latino College Presidents: In Their Own Words* (León & Martinez, 2013), eleven college presidents are profiled. Four women are highlighted in the book, three of whom are community college presidents. The women profiled include Erlinda Martinez, President of Santa Ana College; Herlinda Martinez Glasscock, retired president of North Lake College; Leslie Anne Navarro at Morton College; and Mildred Garcia, who had moved from Dominguez Hills to serve as President of California State University, Fullerton. Common themes in the work include strong parental and family support for education; a personal commitment to education at an early age; a deep commitment to the Latino community; overcoming gatekeeper's discouragement; and other unique hurdles faced by Latina presidents based on their race and gender status (León & Martinez, 2013, p. 38).

These are the only two books that address women of color presidents, even though neither work is exclusively about women of color. There are, however, several dissertations that have explored the journeys and experiences of women of color administrators, including senior administrators and presidents. Most of the work is about women community college presidents and women at minority-serving institutions. These dissertations represent important contributions to the scholarship about women of color presidents. The dissertations often involve a qualitative approach that uses storytelling, narrative analysis, surveys, and interviews. The incorporation of storytelling as a methodology for women of color in the academy has become an important technique for understanding the role of the education system in "reproducing and sustaining racial, gender, and class oppression, as well as the myriad of ways in which people of color respond to different forms of oppression" (Jean-Marie & Lloyd-Jones, 2011b, p. 172).

The dissertations are usually grounded in theoretical foundations based on leadership theory, organization theory, race, class and gender scholarship, Black feminism, critical race theory, Latino critical race theory, and critical race feminism. The primary limitation of most dissertations is that because of the necessity of privacy, confidentiality, and the protection of individual identity and institutional identity, pseudonyms are often used, resulting in the continued invisibility and marginalization of women of color. This is most evident in Bucklin's (2010) dissertation about women presidents. Bucklin interviewed 8 out of the 40 women presidents from doctoral granting institutions as of June 2008. Although it is unclear if any were women of color as race is never mentioned, her work illustrates the key challenge related to research involving women and women of color presidents. As Bucklin (2010) noted in reference to illustrations relating to issues of gender,

> I cannot share many of those stories in this analysis because they would easily identify the president and the other parties concerned in the incidents or they were shared as "off the record." ... During every interview, at one point or another, I was told something similar to "but you can't print that!" (p. 55)

Similarly, Fong-Batkin (2011, p. 22) in her dissertation noted that "many participants indicated that they wanted their identity kept confidential, as well as the name and area of their college." She indicated that she attempted to even further protect their identities by not using the actual title and area of each participant. She states, "For example, I did not indicate if I interviewed an Assistant Dean or Associate Vice President. Instead, they are listed as Dean or Vice President."

Despite these limitations which reinforce the invisibility of women of color leaders, consistent themes emerge from the scholarship. The general themes from these dissertations are that women of color presidents must be prepared to address racism, sexism, and classism, as well as work-life challenges. Successful journeys to the presidency and tenures within the presidency require a combination of external factors, as well as internal and intrinsic qualities. External factors include having appropriate preparation, often through leadership development programs and strong mentoring. Internal qualities include resilience, a strong sense of self-identity, self-esteem, and purpose.

The most comprehensive dissertation is Huang's (2012) *Navigating Power and Politics: Women of Color Senior Leaders in Academe*. She examined the experiences of nine women of color, including seven presidents, a vice-provost, and a provost at four-year institutions. Five participants were at predominantly minority-serving institutions. Three women were African American, two were Asian American Pacific Islander, two were Latina, and two were American Indian (Huang, 2012, p. 188). As Huang noted in her literature review, women of color in the academy have experienced common themes: hostile climates, isolation, racism, prejudice, discrimination, and gender bias (Huang, 2012, p. 39, 179). They must navigate the "insider/outsider/other" status and the glass ceiling (Huang, 2012, pp. 39–40). In addressing these challenges, they have relied on mentoring and networking, support groups, women's commissions, their family, and their faith. The important role of their families in developing self-confidence and creating a commitment to service is also a common theme (Huang, 2012, pp. 39–40).

Her work drew upon multiple theoretical frameworks. She incorporated theories from critical race scholarship; scholarship on the use of power and politics in organizational decision-making; research on the bases of social power; and work on connective leadership and intersectionality (Huang, 2012, pp. 12–13). Using the case study approach and semi-structured interviews, four themes emerged. The first theme was "advancing women through opportunity and experience," which focused on the importance of women being prepared, having mentors, being encouraged by parents and partners, and participating in networking (Huang, 2012, pp. 250–263). The second theme was "challenges of race and gender: inviting partnership with community" which involved recognizing the role of racism and sexism; understanding institutional culture; and building partnerships and alliances with the external community (Huang, 2012, pp. 263–277). A third theme was "inclusive and persuasive leaders: creating positive change" which addressed having an assertive, collaborative, flexible, transparent, and inclusive leadership style; creating the right team; learning from role models; and being willing to take risks and be courageous (Huang, 2012, pp. 277–299). The final theme, "using power and politics to achieve goals" addressed the ability to effectively use influence, privilege, and identity to understand institutional and external politics (Huang, 2012, pp. 299–313).

Another significant dissertation is that of Wise (2013) in *No Crystal Stair: Narrative of Female Community College Presidents of Color*. Wise (2013) examined the career paths and the personal, professional, and organizational challenges of eight women of color community college presidents within the California Community College system, using critical race theory and narrative counterstories, as well as scholarship on career paths and organizational culture. The women included three African American, two Latinas (Mexican American and Nicaraguan American), one Hispanic, and two were Asian Americans (one Chinese American, and one Filipino American) (Wise, 2013, p. 44).

Key findings were that women of color often had a non-traditional career path to the presidency through student services and other auxiliary units (Wise, 2013, pp. 110–111), rather than the traditional scholar-president route. In addition, women of color experienced a range of racial microaggressions, including socioemotional, intellectual, physical, positional, and verbal. These experiences included being excluded from meetings, being subjected to stereotypes, having their authority questioned, and being urged to get "second opinions" (Wise, 2013, p. 114). Women of color were often over-looked for opportunities and viewed as not being "presidential material," and thus needing to be "twice as qualified, twice as credentialed, and twice as politically/collegially connected" compared to White males to be considered for senior opportunities (Wise, 2013, pp. 114–115). Other challenges for women of color include balancing work and family, navigating cultural expectations and intraracial conflict, maintaining cultural pride, and continuing a commitment to an activist/advocate stance on behalf of students (Wise, 2013, pp. 116–117).

Wise's findings also emphasized their survival strategies, noting their resiliency, their professionalism, and their ability to use "counter-transgressive grace" in response to microaggressions (Wise, 2013, p. 125). Wise (2013) defines "counter-transgressive grace," as

> a form of emotional intelligence demonstrated by women of color in which unrequited gracious behavior, which is not necessarily merited, is granted to the transgressor(s) by the recipient in light of dysconscious microaggressions of a racial or gender bias nature. Such grace is generally demonstrated through language and behavior that corrects and/or educates the transgressor so he or she is made aware of their slight and is discouraged from repeating it. The grace is presented in a dignified manner that is professionally acceptable and maintains the dignity of all involved. (p. 125)

Wise also found that women of color must be willing to take risks for advancement, participate in professional development, and find strong mentors in order to advance to presidencies.

Fong-Batkin's (2011) dissertation, *Traditionally Untraditional: The Career Trajectory Navigation of California Community College Women of Color Administrators*, also examined the career trajectories of women of color community college administrators. She looked at thirteen administrators, including the dean, vice president and president levels. Four presidents are included (Fong-Batkin, 2011, p. 69). The interview group consisted of five African Americans, five Latinas, and three Asian Americans. Two presidents were African American, one was Asian, and one Latina. Three key themes emerged through her analysis of interviews through a feminist and critical race theory lens. The first theme, "traditionally untraditional career path" was the reality of their non-traditional career paths through student services based on their intersecting race, class, culture, and gender status and being "accidental administrators" (Fong-Batkin, 2011, p. x, 154). The second theme, "strategic connections: strategies and sources of support" involved the strategies used to navigate their experiences, including mentoring and networking

(Fong-Batkin, 2011, p. x). The third theme, "leading as a gender and racial-ized administrator" reflected experiences of racial microaggressions, and the pressure to assimilate within a White male culture (Fong-Batkin, 2011, pp. x, 98). She notes that women of color experience barriers such as race and gender intersectionality, the "chilly" environment, tokenism, overutilization, and the presumption of being underqualified and not good fits. Leadership programs, however, are helpful to address issues faced by women of color administrators (Fong-Batkin, 2011, pp. 142–143).

Research has also been done on the leadership styles of women of color senior administrators. Wardell's *Leadership Behaviors and Practices among Executive Women of Color in Higher Education* dissertation (2010) examined the use of the five leadership practices scales of Kouzes and Posner (1997). These practices include challenging the process, inspiring a vision, enabling others to act, modeling the way, and encouraging the heart. Challenging the process relates to focusing on change, taking risks, and displaying courage and conviction. Encouraging the heart relates to appreciating others, creating a community, and celebrating successes (Wardell, 2010, pp. 10–11). Inspiring a vision involves a leader setting a vision and enlisting others in support of the vision (Wardell, 2010, p. 38). Modeling the way involves a leader clarifying values, finding voice, and using herself as a model for others (Wardell, 2010, p. 38). Enabling others to act is about collaboration, building trust, and shar-ing power (Wardell, 2010, p. 38). Through a survey of 34 directors, deans, and vice presidents, Wardell (2010) found that women of color administra-tors self-identified as using all five practices, but that challenging the process and encouraging the heart were the two highest practices.

Other notable work on women of color faculty and administrators in the academy includes edited volumes by Jean-Marie and Lloyd-Jones (2011a, 2011b). Their work explored issues related to mentoring, paths and barriers to professional advancement, the agency of women of color and their impact within an institution, and retention and promotion. The impact of race and gender on the experiences of women of color is a clear theme. There are also other dissertations on the specific experiences of Latina presidents and African American women presidents (Aschenbrenner, 2006; Ausmer, 2009; Edwards-Wilson, 1998; Humphrey, 2012; Latimore, 2009; Maes, 2012; Martinez, 2008; Smith-Ligon, 2011). These works generally reveal common themes related to the role of family and cultural background; experiences of racism, sexism, and classism; and the traits of perseverance, resiliency, and determination.

The existing scholarship, while limited, demonstrates the difficult jour-ney of women of color presidents in the academy. Given the prominence of issues of race, class, and gender in the journeys of women of color in higher education administration, it is critical to see their journeys as journeys of social justice. They are journeys about claiming space, claiming belonging, asserting rights, claiming voice, and claiming power and authority. They are journeys that challenge the existing status quo. The journey to a presidency of a four-year institution often involves a journey through the academic ranks from assistant professor, to associate professor, to full professor. Once a faculty member moves into administration, the typical pathway includes serving as a department head, then as a dean, then a provost, before the presidency. At each step along the way, women of color are confronting and challenging the hegemony of the academy. They are fighting masters on a plantation: masters who control access to advancement, who make tenure and promotion decisions, who control search committees, who control policies, practices, and procedures, and who can perpetuate systems of thoughts, ideas, and values.

This fight requires a weapon and tool to engage in this battle of social justice. The Transdisciplinary Applied Social Justice (TASJ) model (Pratt-Clarke, 2010) is a tool that facilitates understanding the experiences of women of color presidents in higher education. It is a tool of empowerment. It uses theory, methodology, and praxis with the goal of transforming society.

The Transdisciplinary Applied Social Justice model

The Transdisciplinary Applied Social Justice model (Pratt-Clarke, 2010) is designed to help increase the likelihood of successfully addressing and responding to systematic and institutional oppression. The model encourages an interrogation of the elements that perpetuate oppression: power, philosophy, people, processes, practices, policies, perceptions, and privilege. The model incorporates concepts from social movement theory, Black feminist thought, and critical race feminism. It argues that responding to issues of social justice and the traditional and historical marginalization of populations based on their intersecting identities requires a strategic approach influenced by multiple disciplines (Pratt-Clarke, 2010, pp. 37–41).

The model allows us to define the underrepresentation of women of color presidents as a moral imperative. The model then requires attributing responsibility for the cause of underrepresentation and identifying actions to address the causes. The power domains from Black feminist thought provide a lens to understand the myriad and complex issues women of color face in ascending to and leading institutions. Collins (2009, pp. 295–309) identifies four power domains: structural, disciplinary, hegemonic, and interpersonal.

Higher education institutions exist within the structural domain. This is the domain of macro level social structures, such as the education system, and their micro level manifestations including colleges and universities. In the context of higher education, the structural domain includes the organizational hierarchy of departments, colleges, units, and programs. Because of the structure, each level can become a barrier to advancement.

With respect to the structural domain, Bernal and Villalpando (2002, p. 170) noted that there is a "current de facto segregation in higher education." They found that faculty of color tend to be "concentrated in institutions of lesser prestige with fewer resources" (Bernal & Villalpando, 2002, p. 170). There is segregation by institutional type and by rank with community colleges having the highest percent of women of color faculty and with women of color being disproportionately represented in the ranks of instructor and lecturer (Bernal & Villalpando, 2002, p. 170). In addition, there is segregation by academic department with faculty of color and women of color represented in units that are typically considered less prominent and prestigious, and undervalued, including humanities, ethnic studies, women studies, education, and the social sciences (Bernal & Villalpando, 2002, p. 170).

The segregation of women of color in higher education institutions is often the result of the operation of the hegemonic domain. Hegemonic domain is the domain of attitudes, values, and beliefs. It is the domain of racism, sexism, and classism. It is the domain that reflects deeply held beliefs about qualifications and the ability of women of color to be scholars and administrators. Research has shown that women and women of color must meet a higher standard of excellence and achievement:

> Leaders belonging to diverse identity groups can perform especially well to the extent that they have had to meet a higher standard to attain leadership roles in the first place. In support of this possibility, the requirement that women and racial minorities meet higher standards to be accorded competence and agency has been demonstrated in many contexts. (Eagly & Chin, 2010, pp. 219–220)

As one women of color administrator stated:

> I'm not sure as to why someone making the decision about who would get the job determined that I did not have the readiness that some of my peers had when they were given the same level of responsibility at a younger age or an earlier point in their career. In fact, even now as I think about the years I've put into making sure my readiness for certain things couldn't be challenged, other people learn on the job. They get the jobs; they learn as they go. So I can't say with-let me put it this way—my suspicion is that it has something to do with being a woman and it has something to do with being a woman of color. (Wise, 2013, p. 59)

The hegemonic domain is also the domain that tends to devalue the scholarly contributions of women of color. It is based upon a Eurocentric epistemological perspective grounded in white privilege and white supremacy (Bernal & Villalpando, 2002, pp. 171–172). These values, beliefs, ideas, and ideologies are operationalized through the disciplinary domain. The disciplinary domain is the domain of policies, procedures, and practices that reinforce the hegemonic domain. It is the domain of tenure and promotion policies, hiring processes, and other bureaucratic procedures.

This is the domain of unwritten rules that apply to women of color in the academy. These rules, often stumbled upon during the academic journey, reveal important themes about the complicated and difficult space in which women of color exist in the academy. The rules, as identified by Mitchell and Miller (2011) include "you are assumed to be incompetent, until you prove you are competent"; "the politics of race have no racial boundaries"; "develop your academic persona, but do not let it consume you"; "and prepare to be lonely, professionally, and socially" (pp. 198–210). Understanding the existence of these rules facilitates the development of responses and strategies to counter their operation and to increase the likelihood of success of women of color in the academy in the tenure, promotion, and administrative journey.

While these rules shed light on the operation of the disciplinary domain, they also reflect the importance of the interpersonal domain for women of color, not only as faculty, but also as administrators. Individuals in the interpersonal domain enforce and execute the policies, practices, and procedures of the disciplinary domain, as influenced by the biases and prejudices that they bring from the hegemonic domain. The interpersonal domain involves the day to day interactions and encounters between individuals. It is the space in which racism, sexism, and other biases, including microaggressions are carried out. More importantly, though, it is also a space in which acts of resistance, self-empowerment, and activism exist.

The domains facilitate an understanding of the complexity of challenges women of color face in their pursuit of the highest rung. As Martinez (2008, pp. 217–218) noted there are in fact "forces" which are part of "the policies, configuration and operation of higher education" that impact who can advance in the academy. The role of embedded structures, social reproduction, and "Anglo-male-normed conceptions of leadership and merit" (Martinez, 2008, p. 218) are critical factors in the journeys of women of color. Being able to address these factors requires developing strategies to combat the operation of the power domains. The TASJ model enables the careful consideration of a counter strategy, a counter movement, and a counter narrative to combat the power of the domains. Women of color must assert their individual agency. As

Griffin (2013, p. 89) noted in her journey to pursuing tenure and promotion, "academe is a unique geography requiring a strategy for gaining full expertise of its cultural landscape." Her (Griffin, 2013) tenure journey included a dedicated focus on understanding the policies and procedures for tenure.

> I sought and obtained copies of the department and/or college, and campus-wide policies for tenure and promotion. Inquiries about these policies were made by me, to persons within and outside my academic unit on anything that was not clear. I attended multiple seminars and workshops which focused on my institution's tenure and promotion policies to learn the required criteria necessary for the journey toward tenure and promotion. (p. 89)

She also established formal and informal mentoring relationships within and outside of her institution. She was conscious of the amount of her service and she pursued an aggressive research agenda with strong scholarly outcomes (Griffin, 2013, p. 89).

Women of color must develop a strong interpersonal skill set to survive. They must have an aspirational mindset, be willing to take risks, and adopt a professional and presidential persona (Latimore, 2009, pp. 125–126). Interpersonal domain skills often include strong communication skills, a high level of competency, a commitment to building consensus, an ability to be strategic and resilient, a focus on collaboration and collective results, a strong sense of pride, and a deep dedication to their culture and community (Huang, 2012, pp. 72–74; Martinez, 2008, p. 219). Women of color presidents must be confident, well-prepared, and assertive. They must have a "diverse, collaborative, entrepreneurial, and inclusive leadership style" (Huang, 2012, p. 348).

Unfortunately, for many women of color, it takes almost superhuman strength to survive. They have to be proficient in institutional policy and protocol and understand that they need to be "better prepared and work harder than their Anglo male and female colleagues to move up the ranks" (Martinez, 2008, p. 220). Constance Carroll, president of Indian Valley College in Navato, California in 1982, noted that her formula for surviving was to tell herself over and over:

> You must be better qualified than the men; you must be more articulate; you must be more aggressive; you must have more stamina to face inevitable setbacks; you must have more patience, since you will advance more slowly. Above all you must remain feminine and not appear threatening. (White, 2007, p. 9)

As the model illustrates, the domains reflect both challenges and opportunities. They are the sources of oppression, but also opportunities for activism. Using the model in the war for inclusion means that we have to challenge institutional structures, ideologies, and individuals who seek to inhibit the advancement of women of color in the academy. Women of color are able to successfully journey into presidencies because they are able to negotiate multiple domains. This battle for inclusion, however, cannot be fought be women of color alone.

The war requires allies: men of color, White men, White women, and existing faculty members, deans, department heads, and governing board members. Current administrators and faculty members on search committees, promotion and tenure committees, and admission committees must be willing and able to identify and recognize talent in non-traditional forms; must be willing to support, mentor, and nurture that talent; and must be an advocate for the success of students and faculty members of color. They must be willing to join the army and use new and different weapons in the war to diversify the academy. They must have courage and the conviction to stand up and speak out when justice occurs. They must also be willing to share the secret passwords, codes, connections, and relationships that facilitate publications, grants, and promotion. It has to be a collaborative and cooperative battle. Successful social movements, which transform societies and social institutions, are able to garner support across large and diverse populations in support of a common, moral, and just cause. The advancement of women of color into presidencies is such a cause.

Conclusion

This book represents an act of social justice. It represents a strategic effort to target the hegemonic domain. Its goal is to address the invisibility, the silence, and the marginalization of women of color presidents by providing visibility, affirmation, and legitimacy of their experiences, journeys, and lives. This book is a tool and weapon in the battle for inclusion. It documents the success of women of color presidents and signals to those of us beneath the adobe ceilings, the bamboo ceilings, and the plantation roofs, that it is possible to break through the layers of mud, dirt, and filth of the "system" to lead institutions of higher education.

References

American Council on Education. (2012, March 12). *Leading demographic portrait of a college president reveals ongoing challenges in diversity, aging.* Retrieved from http://www.acenet.edu/news-room/Pages/ACPS-Release-2012.aspx

American Indian Higher Education Consortium. (2015). *About AIHEC.* Retrieved from http://www.aihec.org/who-we-are/about.cfm

Aschenbrenner, L. L. (2006). *Rising to the top: The personal and professional journeys of four Hispanic women leaders in higher education* (Doctoral dissertation). Retrieved from ProQuest Dissertations and Theses database (UMI No. 3229049).

Ausmer, N. (2009). *Redefining leadership: Examination of African American women serving as presidents in institutions of higher education* (Doctoral dissertation). Retrieved from Proquest Dissertations and Theses database (UMI No. 3367679).

Bernal, D. D., & Villalpando, O. (2002). An apartheid of knowledge in academia: The struggle over the "legitimate" knowledge of faculty of color. *Equity & Excellence in Education, 35*(2), 169–180.

Bucklin, M. L. (2010). *Madame President: Examining the influence of gender on women university presidents' leadership* (Doctoral dissertation). Retrieved from Proquest Dissertations and Theses database (UMI No. 3419937).

Chen, E., & Hune, S. (2011). Asian American Pacific Islander women from Ph.D. to campus president: Gains and leaks in the pipeline. In G. Jean-Marie & B. Lloyd-Jones (Eds.), *Women of color in higher education: Changing directions and new perspective* (Diversity in Higher Education, Vol. 10, pp. 163–190). Bingley: Emerald Group Publishing Limited.

Collins, P. H. (2009). *Black feminist thought: Knowledge, consciousness, and the politics of empowerment.* New York, NY: Routledge.

Cook, S. G. (2012, May). Women presidents: Now 26.4% but still underrepresented. *Women in Higher Education, 21*(5), 1–3. Retrieved from http://wihe.com/women-presidents-now-26-4-but-still-underrepresented/

Eagly, A. H., & Chin, J. L. (2010). Diversity and leadership in a changing world. *American Psychologist, 65*(3), 216–224.

Edwards-Wilson, R. (1998). *The leadership styles of African-American female college presidents* (Doctoral dissertation). Retrieved from Proquest Dissertations and Theses database (UMI No. 9822137).

Fong-Batkin, L. G. (2011). *Traditionally untraditional: The career trajectory navigation of California community college women of color administrators* (Doctoral dissertation). Retrieved from Proquest Dissertations and Theses database (UMI No. 3474384).

Fournillier, J. B. (2010). Plus ça change, plus c'est la même chose: An Afro Caribbean scholar on the higher education plantation. *Creative Approaches to Research, 3*(2), 52–62. doi: 10.3316/CAR0302052

Griffin, K. L. (2013). Pursuing tenure and promotion in the academy: A librarian's cautionary tale. *Negro Educational Review, 64*(1–4), 77–96.

Huang, B. J. (2012). *Navigating power and politics: Women of color senior leaders in academe* (Doctoral dissertation). Retrieved from Proquest Dissertations and Theses database (UMI No. 3517678).

Humphrey, M. (2012). *Experiences of African-American female community college presidents using a student affairs pathway: a phenomenological study* (Doctoral dissertation). Retrieved from Proquest Dissertations and Theses database (UMI No. 3551624).

Jean-Marie, G., & Lloyd-Jones, B. (Eds.). (2011a). *Women of color in higher education: Changing directions and new perspectives.* Bingley: Emerald Group Publishing Limited.

Jean-Marie, G., & Lloyd-Jones, B. (Eds.). (2011b). *Women of color in higher education: Turbulent past, promising future.* Bingley: Emerald Group Publishing Limited.

Kouzes, J. M., & Posner, B. (1997). Leadership practices inventory: Participant's workbook. San Francisco, CA: Jossey-Bass.

Jones, S. R., & Komizes, S. R. (2001). Contemporary issues of women as senior student affairs officers. In J. Nidiffer & C. T. Bashaw (Eds.), *Women administrators in higher education: Historical and contemporary perspectives* (pp. 231–248). New York, NY: State University of New York Press.

Latimore, R. S. (2009). *Rising to the top a national study of Black women community college presidents* (Doctoral dissertation). Retrieved from https://getd.libs.uga.edu/pdfs/latimore_robbie_s_200905_edd.pdf

León, D. J., & Martinez, O. R. (Eds.). (2013). *Latino college presidents: In their own words.* Bingley: Emerald Group Publishing Limited.

Lloyd-Jones, B. (2011). Diversification in higher education administration: Leadership paradigms reconsidered. In G. Jean-Marie & B. Lloyd-Jones (Eds.), *Women of color in higher education: Changing directions and new perspective* (Diversity in Higher Education, Vol. 10, pp. 3–18). Bingley: Emerald Group Publishing Limited.

Lum, L. (2008). Forming a pipeline to the presidency. *Diverse Issues in Higher Education, 25*(7), 12–14.

Machado-Casas, M., Ruiz, E. C., & Cantu, N. E. (2013). "Laberintos y Testimonios": Latina faculty in the academy. *Educational Foundations, 27*(1–2), 3–14.

Maes, J. (2012). *The socio-cultural and leadership experiences of Latina four-year college and university presidents: A través de sus voces (through their voices)* (Doctoral dissertation). Retrieved from Proquest Dissertations and Theses database (UMI No. 3509591).

Manuelito-Kerkvliet, C. (2005). *Widening the circle: Mentoring and the learning process for American Indian women in tribal college administration* (Doctoral dissertation). Retrieved from Proquest Dissertations and Theses database (UMI No. 3181109).

Martinez, S. R. (2008). *Latina presidents of four-year institutions, penetrating the adobe ceiling: A critical view* (Doctoral dissertation). Retrieved from Proquest Dissertations and Theses database (UMI No. 3341931).

Mitchell, N., & Miller, J. (2011). The unwritten rules of the academy: A balancing act for women of color. In G. Jean-Marie & B. Lloyd-Jones (Eds.), *Women of color in higher education: Changing directions and new perspective* (Diversity in Higher Education, Vol. 10, pp. 193–218). Bingley: Emerald Group Publishing Limited.

Nidiffer, J. (2001). Crumbs from the boy's table: The first century of coeducation. In J. Nidiffer and C. T. Bashaw (Eds.), *Women administrators in higher education: Historical and contemporary perspectives* (pp. 13–36). New York, NY: State University of New York Press.

Pratt-Clarke, M. (2010). *Critical race, feminism, and education: A social justice model.* New York, NY: Palgrave Macmillan.

Reid, P. T. (2012). Black and female in academia. *Back to the Presidency Spring Supplement 2012, Diversity in Leadership.* Retrieved from http://www.acenet.edu/the-presidency/columns-and-features/Pages/Black-and-Female-in-Academia.aspx

Sanchez-Hucles, J., & Davis, D. D. (2010). Women and women of color in leadership: Complexity, identity, and intersectionality. *American Psychologist, 65*(3), 171–181. doi: http://dx.doi.org/10.1037/a0017459

Smith-Ligon, P. (2011). *An examination of African American female college presidents' professional ascendancy and mentoring experiences* (Doctoral dissertation). Retrieved from Proquest Dissertations and Theses database (UMI No. 3506921).

Turner, C. (2007). Pathways to the presidency: Biographical sketches of women of color firsts. *Harvard Educational Review, 77*(1), 1–38.

Wardell, M. J. (2010). *Leadership behaviors and practices among executive women of color in higher education* (Doctoral dissertation). Retrieved from Proquest Dissertations and Theses database (UMI No. 3397951).

White, D. G. (2007). "Matter out of place": Ar'n't I a woman? Black female scholars and the academy. *Journal of African American History, 92*(1), 5–12.

Wilson, R. (1989). Women of color in academic administration: Trends, progress, and barriers. *Sex Roles: A Journal of Research, 21*(1/2), 85–97.

Wise, C. B. (2013). *No crystal stair: Narratives of female community college presidents of color* (Doctoral dissertation). Retrieved from Proquest Dissertations and Theses database (UMI No. 3568307).

Wolverton, M., Bower, B., & Hyle, A. (2008). Women at the top: What women university and college presidents say about effective leadership (Journeys to Leadership Series). Sterling, VA: Stylus Publishing.

3. *The Adobe Ceiling over the Yellow Brick Road*

GABRIELLA GUTIÉRREZ Y MUHS

Editors' Note:
Dr. Gabriella Gutiérrez y Muhs is a multilingual, bicultural Chicana poet and academic cultural worker. She is the daughter of migrant workers and grew up in México, Texas, California, and Chicago. Dr. Gutiérrez y Muhs received her doctorate in Spanish from Stanford University, and is a full professor in the Departments of Modern Languages and Women & Gender Studies at Seattle University. She is also Director for the Center for the Study of Justice in Society. In 2006, Dr. Gutiérrez y Muhs was named the 2007–2009 Wismer Professor for Gender and Diversity Studies at Seattle University. Her research interests lie primarily in the areas of Chicana/Latina and Latin American literatures, theorizing Chicana/Latina/Mexicana subjectivity, Chicana/Latina spirituality, cultural studies, and feminist theory.

The Adobe Ceiling

I want to remember Cecilia Burciaga, Dr. Victor Rodríguez, and Dr. Lora Romero. I dedicate this work to the memory of my dear friend Cecilia Preciado Burciaga and her husband José Antonio "Tony" Burciaga, our legendary "Chicano power couple." Cecilia died at age 67 after a seven-month battle with cancer. A native of California, she was a nationally respected leader in civil rights and higher education. She became one of the first high-ranking Latina administrators to serve at a top United States private university. Cecilia was a mentor to me and to hundreds, perhaps thousands of students and faculty members during her 20 year career at Stanford University.

While I was a doctoral student there in 1994, her leadership position was eliminated and she was fired by the administration. The administration who made Condoleezza Rice—herself a beneficiary of affirmative action and who was mentored by Burciaga when she came first to Stanford—their hatchet lady to the outcry of students, faculty, and staff who staged protests in support of Cecilia. The statement of Dr. Francisca James Hernández in response to Cecilia's untimely death captures so much of who she was:

> Mi Querida Mentora, There are so few who have inspired my life as you. Sobre todo por tu integridad. I witnessed you struggle against injustices at Stanford on behalf of us the students, people of color, women, queers, and working class people, sometimes winning, sometimes losing. Painful shit. You paid the price. Pero NUNCA te quedabas callada. Mujer osicona. I loved and LOVE that about you. They could never control your tongue y menos tu mente! You touched so many and made us feel of your inner circle, as if, yes, we could aspire to your courage. Daring to walk in your shoes is an awesome challenge. Yet, you inspire as a living example of how social justice work is done ... with love and truthtelling and persistence y manos a la obra! I work to honor this legacy every day in classrooms filled with the working class poor and the heavy challenges this presents to us collectively. To you, I lift a shot of Patrón (and many more) y grito, Ajua! Que Viva Cecilia! Que Viva Tony! Que Viva la Chicanada! c/s. (Hernández, 2013)

The firing of Cecilia and her husband Tony, who also worked for the university, caused so much pain and Cecilia was forced to leave Stanford, but that never stopped her. She went on to work at other institutions and led various efforts to support not only Chicana/Latina students and other minorities but also Whites in higher education, particularly those students who were first generation college attendees. She, in fact, secured scholarships for Latina and minority students at Stanford and CSUMB (California State University Monterey Bay), as part of her settlements with them. Cecilia was what many of us are, *indomables, indomitable*. Rest in Power, Cecilia Preciado Burciaga.

No, it was not during my academic trials and tribulations, otherwise known as a tenure track, that I first learned the nuanced meaning of the term "tenure." When I was a senior at Occidental College in the late 70s, one of my professors, Dr. Victor Rodríguez, had not received tenure and committed suicide. He was a man of color. Dr. Rodríguez was labeled as a Spanish-speaking Black man, a gay man, from the Caribbean. Everybody said "there was just something not quite right about him," and dismissed his life and passing. He taught Spanish and was a beautiful and well-mannered man who worked at my private university. I never forgot that he was the only Black Latino at our campus, and one few Black faculty.

Along the way, I also met other people who were denied entry into the Academy. They often were the kindest professors to me by making time for my academic and personal needs outside of the classroom. These exceptional professors embraced me, a migrant young woman with few material resources, who almost never wore shoes, who owned very few changes of clothes, and who had never seen a check book in her life before going to college.

In graduate school in 1997, another one of my professors, prior to undergoing the tenure process, killed herself. This time it was a Chicana, a lesbian, named Lora Romero. I was angry at her. How could she, an elite intellectual at a first-rate university, kill herself? At the time, I did not understand that both of these individuals would choose to fight by ending their lives—but I could, like most human beings, feel their anguish, desperation and painful acceptance of their circumstances.

It was then that I fully realized that by not supporting and fully embracing people of color in the Academy, we were acting irresponsibly—and that the best antidote for this disease is to be communal and transparent. Most recently, social science and economic research as well as anthropological cross-cultural studies focusing on the individualistic nature of United States society have gained national attention through popular articles published in *The New Yorker*, *The Atlantic*, *The Nation*, among other news magazines. For better or worse, we still live in the wealthiest country in the world— something the powers that be would have us forget, and which we ourselves tend to forget as we struggled for years in the greatest economic recession since the Great Depression.

We also continue to experience unstable employment and unrelenting attacks on what is left of our social safety net. Much of what many of us— who grew up working-poor in the United States and/or came from developing countries in the Global South—knew all along was finally confirmed by social research. According to a report by Kolbert (2012), non-poor contemporary U.S. children may represent the most self-indulgent young people in the history of the world. It was also found that the "weird" Western mind, and people in the U.S. championing all other Western nations, is "the most self-aggrandizing and egotistical on the planet" (Kolbert, 2012). Simply put, we are more likely to promote ourselves as individuals versus advancing as a group and have the "tendency to telescope in on an object of interest rather than understanding that object in the context of what is around it" (Watters, 2013).

It is then not surprising that these social and psychological behaviors and dynamics, major psychological blind spots and gaps in our emotional intelligence, are most often reproduced and overly accentuated within the confines of the most elitist and prestigious institution outside of government in the United States: the Ivory Tower. Research on emotional intelligence has long suggested that we all need a high level of emotional acuity in order to meet the demands of any given profession, regardless of its prestige or status. This is often overlooked in academia where a high level of cognitive acuity is often valued more over traits of emotional intelligence. This pattern is typified by the archetype of the academic who possesses a wide range of intellectual interests and abilities. In our collective consciousness, this has further racial and gendered implications.

We usually picture the caricature or stereotype of the high IQ academic as a White male, who Goleman (1995, p. 44) characterized as "intellectually adept in the realm of mind but inept in the personal world." In some of the early books published on emotional intelligence, descriptions of such individual ranged from ambitious and productive to not so flattering character traits such as critical, condescending, fastidious, emotionally bland and cold. Even then it was suggested that women with high IQs but perhaps low emotional intelligence observed more positive character traits than men with the peculiarities that women, largely due to socialization, tend to be introspective, prone to anxiety, rumination, and guilt, and hesitate to express their anger openly though they do so indirectly. Remember, these are mere archetypes, borderline caricatures. Since there are no people who are high IQ-PURE types, any similarity with any of our colleagues is mere coincidence.

Yet, as González and Harris (Gutiérrez y Muhs, Niemann, González, & Harris, 2012, p. 5) maintain, "Among researchers and scholars, the romance of the brilliant, lonely genius in pursuit of Truth—even if the heavens should fall—still lingers around promotion reviews." Thus, the Academy is the kind of place that "naturally" attracts this type of intellectually gifted individual or at least so the story goes. However, if we extrapolate, the disinterest in individuals who possess high levels of emotional intelligence results in faculty and staff who fall short of being socially poised, lack the capacity for commitment to people or causes, for taking reasonability, for having an ethical outlook; and who are not gregarious and do not know how to express their feelings appropriately, all of which are characteristics of high emotional intelligence.

Similarly, like any other social institution, academia mirrors our capitalist economic system. It reflects and reproduces existing social hierarchies that are deeply rooted in a legacy of colonization, institutional patriarchy, misogyny, economic exploitation, and White supremacy. These things gave birth to the United States. The Introduction of *Presumed Incompetent* details that,

> The restrictiveness of American academic culture has its origins in the history of American education. The nation's most prestigious universities were not established to educate women, people of color, or the working class. On the contrary, they were designed to serve the interests of wealthy White men. (Gutiérrez y Muhs et al., 2012, p. 7)

In the Afterword to *Presumed Incompetent* (Gutiérrez y Muhs et al., 2012), I write:

> It is in this larger context that as a twenty-first-century Latina I, myself, came across many obstacles in my quest for tenure and particularly an epistemological gap in academia: an emptiness in the journey from graduate school to an assistant professor to full professor. To my knowledge, there was no one document readily available for new PhDs that defined, deconstructed, described, or clarified the evolution of terminology in academic settings about acquiring tenure. Although these documents perhaps exist in some institutions, they are purposefully written to possess certain levels of mystery, obscurity, and avoidance, depending on the university. (p. 501)

In 2004—after four years of working at my current university—through reading about Cecilia Burciaga's concept-metaphor of the dense, impenetrable "adobe ceiling" in academia for Latinas, as opposed to a more penetrable, see-through "glass ceiling" encountered by White women, I became more aware that in fact there was a difference in how the intersection of gender, race, and class came together in our professions. I, like one of the contributors to *Presumed Incompetent*, felt that my credentials and skills were erased in Latin American social circles in the Modern Languages Department at my university. And so, when I first told Cecilia Burciaga that I had problems at my institution, because I was considered "non-collegial," she flew up to Seattle to assess the situation, and to share and support. Era mujer de acción, she was a woman of action: unstoppable, intrepid, and marvelously powerful. She said to me when she arrived, "Hey, are you having fun yet? We are going to have a lot of fun on this ride" she stated this, turning the tortilla around and letting me know that I was in charge of my own situation, and not the others, not the institution, not the men, and that I could make out of it whatever I so well pleased, absolutely empowering. Because of her, I took the sartén por el mango (the frying pan by the handle), all in great part because of her guidance and unconditional support, as well as her intrepid intervention in my life and the lives of many other people, particularly women, because she was quite a feminista.

I was raised in the Bay Area by feminists and very strong women such as Bettina Aptheker, Adrianne Rich, Tillie Olsen, Shirley Flores Muñoz, Mary Louise Pratt, y la misma Cecilia Burciaga. My mother was a cannery worker and a resistance leader among those in her cannery. Seeing her exit the workforce because of the incredible 1985–1987 Teamsters' strike in Watsonville, California, I knew that the best way to resist is to put all your chips on the table. At the time of the strike, I watched as supporters donated canned goods which the leaders distributed openly and evenly among the strikers, instead of secretly bestowing more on some than others to gain a political or social advantage. In this case, it is only by including all the voices of women emerging from various experiences in academia, including the positive ones, that we can comprehensively analyze and correct the institutional process. As a junior faculty member, I knew very well that victimization and acting like a victim did not work. Those behaviors and mental pathologies only make the oppressor stronger. I did not want to reproduce that way of acting, even in my own struggle for tenure and promotion to full professor.

Mid-Career Muddle

While *Presumed Incompetent* (Gutiérrez y Muhs et al., 2012) focused largely on pre-tenure, I have recently been reflecting on the post-tenure world and the connections between the two worlds. Mid-career in academia means that you will no longer be fired, but that you must prove to your institution and the academy, especially as a woman, a Chicana, a multilingual person who may come from a previous teaching or service career, that you are worthy of being called a professor. This is where you show "THEM," the them that did not want you to be their equal, to acquire tenure, because they did not see that "you could contribute as much as them to the academy" that you are in fact invaluable, and that you are not an "affirmative action hire," an "opportunity hire," a "gender hire," an "international hire," a "diversity hire," and, that you undoubtedly are part of the intellectual class, whatever that may be at your university. However, the fashion by which we integrate ourselves into what our future career will consist of is essential to erect during the pre-tenure years. (I use the word erect purposefully here.)

We are in fact the person who will be constructing our professional persona and need to be conscious of this at all times during our pre-tenure years. I learned as I proceeded that I had a lesson to teach the academy about valuing my assets, because I did value them myself. I wish I had already known that the power that I acquired post-tenure would not be an immediate click and save, but an "erecting" of a reputation that I had a large part in building for myself. We also oftentimes are seen as representing our ethnic group, particularly where we are the only Chicana/o Latina, African-American, Asian-American, Native woman in sight, for that institution. There is a lack of understanding on behalf of the academy of what minority intellectuals in the academy have to give up and sacrifice in order to remain as respected academics both in their discipline and institution and in their representative community(ies).

I will never forget the disparaging look the Latina student, who did not work for me but filed papers outside my office, had while watching the amount of work that I prepared for every day. She saw me working intensely every day: direct programs, go in and out, meet with students, print, copy and go out loaded with books and materials to teach, for meetings, for presentations. She witnessed the papers placed in my box for correcting, and how I rushed home at six most days. She once looked at me straight in the face and said to me in a sorrow filled tone: "Professor, I don't want your life." Perhaps because she was so sincere, her words impacted me greatly. She said clarifying: "I don't want to work like you do."

In one of the essays in this collection of *Presumed Incompetent*, De la Riva-Holly eloquently stated:

> I truly do not know that I would take this road again in life. I cannot say that it is worth having the job that I now have—and profusely enjoy—because chipping away at your soul for six years is not something I recommend to anyone. Nonetheless, it is extremely important for me to document this territory, the rhetorical geography of this jumbled administrative language: the turns and twists, the stop signs, the obscure hand signals of the country of academia; the rivers of silence and continuation, especially because so few of us are working here, so few members of underrepresented and historically oppressed groups triumphing in these obscene waters of fate through hard work, perseverance and endurance. ... (Gutiérrez y Muhs et al., 2012, p. 295)

The passing of Cecilia Burciaga and others mentioned earlier who committed suicide, and my own health problems and those of many of my colleagues, solidify for me the gravity of our work. Our bodies sometimes take a toll from the unwelcoming, hostile, and toxic environment of academia. To what extent are we willing to sacrifice our own well-being and that of our loved ones to remain in the Academy? How, where, how long and under what conditions you wish to work is essential to the notion of having the power to create the ideal working conditions for your particular situation, demands, and expectations.

For most workers, this is a fantasy, something that will never occur, that they will never be able to have input or say about. But for some people for whom a work climate and working conditions are essential to well being and quality of life, this ability to evolve within your position while enjoying your profession is essential. As a Latina woman I knew early on that I needed to be able to produce three times the amount of work White men or women had to produce in order to become a respectable person in my area—this was a given, but how I presented myself while doing this, was to be the drafting of my professional persona. And, if I did not actively construct the persona that I wanted to represent me, other well-meaning, or not so well-meaning colleagues would. Thus, we must be active participants of the construction of our professional persona pre-tenure.

Conditions for Latinas in the Academy have somewhat improved in recent years, but not to the extent to where we can relax totally about expectations and conditions. Nonetheless, we must not look like victims while we are on our way to hopefully not becoming gatekeepers but instead those professors who welcome others like us into the academy. My mother always says: "no hay que ir al cielo llorando" (we must not be on our way to heaven and crying). Working class women have always had to be superwomen by having to survive adversity and communal living "conviviendo" supporting others and being supported into a "livable" life. We contribute enormously to the type of climates that exist in our work place and some companies, chairs, bosses, and managers are able to acknowledge and value this, and in the academy we must know how to present our value to others as we proceed towards tenure and navigate post-tenure.

It is particularly important that we pay attention to potential post-tenure obstacles that might not become obstacles and make the task of surviving the tenure process almost insurmountable if we don't address them early on. We need to reflect on post-tenure when some of the issues that pushed our colleagues to support us are gone. After tenure the political monopoly to possess you is gone, you are a "played card," people know where you stand politically. In post-tenure, most pre-tenure groups might not want you in their corner any longer, as you might be a loose canon, if you:

(a) Felt you "told the truth"—were in your opinion honest throughout your pre-tenure process, your commitment to speak your mind scares your colleagues now, because as an insider, an "associate professor," you might also challenge them and "tell the truth" to others about them.

(b) "Play a certain identity role" to which they cannot subscribe: i.e. Chicana, Marxist, African-American, feminist. ... You are a dangerous element for you are openly identified as standing for the rights of these groups. You might be possibly identified as a person who engages in "identity politics."

(c) "Associate ONLY (exclusively) with the rebels." Here it is essential to also participate in developing connections with other groups pre-tenure who will be there for you after tenure. (i.e. poetry club, advisor to student clubs not necessarily linked to your race, ethnicity, gender).

(d) Are more successful publishing and acquiring grants and awards. Competititiveness is what allowed you to be successful, because most academics have to compete for the very few resources available. However, it is important not to brag about your accomplishments constantly. There are venues such as annual professional reviews, submission to the university news, etc. where this is acceptable, but although unsaid, this type of continual mention of your successes is not embraced by most of your colleagues.

(e) The students support and love you, and you in turn publish with your students or support them into acquiring PhD's, positions in academia, excellent jobs, or internships. This is wonderful work, however, your students will be gone in four years, and it is important that you connect with staff and other institutional people who will be there for you post-tenure.

Also, amazingly enough, most of the tenured women I met—especially if they were working class or were unmistakably identified by others as women of color—had walked a treacherous road that was never discussed post-tenure or even spoken about along the way. Most experienced a tumultuous and even surrealistic journey—which a couple of them described to me as "hazing"—seen as part of entering the fraternal and paternalistic institutions that they had chosen to join. Many women professors on my voyage dropped out of the process, precisely because acquiring tenure became an obscure procedure. They were often described by colleagues as the casualties of an intellectual war.

Mid-career is truly a difficult terrain—your family and friends think you must be grateful for your job, having acquired tenure-the stability of employment and benefits, etc. But, if you are a woman of color, and have been undermined, never truly given credit for your accomplishments, academic or otherwise, you feel the need to prove to all that you are at least as deserving as them in the academy and that you will become renowned outside of your university and even your discipline. Because of the above mentioned issues and many more not addressed in this paper, after acquiring tenure, you could become completely isolated from the academy, your institution, and your family. There are also other emotional issues you must confront post-tenure, for which you can prepare pre-tenure.

So you can either vegetate in isolation as a person of color post-tenure, as many colleagues of all backgrounds do and teach to the best of your ability, simply being present after acquiring tenure to fulfill your responsibilities, or you can embark on a quest for fame. The first thing one of my Ph.D. mentors and ex-professors told me when I notified him that I had received tenure was: "Well, I do hope depression doesn't get you now." As my friend and colleague stands in front of me and states: "I don't want your life, this is why I don't buy a house," or "I am glad I didn't have children, when I see you dealing with yours." Although her intent is to let me know that she understands my pain, my life, my struggles—what she really does by saying this is to tell me that I have chosen wrong, that I am not as smart as her, because she could foretell what it would cost her health and life to have a house, to have children, that I should have taken the example given to us by the childless women from the generation before us, before Adrienne Rich gave feminists permission to have children, and that we cannot do it all, I depress her, and she can no longer see me, because she too is post-tenure depressed. Neither of us fully established links with colleagues that are willing to continue supporting us post-tenure, we, according to them have too many liabilities.

When I think of all the professors/colleagues who could not have coffee with me, who would not attend the events I invited them to, where some of them would have been honored by junior faculty, I now understand why they did not care to support me or my family on my quest for tenure. And the handful of people who did support me unconditionally, are now my heroes, because they truly had no reason to do so, other than their political commitment to me and my cause. There was no carrot at the end of their path, helping me was inconsequential. There was no incentive either professional or personal for many of them to wish to spend time with me or on me, giving me advise or reading my work. They had tenure, they had their problems and their families to raise, their books to write and they did not need to associate with me, plainly.

The academy is one of the most selfish arenas for professionals. It does not provide incentives for professors to support junior faculty, and oftentimes after they have been supportive, or if they did support that person, that person gives them no credit, does not list them in their acknowledgements, or nominate them for awards, or simply states to their dean that this person had been instrumental in supporting them, because they do not want to use their chips, conversation, sympathy on that issue. We all want to be exceptional. Unfortunately the resources in academia are few, especially for women and minorities, and oftentimes, especially our newly minted associate professors will not use them on other women. This is difficult to witness, and something that I hope we remedy in the academy, by ascribing some type of credit towards promotion or remuneration for associate and full professors for actively supporting junior faculty members.

Being a professor is truly a privilege, and while we have heard this many times, we have not yet unpacked why. I would like to list the different types of privilege that working class academics lack when they enter the academy, and also to underline that the academy does not understand the complicated lives of assets and liabilities that impact its professors. There are various forms of capital involved in the life transactions of most individuals, especially when we look at them intersectionally: while culturally having 173 cousins is for me, as a Mexican woman, an asset, in academia and in society, my mostly working class cousins, some of them undocumented, are liabilities.

The culturally correct etiquette for my social class and culture, my barrio, my mother, and where I come from is that I give each of my relatives a book when my books are published, nonetheless academia would never understand this. "Your books are expensive," says my cousin Adela. "Do you get half of that money?" To her, as a working class factory worker, who began this job at age 16, after marrying and coming to the United States, to work and raise three children, there is no meaning or value to my bookwriting if I am not getting any or much of the money that the press charges for my book, and most importantly, if I am not given books for my relatives, no matter how many relatives I have. In her eyes, I am a Ph.D. and a sap. Although this goes unsaid, I understand that am not truly worthy of much respect if I am letting the press get away with this barbarity. Publishing a book, is thus, a liability for me.

In academia being a professor implies that I have certain assets that others do not have, that is, different types of currency or privileges. In the interest of this paper, I would like to divide these types of privileges into three types of assets: financial, social, and cultural. Realistically, the financial issue is thus essential in order for the other two to be enjoyed, nonetheless for working class professors, no institution or organization subsidizes this. Once we become Associate Professors, we acquire a rank, almost like in the army, whereby we become equal to other Associate Professors, although in reality, we will never have the same currencies. I must be able to subsidize my travel, books, and cultural life in order to continue to navigate in academic settings professionally, socially and culturally, successfully ... and in order to be truly able to promote my books.

I recently received a tip from Professor Richard Delgado on what it means to be an academic in today's world. He said to me, "Publishing a book or two is no longer enough Gabriella. Being a real academic now, means traveling to conferences, and presenting your work, exchanging ideas about your research with other super stars." Reflecting on this, I realize that that type of life, for women for whom their local communities and families are central to their lives, is almost an impossibility. And I found through this, as a woman of color and particularly a Chicana, that my tenure and promotion is being devalued even more, if this is the new standard for intellectual. Without inheritances at my disposition, trust funds and investments that my relatives have left for me, the bar that guarantees my success as an intellectual, has once again been raised, right after I arrived. Many years of education, from various institutions, a Ph.D. from a renowned private institution, the publication of several books and multiple articles, poems and essays, a permanent job, which in the 21st century becomes more rare, my keynote speeches, public speaking skills, multiple languages, and prior travel as well as connections mean little, if I cannot compete with the economic meaning of success, liquidity to expose others to my presence and scholarship. Thus, I am lacking social capital and social entitlement and because of this, am unable to influence ongoing cultural narratives.

In order to acquire this social capital, I would have to incur debt, and be married to a similar intellectual who agrees to give up camping and family vacations for conferences and symposiums, for which s/he is willing to borrow and invest, in order for me to become a top intellecutal in my discipline, in the American academy, in the world, since all of us are globally colonized by the established academic norms of Western universities. Or, I need to obtain a position in a rich private instititution whereby my institution is willing to subsidize my travels and other intellectual endeavors as part of my work package. This reflection is worthwhile in looking at equity and equality, can one happen without the other, which comes first the equality egg or the equity chicken?

Social Class Captives

(For Women Academics from the working class)
Unable to run from our lives
we construct rubrics
to measure the assets
of our possessions
since the debits are greater than the credits
we think. ...
but how do you count a hug, at a university, in pounds or letters,?
the hope a student has inside
the tear they reversed into a smile,
because you were the mathematician of their assets ...

How many universities become accordions, because someone read you?
Because your music played in barns, reservations, hoods and buses?
Because while you carried your daughter on your back
and held a book with one hand and your breast with the other, you cultivated
the future
in someone

What do we call the thoughts that couldn't happen?
lapsed truth,
or inclusive matter?

Perhaps only they,
the future intellectuals,
can escape
these captive lives
that social class thought
imposes on us
Gabriella Gutiérrez y Muhs

Closing Thoughts and the Yellow Brick Road

As the daughter of migrant/immigrant farm-working parents, who lived their lives in fear of their *patrones* firing them—or of someone else at the migrant camps making up something about them to steal their highly desired manual-labor position—I identified similar patterns of external and internalized oppression and undermining feelings of paranoia in academia. I recognized this as unsettling, particularly coming from the educated and privileged lot that ran these institutions. However, growing up I had practice by enduring difficult situations. I had been forced to redefine high school and college for my population of children of farmworkers who attended major universities, only to graduate and become the "Other." Similar to the role of an assistant professor of color or a professor from a background of poverty who now holds a position romanticized by the outside world, at times, my goals and achievements have been challenging to navigate without support and instruction.

I am a language, literature, culture professor, and cultural worker. I teach Chicana, Latina, and Latin American Literature. One of the books I teach is *Caramelo* by Sandra Cisneros from where I copied this quote:

> People said, [...] Take care of yourself. But how was Soledad to know what they meant? Cuidate. Take care of yourself. Hadn't she taken care of her stockings, polished her shoes, washed her ears, brushed her teeth, blessed herself when she passed a church, starched and ironed her petticoat, scrubbed her armpits with a soapy cloth, dusted off the soles of her feet before getting into bed, rinsed her bloody rags in secret when she had "the rule." But they meant take care of yourself "down there." Wasn't society strange? They demanded you not to become ... but they didn't tell you how not to. The priest, the pope, Aunty Fina[...]—Take care of yourself. But no one told you how to ... well, "how" exactly. (Cisneros, 2003, p. 250)

The beautiful painting on the cover of *Presumed Incompetent* is "Color Block Face" and was painted by Bernadette Elszy-Perez. I use "the Yellow Brick Road" as a powerful metaphor for the path that women, particularly women of color, have to travel by and through in the Academy, much similar to the mysterious road that young women like Celaya in the previous quote have to navigate as they enter womanhood. Of course, the reference to "the Yellow Brick Road" is from *The Wizard of Oz*. Like administrators and colleagues, the munchkins tell Dorothy to follow the Yellow Brick Road. They encourage her, but no one tells her where to go at the crossroads. Likewise, during the tenure-track process in academia, there are no signs telling you where to go from here. As I often found, paths diverge and there is no one there to guide you.

As a minority and a working-class feminist, I also observed that most of the women I knew were forced—if they wished to become part of the Academy—to blindly follow a yellow brick road without road signs. It was an imaginary and supposedly ethical yellow brick road, at best only described peripherally by others. This interminable road was supposed to lead us into a permanent position in an institution that was part of the U.S. Academy. I felt that academia's bedside manner was lacking, to put it mildly. It was lacking in providing a manual for new users, particularly for those who had invested deeply with high stakes, especially if they were women or came from the working class. Often new professors from the working class did not have the hidden agendas that other professors, a majority of them coming from the middle class and university-educated parents, possessed or could rely on for advice.

My advice for women of color is to nurture personal relationships with those who love you, and listen when they express concern for you. Sometimes loved ones know better than we do what is best for us. Be aware that, when psychologically injured at work, you may experience the stages of grief identified by Kübler-Ross (1969)—denial, anger, bargaining, depression, and acceptance. Awareness and understanding of these stages will facilitate your healing. Do not hesitate to receive support from a counselor or psychologist, especially when trusted friends are not physically accessible to you in your current location. Try not to take things personally. Finally, remember to laugh. Remember to take care of your body and your spirit. Enjoy the moments that make an academic's life worthwhile and gratifying. Remember that, even under the most challenging circumstance, ours is a noble profession and we can transform minds and lives daily. We are privileged to be where we are. We may have to change work locales, but there is a place where our contributions and skills are valued.

References

Cisneros, S. (2003). *Caramelo: A novel.* New York, NY: Vintage Books.

Goleman, D. (1995). *Emotional intelligence.* New York, NY: Bantam Books.

Gutiérrez y Muhs, G., Niemann, Y., González, C., & Harris, A. (Eds.). (2012). *Presumed incompetent: The intersections of race and class for women in academia.* Boulder, CO: Utah State University Press.

Hernández, F. (2013, March 26). *Remembering Cecilia Preciado Burciaga.* Retrieved from http://www.queridacecilia.com/

Kolbert, E. (2012, July 2). "Spoiled rotten: Why do kids rule the roost?" *The New Yorker.* Retrieved from http://www.newyorker.com/magazine/2012/07/02/spoiled-rotten

Kübler-Ross, E. (1969). *On death and dying.* New York, NY: Macmillan.

Watters, E. (2013, February 25). "We aren't the world." *Pacific Standard: The Science of Society.* Retrieved from http://www.psmag.com/magazines/magazine-feature-story-magazines/joe-henrich-weird-ultimatum-game-shaking-up-psychology-economics-53135/

4. The Labyrinth Path of Administration: From Full Professor to Senior Administrator

IRMA MCCLAURIN, VICTORIA CHOU, AND VALERIE LEE

Editors' Note:
    This chapter explores the journeys of three women who became senior adminis-trators. They share their reflections on their journey and the challenges and oppor-tunities of being a senior woman of color administrator in higher education. Dr. Irma McClaurin is Chief Diversity Officer at Teach for America (TFA). Prior to the appointment as Chief Diversity Officer, Dr. McClaurin held multi-ple administrative and faculty positions in higher education. After becoming a tenured professor in the study of Anthropology at the University of Florida, Dr. McClaurin entered the administrative realm of higher education by becoming Deputy Provost of Fisk University. Dr. McClaurin also served as the President at Shaw University and the Associate Vice President at the University of Minnesota. Dr. McClaurin received a Bachelor of Arts in American Studies from Grinnell College, a Master of Fine Arts in English with a specialty in Poetry, and a Doc-torate of Philosophy in Anthropology, both from the University of Massachusetts, Amherst.
    Dr. Victoria Chou is Interim Dean for the School of Education at Domini-can University and serves as Dean Emerita for the College of Education at the University of Illinois at Chicago (UIC). She was also the interim Executive Asso-ciate Chancellor for external and government relations. A former school teacher, Dr. Chou became a reading specialist in teacher education. Her research focus has been on reading competency and how to enhance the quality of teaching in Amer-ica's inner cities for people of color. She chaired UIC's Council for Excellence in Teaching and Learning, along with the Academic Affairs subcommittee of the Chancellor's Committee on the Status of Women. Dr. Chou helped co-found the Chancellor's Committee on the Status of Asian Americans, and the Institute for Research on Race and Public Policy. Dr. Chou earned her master's and doctorate degrees from the University of Wisconsin-Madison, and joined the UIC faculty in 1978.

Dr. Valerie Lee retired in 2015 from holding three administrative appointments at The Ohio State University. She served as Vice Provost for Diversity and Inclusion, Vice President for Outreach and Engagement, and Chief Diversity Officer. Prior to these appointments, Dr. Lee served both as Chair of the Department of English and the Department of Women's Studies. Dr. Lee was professor of English at Denison University from 1976 to 1991. She joined Ohio State University in 1991. Dr. Lee earned a Doctorate of Philosophy in English from The Ohio State University. In addition to several books and journal articles, she has served on the MA thesis, MA examination, and PhD dissertation committees for over 100 students.

This chapter begins with Dr. McClaurin's reflections on her senior leadership positions, including a presidency, a deputy provost position, and an associate vice president position.

Irma McClaurin

How did we women-of-color get here in the Academy? How did we transition from our roles as Associate Professors to Full Professors to becoming high level administrators in higher education: i.e., deans, provosts, vice presidents, and even university presidents? It is important to understand that in the Academy, there is an assumption that we, women of color, are not supposed to "get" into these positions as high-level administrators. In actuality, too often the roads that lead to these professional paths are those less traveled by women of color. So consider these facts: although women represent over 50% of students who enroll in and matriculate through college, and while students from racial and ethnic minority groups are now 34% of all college students, 75% of all college presidents are men, and mostly White men (Cook, 2012). This speaks about privilege and access to opportunity.

In 1961, President John F. Kennedy signed Executive Order 10925 which mandated anti-discrimination in government and ordered federal contractors to "… take affirmative action to ensure that applicants are employed, and that employees are treated during employment, without regard to their race, creed, color or national origin" (Kennedy, 1961). Moreover, 42 years after the passage of Title IX, and 94 years after the passage of the 19th Amendment that guaranteed that "the right of citizens of the United States to vote shall not be denied or abridged by the United States or by any State on account of sex," White men continue to overwhelmingly represent the face of university presidents nationwide (Cook, 2012). These major legislative and legal milestones were crafted to ensure equality in access and opportunities for women and historically underrepresented groups often referred to as ethnic and racial minorities. However, women today, and women from those historically disenfranchised ethnic and racial groups in particular are still disproportionately underrepresented in leadership positions that reflect arenas of power.

Ironically, where we expect to see the most progress is in our institutions of higher education. Yet, the numbers here are often worse than what we would expect in the corporate world. Upward mobility to leadership positions for women of color remains elusive and the successes dismal in the Academy. According to the American Council on Education (ACE) study of American college presidents, the key route to a college president is serving as a senior administrator. In 2008, only 16% of senior administrators in higher education were people of color with only ten percent being Chief Academic Officers (Cook, 2012). And so, in this post-Affirmative Action, post-Roe vs. Wade, "post-feminist," and supposedly "post-racial" moment, women still rarely sit at helms of power. Yet, when women are offered the opportunity to lead in the grand capacity of assuming the role of University President we marvel because they are the exceptions and not the rule. For women of color in particular, our presence as leaders is even rarer. If we do finally get to play in the power sandboxes, we are viewed and treated as the "exceptional" person of color rather than normative. As leaders, women of color often get one shot at the sand box to get it right.

Unlike White men or White women presidents, we often do not get a second chance, should our first try fail. There are no future job offers waiting for us in the wings. And, we must excel at even greater heights than our White male and female counterparts to simply be viewed as an equal. Regardless of our scholarship or prestige in the field, women of color in the Academy are consistently under scrutiny and observed for what we do wrong, yet rarely praised for what we do right. As Pamela Reid contextualized when referencing Ntozake Shange, "Being Black, a woman, and an academic is a metaphysical dilemma" (Reid, 2012). And so, some of the questions that we might ask ourselves—once we arrive in these power spaces that are not expecting us—are the following:

> What was I thinking? What can I, as a woman of color, accomplish? How do I create a work/life balance? Are there any further leadership opportunities? Who do I owe and to whom am I accountable in this leadership position—my institution, my community, my racial/gender group, myself, or, quite possibly, all of the above?

Given my experience as a former university president, I believe that women of color administrators can participate in significant institutional transformation. We can open up new spaces. We can also serve as mentors and support other people like us who represent the vulnerable and underserved ranks in high-level administrative positions. Because we actually embody diversity, people have to pay attention to the fact that we exist and are here to stay. There are, of course, historical reasons why people of color in the United States who have historically been excluded are just now being included in traditional institutional spaces of higher education.

This movement of inclusion was originally captured under the term of "multiculturalism," now "diversity." The terms "diversity, equity and inclusion" are the words and phrases that have captured the imagination of the Academy. But such terms do not necessarily translate into "authentic" power sharing. While there has been inclusion, simply adding diversity to the mixture is not enough, if such inclusion comes without authority, power, respect, and support. We must proceed cautiously when embracing the idea that "diversity" means anybody and everybody in our rush to be "inclusive." Diversity of thought, diversity of politics, and diversity of geography all have very different ramifications and possibilities than diversity of race/ethnicity, gender, abilities, or sexual orientation.

Racism and oppression are historical circumstances that created the need for diversity. However, what we are witnessing is that, while those historical circumstances may have generated the need and demand for inclusion, they did not necessarily translate into hiring practices that include individuals who have lived through exclusion or whose background and experiences are rooted in historical oppression and discrimination of their race or ethnic group. Further deceiving is the term "people of color" which has come to dominate the nomenclature, yet often it is totally unrelated to historical circumstances. Therefore, the challenge to diversity, equity, and inclusion today is that we now have new forms of marginalization. There are also serious trust issues within the institutions where we find ourselves serving as women of color administrators. And finally, sometimes the gate keepers put in place to delay, derail, or propel us resemble ourselves.

I own everything that I have experienced and I am grateful for each opportunity. My rise to become a high-ranked administrator in higher education began after my journey through the tenure-track process. I received tenure at the University of Florida. I have a Masters of Fine Arts in English, which is a terminal professional degree. I had enough publications to get tenure but when I moved into academic affairs, people would ask, "So, when will you get a real degree?" So, education and professional degrees are not viewed in the same way as a research degree. I also completed a research degree in anthropology. Thus through my work, I was positioning myself to be inside the Academy while at the same time, to be that oppositional voice. Therefore, the question I wrestled with most was: could I be inside the Academy without being a complete "insider?"

Administration fits very neatly into the work that I was doing as an anthropologist, which was looking at structural inequality. This is what I studied yet at the same time I considered myself a systems person, I also considered myself an activist. To me, administration is about the intersection of these two. I think part of the challenge is that some people fall into administration without considering all of its complexities. There is a program within the American Council on Education (ACE) called "ACE Fellows." As an ACE Fellow, people get to practice being an administrator before assuming a full-time appointment. There are also a lot of institutions that offer these diversity initiatives vis-á-vis on-the-job training. Many institutions have opportunities for assistant or associate dean positions prior to higher-level administrative duties.

While a tenured faculty member at the University of Florida, I found myself in Washington, DC on business. One day as I was walking down the street, the first Black woman president of Fisk University, who was also the first Black woman at Grinnell College hired on a tenure track back in the 1970s, was standing in front of me. During my academic pursuits, she had been a teacher of mine. We had a conversation and she offered me the opportunity to be Deputy Provost at Fisk. It sounded interesting. I accepted the offer and took a two year leave of absence from the University of Florida. Just as I was settling into my new position, six months later the Provost stepped down. Six months after he left, the President of Fisk University resigned. So, six months before my term was over I decided to simply resign because it was very challenging.

An opportunity arose at Bennett College in Greensboro, NC. I arrived on campus and founded their Africana Women's Study program. During the process of researching to create the program, I came across a position at the Ford Foundation. I applied and got the position. I became the Program Officer for Education and Scholarship for the Ford Foundation. Thus, because these opportunities continuously occurred as I was journeying through the tenure journey, I took another leave of absence. At that point my University of Florida colleagues, who are used to taking multiple leaves, decided the "colored girl" had enough. The administration said, "We think we've done enough for you." I was subsequently released from my tenured position. University of Florida included my sabbatical and my tenure in their severance package. In their minds, they felt that they had "given these things to me," rather than acknowledging that I had earned tenure and my sabbatical. That was the implication, at least. So, I demanded and received a year's leave of absence instead. When it came time to renew that, the Provost declined my request.

After this career redirection, I contemplated going back to Gainesville or simply staying in New York at the Ford Foundation, where I had the job of giving away $10.9 million. I decided to stay in New York. When I was at Ford, I would have these amazing ideas but I could not give funding to myself. So, being able to "let go" was the most difficult. Due to obvious conflict of interests, if it was a good agenda I basically had to give it over to someone else. As a scholar whose been trained in the highly individualistic mode, that is a difficult thing to do. But, I think in many ways it also prepared me for the work I had to do as a university president, which involved being able to delegate. I learned that you cannot do everything yourself. I have worked at Predominantly White Institutions (PWIs), research institutions, public land-grant institutions, women's colleges—both Black and White, and I have also worked at Historically Black Colleges and Universities (HBCUs). Structure is structure and none of it is perfect.

After my time with the Ford Foundation, I went to the University of Minnesota where I helped with renovating a 21,000 sq. ft. shopping center by transforming it into a university research center to be based in the community—the Urban Research and Outreach-Engagement Center (UROC). This project put me in the foray of community engagement and in some ways was like doing anthropology work again. Through my work with UROC, I had one foot in the community and the other foot inside the institution.

Titles do matter. They can be strategic and they tell you to whom you report. At the University of Minnesota, I was both an Associate Vice President and the founding Executive Director. I could go to other offices and leverage my title in order to get things moving. Titles speak about access to power. You should not keep interim titles for more than a year because they are a dead end. As people are reviewing you during a search process, if you have been "Interim" for too long, you are not seen as someone who has actually held that position. It is a great entrée point into administration, but if you hang on for too long it can pigeonhole you in the wrong direction.

Some administrative positions do not come with tenure. It took a year before I got tenure at the University of Minnesota. It is important to get tenure when you have the opportunity. Once you have tenure, there are more opportunities. Joining administration after having been a tenured faculty member provides a place or position to return after you have completed your appointment as administrator. In the back of your head you may desire to stay there for five years or twenty years, but you also have to remain cognizant of your willingness to walk away. If there is a change in administration, they may decide that you are not the person they want in that position. Therefore, it is always beneficial to have a second plan of action. Aim to achieve "Plan A," but also have a "Plan B" ready as well.

Sometimes you are brought in because the administration does not know what they want to do and you are the guinea pig. You are also supposed to be the "Superwoman of color," the "Super Black woman," the "Super Latina," or the "Super Asian woman" because they want you to be accountable. Then, when you do make the changes, they no longer need you around. From my experiences, fellow administrators would rather work along someone who looks more like them and that they are more comfortable with. So, one of the things that you have to know is that as you move into these positions you have to be willing to walk away. I have been tenured twice. And, I have also walked away from it twice.

After three years at Minnesota, I left to become President of Shaw University. My time as President of Shaw University was short-lived. That love affair lasted eleven months, and then we had a divorce. I had a five-year contract at Shaw and I only served eleven months. As you ascend in administrative positions, make sure you have a good attorney who understands the kinds of contracts that are needed and where it is possible to negotiate, otherwise you can get screwed.

As higher educational administrators, we have accumulated new knowledge bases that we had to figure out in order to be successful. We each had to learn how to leverage challenges, not only in terms of doing the work before us, but also in being consistent and faithful for why we, as women of color, got into the Academy originally. The word transformation is really not in the vocabulary at academic institutions. As an administrator, you can make some changes, you can tweak protocols, and you might get a little innovation, but these institutions are rooted in historical tradition. They were here before we arrived and they will be there after we are long gone. You have to be clear and realistic about what is really possible, if you go in with a vision of being a change agent. To effectually do this, I have some tips for future women of color administrators.

As a president, you are required to administratively network. How you network, as well as what positions you accept, primarily depends on where you want to go. If you see yourself moving up the ladder to a presidency or vice presidency, particularly if you are in charge of external community relations, having some knowledge of what those sectors are and how they operate is important. As president, I used a search agency to build relationships. I got an invitation to what they called the "50's Club," which historically included 50 White men who were there because of the positions they had. Different kinds of organizations will give you exposure and access to resource and knowledge bases. This is a form of capital because it opens up opportunities to move in other arenas. Administratively networking is resource building.

Second, make sure that change is what the institution/department/office actually wants versus what they said they want, because what they said and what they mean might be two different things. Read the landscape of your environment very carefully. Also, be clear about what cultural changes you will be able to impact. Finally, you will have to be willing to walk away from any position that does not value your input. The higher up you get in administration, the more challenging the profession becomes. It does not matter what race you are—most of the administrators and powers of authority are men, and their understanding and the perceptions of women and women leadership can be very different. Many men have an expectation of how you should present yourself as well as what you should present. So, when you take that step to move into senior administrative positions, some of us know it is a stroke of luck if you get to retire from them because you serve at the will of whatever power there is.

One of the challenges a faculty person has when stepping into administration are the different layers of collegiality. As faculty, your colleagues and you operate in a certain kind of relationship. As you move into administration, it is a job. It is not your family, and they are not your friends. They are colleagues. You have to be clear about what kind of relationship you want with other administrators before you find ways to be successful in the culture. Then, we must all deal with the "likability factor." Our clothes matter, how you present yourself matters, and how we relate to people matters. The higher you climb the administrator's ladder, the more it matters. Likability is something you have to count in with your attitude. Other factors to consider are how you respond to conflict, team playing, and collaboration.

Administrators have journeys of transition. Some of us are more accidental administrators than others. Many of us did not plan on becoming administrators. Yet, some of us have very strategically moved through layers, individually, while some of us have probably been very collective. I have been told that I do not fit the paradigm by individuals who work with senior administrators, but each of us has a story that talks about the path by which we arrived in our current position.

Victoria Chou

Editors' Note: Dr. Victoria Chou's reflections build upon Dr. McClaurin's. Dr. Chou describes her journey into administration and shares the identity shifts she had to make to be successful. She also provides advice and suggestions for women considering administrative paths.

I was getting ready to leave for China for my first sabbatical in 1989 when the Tiananmen Square massacre happened a month prior to our leaving. It stopped me and my family, including my then one-year old daughter, in our tracks. It was the same year that our dean and two college associate deans retired. Because I was foregoing the sabbatical, the acting dean invited me to be associate dean, which is what started me on the path of administration twenty-five years ago. I have now served as dean in the University of Illinois at Chicago's College of Education for seventeen years.

In 2013, I took on an additional administrative role and agreed to serve as Interim Executive Associate Chancellor for external and government relations. As with a deanship, the role deals with external relationships, albeit with different constituencies and their unique issues and problems. I have learned more about public transportation and advanced manufacturing in a short few months than in all of my previous years. I convene and am involved in networks of communicators in other units. The work has presented me with new challenges to unpack and understand, several new vocabularies, and expanded understandings of administrative roles in general.

I thought it would be useful to share the personal identity shifts I made as I grew into the administrative role. I learned these lessons organically through the experience of being an administrator. They may be useful for those considering a move to administration in the academy. The first shift is from "we" to "they." One of the shifts I found I had to make was moving from being a member of "we," as in "labor," to being a member of "they," as in "management." When you make this journey, or when this is made for you, you are "othered" in a whole new way by your former compadres. Your actions will be read as *their* actions. You are no longer an inner circle member of a unified body, and so all the folks you thought you had in your trust group are now on the other side of the wall by virtue of their roles vis-à-vis your role. You now must make consequential decisions about your former mates. They may be afforded input, but only you have the authority to make the decision. Those faculty colleagues and friends who do maintain relationships with you may get read as currying special favors with you or you may be perceived as granting special favors, which is something you have to watch for. Even those you thought were your most trusted friends may now have you in a box labeled "boss," and that changes the nature of the relationship.

Succeeding at administration requires discretion and treating confidences as sacred, even when doing so ensures that full information that might have created understanding cannot be divulged. As a result, distrust, the exact response you do not want, can be created. This can be frustrating, as most administrators know. While two-way disclosure and free flow of communication generally can and will foster greater understanding, you are prohibited from sharing or disclosing information because of the promise of confidentiality. When you cannot always reveal all that you know about a personnel issue or various matters, the other party will naturally respond in kind. In a low-trust context, the other party may understandably respond incompletely, tentatively, and mistrustfully. Trustworthiness has to be earned and demonstrated over and over again, over time. Even then, trust-worthiness is still fragile, provisional, and not guaranteed.

It is important to learn fairly quickly whom you can trust. To ensure trust, you need to have your own circle of trusted colleagues who can provide you with honest feedback. These colleagues should also be individuals who allow you to safely vent. When fine-tuning your thinking, you will see that some folks will be more trustworthy than others. Figure out who your allies are. Because you have to pay special attention to your own power and privilege when dealing with others with less or more power and privilege, ideally you would like to find another "we" at a similar level of authority and power who is capable of giving you straight feedback that you are willing to listen to.

The second shift is from taking care of number one to taking care of others. As an academic you are responsible for yourself. You theoretically are supposed to earn tenure on your own merits and, in many disciplines, you cannot be viewed as collaborating too much. But going from being responsible for creating merit for you, as an academic, to being responsible for supporting others' accomplishments requires a second necessary identity switch. As an administrator, you are responsible, depending upon your position, for the success and welfare of the unit, the department, the university, whichever unit you are assigned to. Whether you like folks or not or whether they like you or not; whether you trust folks or they trust you, you are responsible for their well-being. Moreover, you have to understand that your boss is your boss and manage that. Also, your boss's boss is your boss's boss and cannot be managed by you. You also have to know how to manage down and support others and mentor. Your new identity often has little to do with your own hard-won scholarly identity. Personally, it gave me a little boost of credibility among the faculty to start with but that dissipates quickly, if you cannot help faculty meet their own professional goals.

As a full professor you are invited to author a chapter here or deliver a presentation there and it gives you that sense of still being a scholar, but you would be kidding yourself if you thought you could maintain the same active research life as an administrator that you enjoyed as a faculty member. Your time is no longer your own: the time demands are significant, including in meetings not of your making. There is also unpredictability in administration because of the way things come up that have to be addressed at the moment. You lose those blocks of time where you can really think and reflect about ideas or stay with a paper until it is finished. Scholarship is simply very tough to maintain at a high level of quality. Right now I cannot say that I am an active researcher or scholar, though it was an integral part of my faculty identity that I found very satisfying. It may be pure rationalization, but I believe I continue to bring that critical, questioning, analytic consciousness to everything I do as an administrator.

Other administrators understand better than most what counts as success in administration. You are evaluated and rewarded on an utterly different basis. It is no longer about toting up grant dollars or racking up top-refereed journal articles or academic honors. Other factors are taken into consideration for the metrics that are now so all-important in administration. You have to make the time to learn the new landscape well (i.e., deep structure, assets, challenges, scope of responsibilities, politics and especially the people). You have to be able to forgive yourself for making mistakes and learn from them.

The third shift is from talk to walk in transforming the academy. Why do we do all of this? Why would you want to make this transition? From my standpoint, it is because you can transform the Academy from within all of these administrative places. If we open it up by virtue of who we are, we have a different kind of consciousness that we bring to the table. We can invite others inside by accepting positions of decision-making to make sure voices are heard. Future women of color administrators can speak on behalf of those who have not been included and you can keep hammering about needing to get excluded people included. You may not be able to spend all of your time every day speaking truth to power, but you can figure out how to do it well and very smoothly. You can model different, more collaborative, and inclusive forms of leadership. There are other ways of being a leader and we really need to see these other ways. I still find that the higher up in the hierarchy you go, the more you find that the White alpha male form of leadership is still holding sway. You have to be part of the solution, and you have to pick your battles. Pick your battles rather than fighting every war so that you do not burn yourself out trying to fix everything for everyone.

As a learner-administrator, you can learn more than you ever thought you could because it is authentic practice. Administration is a space where you can see how theory actually translates to practice. Most importantly, you see firsthand how you are a part of that change.

I want to say encouragingly that we need that critical mass inside administration so that you change the structure. But it is really a personal issue that you wrestle with. I would also think that you can try out leadership roles; whether it is taking on a major committee, chairing a search, or accepting an interim vice provost or temporary two-year cycle position to see how it suits you. You should know what your job description is and the metrics used to evaluate you. You can also find the spaces where something needs to be done and push the agenda yourself in the same way you would working as a team. The job descriptions do not have to be personal.

You can be invited to almost any other administrative position, under the position of a dean, without having been a faculty member. Depending on what your discipline is, you can bring some of that scholarship into your administrative work. As you have found with the literature, you can maintain your interest in research, but it is not the same as authoring and publishing original work.

In terms of networking and professional organizations, it is important to keep your original set of professional organizations so you can maintain the number of networks you are in. As a dean, I am a member of other "dean-alike" groups. Professionally, I have found them to be very useful. There are some organizations that are better than others. Again, select those that fit with your professional goals.

Finally, in terms of negotiating, some organizations have information on the web that you can actually find so it is important to do your homework. I would also call networks and find people in similar roles, and ask around. There are more of us in these roles and we would be happy to offer information and advice.

Valerie Lee

Editors' Note: Dr. Valerie Lee provides some closing thoughts about the challenges of administration, including managing teams, making difficult decisions, and leveraging resources.

When associate professors at my university are promoted to full professor, we are invited to give an inaugural lecture to thank the Academy for making such a sound decision. During this lecture, we celebrate our past accomplishments and outline our future scholarly trajectory. Although as grateful as any colleague who has weathered the rigorous process from assistant to full professor, I, nevertheless, wanted the Academy to understand that I managed the system with the same ambivalence, and sometimes mask-wearing, as Ralph Ellison's protagonist in *Invisible Man*. That is, although I had reached the final frontier, I was always a pioneer with another roadmap. I titled my tenured talk "Smarts" and argued that historically African Americans often have shaped knowledge from an interpretative standpoint different from the traditional Academy's paradigm (Lee, 2005).

The larger point of my talk was that although earning full professorship was a rewarding goal, some of us come from communities where those who are formally educated are expected to give back, reach back, and talk back to those upon whose shoulders we rose. Administration has allowed me to give more comprehensive and hands-on, direct-impact service. I have done this by first serving as an elected chair of a fifteen tenure-track and tenured faculty Women's Studies Department and then as a two-term, 102 tenured and tenure-track Department of English. These chairships led to my current positions as Vice Provost of Diversity and Inclusion, Vice President of Outreach and Engagement, and Chief Diversity Officer.

My titles are not honorific. They represent a lot of work. As night settles on our campus oval, others often ask, "Why don't you go home? You do not have to do all that you do." Well, I do not want to do too much sitting down at the very stage of transition when I have the power and the authority to stand up for structural change. If racism and sexism and all the other "isms" are still hurting us, am I supposed to take a sabbatical from a social justice agenda? The transition from full professor to administrator has allowed me to create the changes that I have wanted to see from the earliest days of my career. As I admitted in an essay,

> There is the administrative pleasure of actually getting things done. It is not nearly the same joy as reading a Toni Morrison novel, nor is it as provocative an experience as discussing the future of the humanities. What high-level administration provides is the opportunity to revise the rules, reclaim what and who has been marginalized, and renegotiate terms of engagement. (College English, 2011)

My most difficult decisions are the ones when I have to down-size staff. How can I look at the reduction-in-force papers in front of me and not acknowledge that I am affecting people's lives, their health plans, their children's educational costs, and their ability to regain selfhood? As an administrator, I have prided myself on getting better and better at delivering bad news. Yet, it is the good news of student access and achievement that I most want to share.

Leveraging resources is very important. I could not do my job well if I did not work with a range of different administrators. Diversity is everyone's business. I do not want my office to be a silo for diversity. I believe in moving from silos to solidarity. When I'm hiring, for certain positions I prefer a faculty background. For other positions, a corporate or industry background is desirable. Institutional history and goals should be considered. I have learned from working with people from a variety of backgrounds.

My faculty appointments in English, Women's Gender and Sexuality Studies, the Center for Folklore Studies, Comparative Studies, African American and African Studies, and the Center for Interdisciplinary Law and Policy Studies have taught me a lot about working in the intersections. Interdisciplinary scholars are used to focusing their time and talents in strategic ways.

Additionally, I have great teams that help to support and execute the visions and missions of my respective offices.

Although I have not given up my research agenda, I have had to change it. I am in a department where single-authored books are respected, but it is hard for me to have the kind of sustained time that it takes to produce a scholarly monograph. I now do more book chapters, journal articles, and scholarship on administration itself rather than on literary theory. Many people do not understand that when you are doing "diversity," this is a field you just cannot get up and "do" because you are a person of color. It is a field of research, theory, and practice. As a senior administrator, I now engage in diversity research and I facilitate the research of others. For example, my office sponsors a dissertation writing boot camp for underrepresented students and a writing retreat for junior faculty of color.

I've learned it is important for us to know that we really need to be able to walk away because sometimes we work with people who do not share the same values. I remember at the beginning of my career when I was teaching at a private institution where everyone was supposed to live in that small town, never mind that doing so would have made me the only minority resident. I promptly decided that I would be the first junior faculty to move away to the closest city. The chair called me in and asked, "Do you realize that by moving to the city you could jeopardize your tenure? Tenure is your job security and you could lose it by not staying in this community." At twenty-six years old and oblivious to what lifelong job security meant, I blurted out, "I come from a long line of unemployed people. If this job ends, I'll just pick up another one." Freedom to make my own choices has always been a higher priority for me than stability.

Conclusion

Editors' Note: As the reflections indicate, the path to administration is a unique path for many women of color. It still remains a path on which very few have travelled. The glass ceiling, adobe ceiling, bamboo ceiling, and plantation roof are powerful barriers to the advancement of women of color. Rising to senior administrative leadership positions is indeed a significant accomplishment for women of color. It is often a necessary step in the journey to a presidency.

References

Cook, B. J. (2012, March 12). *The American college president study: Key findings and takeaways.* American Council on Education. Retrieved from http://www.acenet.

edu/the-presidency/columns-and-features/Pages/The-American-College-President-Study.aspx

Kennedy, J. F. (1961, March 6). Establishing the President's Committee on Equal Employment Opportunity: Executive Order 10925. Retrieved from http://www.eeoc.gov/eeoc/history/35th/thelaw/eo-10925.html

Lee, V. (2005). Smarts: A cautionary tale. In J. J. Rosyter & A. M. Simpkins (Eds.), *Calling cards: Theory and practice in the study of race, gender and culture* (pp. 93–105). New York, NY: SUNY Press.

Lee, V. (2011). Celebrating the NCTE Centennial Symposium: How I have changed my mind. *College English, 74*(2), 118–120.

Reid, P. T. (2012, spring). *Black and female in academia.* Retrieved from http://www.acenet.edu/the-presidency/columns-and-features/Pages/Black-and-Female-in-Academia.aspx

Part II

On the Stage

5. *A View from the Helm: A Black Woman's Reflection on Her Chancellorship*

Paula Allen-Meares

Editors' Note:
> Dr. Paula Allen-Meares is Chancellor Emerita and the John Corbally Presidential Professor, Professor of Medicine, and Executive Director of the Office of Health Literacy, Prevention, and Community Engagement at the University of Illinois at Chicago (UIC). She holds appointments in the School of Social Work, the School of Public Health, and the College of Education. She served as Chancellor of the University of Illinois at Chicago (UIC) and Vice President of the University of Illinois from 2009–2015. She is also Dean and Professor Emerita and the Norma Radin Collegiate Professor at the University of Michigan where she served as dean of the School of Social Work for 15 years.
>
> She earned her bachelor's degree at the State University of New York at Buffalo and master's and PhD degrees from the University of Illinois Urbana-Champaign. She rose through the ranks at the University of Illinois at Urbana-Champaign and served as Dean of Social Work there. She holds certificates from the University of Michigan, Harvard University, and the Kellogg School of Management at Northwestern University. She received an honorary doctorate degree in humane letters from the State University of New York. Portions of the narrative below are adapted from a conversation published in the Spring 2015 UIC Alumni Magazine (Smith, 2015) and are shared with permission.

The Journey to Chancellor

If you had asked me several decades ago whether I would become chancellor of one of the largest urban campuses in the nation, I would have said no. But it is terribly strange, life's somewhat independent trajectory. Or, at least, it appears to be independent of my dreams and ambitions. I was content doing a job I loved, and I had little aspiration to lead a twenty-first century campus.

In terms of my family, my father believed that education would be the great equalizer among the races. He, as well as my mother, were deeply engaged in our schooling. My mother took on leadership roles in the school and community. In fact, public school teachers would visit our home for coffee and my mother's special sweets. My siblings and I were to be engaged learners and respectful of our teachers and others. One teacher in particular became my mentor and was another voice in my life space regarding the importance of college. My family integrated in an all "majority" community which over the decades became very diverse.

Perhaps, though, well-timed opportunities that built on each other over a lifetime explain how I arrived at this place. Early in my academic career, I directed the graduate specialization program, then a doctoral program. I became a liaison to the MD/PhD program, and a member of several major university committees. I was elected to the executive committee of the school while an assistant professor and, eventually, I became dean of the school where I had earned my master's degree and Ph.D.

Along the path to the chancellorship I encountered other preparatory opportunities—a CIC Fellowship; time at Harvard's Graduate School of Management Program for workshops on budgeting, compensation, frames for viewing organizations, legal issues in higher education, and university-community relations; time at the University of Michigan's business school for workshops designed to facilitate deans' to capacity to lead the changing landscape of higher education; and most recently, certificate work at Northwestern University on creating a twenty-first century culture of entrepreneurship and innovation.

In addition to these value-added opportunities, I learned on the job. Over the years I was elected and/or appointed treasurer of a national accreditation body; president of a research society; chair of a national publishing organization; board member of the W. T. Grant Foundation; fellow and board member of New York Academy of Medicine; and member of visiting committees such as University of Washington in St. Louis, University of Southern California, and University of Pittsburgh. In 2007, I was elected to the Institute of Medicine (IOM)/National Academy of Sciences where I served on the Membership Committee and now serve on the Awards Committee.

During my tenure in various administrative positions and appointments, I was compelled to contribute to scholarship and research like other noble citizens of the academy, and to serve as principal and co-principal investigator on projects funded by federal, foundation, and state sources. In these endeavors I aimed to model what was expected of the faculty. Perhaps I also feared losing my faculty identity—which, by the way, appears to be more long-lasting than my administrator identity.

Along the way, I have had the good fortune of excellent mentors from various levels of higher education and government. Chancellors, presidents, provosts, and public servants were available to share important ideas and strategize about strategic planning, fundraising, politics, and academic medical centers.

During the "12th World Summit of Nobel Peace Laureates," held at UIC from April 23–25, 2012, my mother died. There sat former U.S. President Jimmy Carter (2002 Laureate), former U.S. President William Clinton, former President of the USSR Mikhail Gorbachev (1990 Laureate), former President of South Africa Wilem de Klerk (1993 Laureate), former President of Costa Rica Oscar Arias, former president of Poland Lech Walesa (1983 Laureate), Kerry Kennedy-President of the Robert F. Kennedy Center for Justice and Human Rights, The Dalai Lama Tibet, Sean Penn, and Professor Jodi Williams (1997 Nobel Peace Prize recipient) to name only a few. Then during the 2013–2014 extensive faculty union negotiations, my fifth year review occurred, and my sister died of an aggressive form of cancer. The bottom line is that life "happens" and the work of the university "happens" at the same time.

A Chancellor's Profile

My physical profile is not typical of most individuals who occupy high-level academic leadership roles in higher education. At a retreat for women deans, one female majority dean contrasted her presence with mine: "I am a very large person with deep and robust voice, which intimidates some of the males on my faculty," she said of herself. She described me as a short African American female with a softer voice. Whereas her profile intimidated some, my profile could go unnoticed and/or ignored. I often wondered if this one conversation at a retreat of women from public and private research institutions could be generalized to others who shared my profile.

During my chancellorship, some were surprised when they met me. Some thought I would be taller. Others were surprised that *I* was the chancellor: I just didn't look like what they had envisioned. Once, someone asked if I were the secretary, and another asked, "Where is the Chancellor?" The so-called typical profile of a chancellor/president/vice president is still majority male, at least six feet tall, and graying or balding. The typical chancellor possesses a disciplinary background—medicine, bench science, business, law, or engineering. Higher education, like the broader society, goes through phases. Earlier, a chancellor needed to be a dean of literature, or arts and sciences. More recently, lawyers were preferred. Today, there appears to be a focus on engaging chancellors who have a background in one of the sciences and/or medicine. As an elected member of the Institute of Medicine and co-chair of the University of Michigan Health Sciences Committee, I brought this discipline, and its association with innovation and economic renewal, to the helm of the University of Illinois at Chicago.

Why UIC?

I was attracted to UIC's rich urban context and the vision of the search committee that recommended my appointment. UIC's strategic plan was impressive, and I was eager to further it—to promote interdisciplinary research and educational programs, cultivate global leadership skills among our students, foster a culture of innovation and excellence, and increase the prominence and recognition of UIC's translational research.

For our faculty, I also sought to create a culture of collaboration, intellectual opportunity, and discipline. I came to UIC from the University of Michigan, where the commercialization of research was common: good ideas led to funding, and academic health centers flourished. I brought this experience to UIC where we created the Chancellor's Innovation Fund and the Chancellor's Discovery Fund, both to support promising research and innovation.

Operating on the assumption that "a culture of discipline is not a principle of business; it is a principle of greatness" (Collins, 2001, p. 1), I was proactive in retaining productive, self-motivated faculty driven to be the very best. As chancellor, I set the tone here, encouraging the provost and deans to hire and retain the very best faculties, and created, in conjunction with the Provost's Office, a campus-level committee to nominate excellent faculty and academic administrators for membership in honorific societies/associations. Such collaboration, discipline, and excellence should be celebrated, so I was delighted to expand the annual faculty achievement awards ceremony to include a robust reception and participation of the president of the system.

I came convinced that improving student success is critical, and that students should come to UIC and graduate. Consequently, we changed our mantra from "Access to Excellence" to "Access to Excellence and Success," and acted to make that mantra reality. When I began my tenure as chancellor, the graduation rate for full-time students was 54% over six years. In 2014, the graduation rate was 60%. I also deepened UIC's commitment and relationship to neighborhoods, communities, businesses, and government agencies, so that students could enjoy robust internships and real-world learning opportunities so that they are prepared when they do graduate.

I came believing that organizational "greatness is an inherently dynamic process, not an end point" (Collins, 2001, p. 9). As Collins (2001) explains, "the moment you think of yourself as great, your slide toward mediocrity will have begun" (p. 9). Thus, when we created the UIC Student Success Initiative we developed a mission-driven agenda and outcomes (e.g. retention and graduation rates, retrospective assessments of time on campus, the quality of teaching, and employability), benchmarked against a peer group as well as an aspirational group. In this initiative and others like it, we aimed to avoid the slide toward mediocrity.

Overall, I wanted to spark conversations about important issues—among them innovation, health equity, massive open online courses, sustainability, collaboration, and diversity. I feel we've made some tremendous gains in those areas. The conversations today are richer and more informed, and in many areas, we have moved from conversation to action in myriad ways. We created new learning opportunities for students, among them the Chancellor's Graduate Fellowship Program and the Global Learning Community Campus Certificate Program. At the undergraduate level, we expanded research opportunities by developing a partnership among the honors college, other academic units, and the chancellor's office. We also created the Cluster Hire Initiative to increase diversity and UIC's interdisciplinary culture. These tangible programs support UIC's pursuit of its strategic plan and its development as a diverse, and collaborative, campus.

Framing Higher Education

During my time at Harvard, I learned to use organizational frames to understand higher education organizations. A "frame is a coherent set of extras forming a prism or lens that enables you to see and understand more clearly what goes on day to day in an organization" (Bolman & Deal, 2008, p. 43). There are four frames: structural, human resource, political, and symbolic.

The structural frame places people in the correct roles/responsibilities. Structures must be designed to achieve organizational goals/objectives; sub-structures within an organization must be coordinated and necessary policies/procedures put in place as controls that provide direction. There is a division of labor. The human resource frame recognizes that organizations serve human needs. For organizations to function, they need ideas, human capital, and vision. In return, personnel receive salaries, careers, opportunities, and a sense of belonging. In higher education, we often provide training and workshops to keep personnel current and informed of new priorities/policies, ensuring that organizational needs and personnel talent pools are congruent.

The political frame recognizes that organizations are political arenas in which considerable drama can occur. Groups comprising an organization may have conflicting agendas, or may embrace divergent preferences for managing an issue confronting the organization. Interest groups and coalitions desire power and control and may use bargaining and negotiation to achieve consensus. Separate unions consisting of faculty and graduate students could form an "interest coalition" during negotiations.

The symbolic/cultural frame recognizes that events, rituals, and ceremonies create shared experiences that foster an organizational culture and express values that bond members. These events and the process that accompanies them are often more important than the actual outcomes. Celebrations of a new building or a major multidisciplinary grant, for example, are proud moments in an organization's history.

Framing at UIC

At UIC I met with diverse stakeholders, sharing hope, vision, and actions we could embrace (human frame); worked with university administration to secure additional resources and support for financial aid and new facilities (political frame); convened gatherings that "showcased" the fruits of our shared labor (symbolic frame); and articulated a vision and work plan for the Student Success Initiative (structural frame).

But it wasn't just these frames that provided a prism. A set of values guided our institutional actions—a search for excellence throughout the organization; an aspiration for additional trans—and interdisciplinary research and educational programs (like the new Department of Bioengineering); and attention to infrastructure needs that support the mission of research, teaching, and service. The creation of expertise in the Office of the Vice Chancellor for Research to support clinical trials was another action to advance institutional excellence.

I worked with constituencies and stakeholders as varied as the faculty senate, student leadership, chancellors, and the president's team to rationally plan for UIC's growth. However, as it often does, "life happened," and we encountered disruptive forces ranging from union strikes to sudden, drastic reductions in revenue. As chancellor, I found myself trying to integrate a specific frame in response to a disruptive force. After all, the ultimate objective is to increase excellence in all aspects of our work. This pursuit of excellence has been my guiding principle across frames and disruptions.

It was in this crucible that I learned, once again, that

leadership is not about being "soft" or "nice" or purely "inclusive" or "consensus building." It is to make sure the right decisions happen—no matter how difficult or painful—for the long term greatness of the institution and the achievement of its mission, independent of consensus or popularity. (Collins, 2001, p. 11)

During my tenure as chancellor, I exercised leadership by hearing the voices of an issue's many stakeholders—unless it was a confidential/legal/personal matter where I was advised not to share and/or discuss information. When unpopular decisions were made, even following extensive collaboration, they were done so to advance the long-term greatness of the institution, with personal/professional risks to me.

There were several key achievements by the team during my tenure at UIC. We secured landmark gifts, including the Department of Bioengineering, the Baseball Stadium, the College of Dentistry Clinic, and the College of Engineering space. We also dedicated and opened the first federally qualified health center in the Chicago area. We established the Chancellor's Committee on Sustainability, the Chancellor's Student Advisory Committee, the Office of Diversity with permanent funding, and the Office of Veteran Services. We initiated recruitment for the African American Enrollment Initiative; created the vision for Student Success Initiative; secured UIC's place as an emerging Hispanic Serving Institution; and supported the Asian American, Native American, Pacific Islander Serving Institution Grant Initiative. We created the Chancellor's Global Excellence Task Force; launched both the UIC Dialogues Initiative and the Chancellor's Initiative in Humanities in Food Studies; and developed the Chancellor's Lecture and Event Series. We achieved US News and World Report Ranking in 2013 of #128, a five-way tie among national universities, an improvement of 19 spots from 2012; and achieved top 25 ranking as an LGBTQ-friendly campus from Campus Pride and Huffington Post, among other achievements.

My Affair with Diversity

My experience as an African American woman; the bold thinking undergirding the University of Michigan's agenda to diversify higher education; my majority mentors deeply committed to diversity; and challenges to affirmative action via the United States Supreme Court have formed my view of higher education's role in educating all Americans. American demography is more diverse than ever, and we must provide access to education for all of our citizens in order to continue *E Pluribus Unum*, "out of many, one." That access should be grounded in a comprehensive, holistic evaluation of a student's potential—not in privilege conferred by birth, skin color, or economic position. National prosperity and advancement are at risk if we fail at this objective.

Nor are these views mine alone. A substantive body of social science research compiled by the University of Michigan, much of it shared as expert testimony in anti-affirmative action lawsuits, indicates that students in diverse settings learn to think in deep and complex ways not always available in a monocultural environment (University of Michigan, 1999). Exploring the value of diversity in an educational setting, Dey, Gurin and colleagues (2004) unpack the layers of diversity we encounter in higher education:

> Structural diversity represents the percentage of a student body that is from an ethnic/racial group other than white. Then there is classroom diversity, defined as exposure to knowledge about race and ethnicity in formal classrooms. Then there is interactional diversity, defined as the extent to which students interact with peers from different backgrounds, different from their own. (p. 116)

As higher education leaders, we desire our students to become comfortable and skilled in engaging all three aspects of diversity. At UIC, we began to address this need by convening a Dialogue Initiative, courses that bring together students from different social identity groups for sustained engagement in credit-bearing courses. These courses allow students to listen, to discuss important social issues, and to learn from and about one another's points of view. This campus wide initiative seeks to capitalize on UIC's structural diversity, deepening students' engagement with a global and pluralistic community, preparing them to thrive in pluralistic professional and social environments.

At each institution I served, diversity of people and ideas was both a value and an objective. In the 1960s, it was a moral imperative that we educate all, in order to thrive in a diverse and democratic society. Over the years, panels on diversity, special committees for recruitment, cluster hires, and collaborations with institutions of color—the list goes on—were employed as strategies to achieve the objectives of diversity and inclusivity. More recently, the moral position has been replaced with concern for reverse discrimination; thus, we are witnessing the emergence of anti-affirmative action. Moreover, while some institutions are numerically diverse, this diversity follows a "plantation model." That is, the institution's leadership team remains majority, setting educational policies and practices, while the student body and lower-level staff are diverse in composition.

As higher education leaders, we must remain cognizant of how the value and objective of diversity have unfolded and strive for true diversity at all institutional levels. As we do, and as we model and provide opportunities for learning, working, and living together, we prepare our students to thrive in the diverse and global twenty-first century.

Facing Challenges

Changes in University Leadership

The University of Illinois is comprised of three campuses located in Spring-field, Urbana-Champaign, and Chicago. Each campus has a chancellor who reports to the president of the system. There is a governed board of trustees who oversees this structure. I did not expect that, during my six years as chancellor, the University of Illinois would have four different presidents, with a fifth joining us in 2015, or that we would have four different board chairs, each requesting to educate the new team. Each new leader needed to learn UIC's history, challenges, and opportunities; each brought a particular vision or charge to the office. Thus we navigated six years of near-constant recalibration and unpredictability.

Some presidents, for example, believed the University of Illinois was a system with three unique campuses; others asserted it was one university with unnecessary duplication of costly infrastructure. One advocated for the centralization of human resources and technology services, suggesting that they report directly to his office with a campus designate liaison. Another encouraged international agreements.

Budget and Facilities

Over a ten-year period, UIC lost about 10% of its general state revenue. However, we continued to receive state-paid benefits for our employees and to negotiate rising costs. In addition, facilities and classrooms continued to age; years had passed with no capital appropriation for campus infrastructure improvements. The state's financial challenges limited UIC's ability to address deferred maintenance.

The team and I worked hard to raise funds and create an entrepreneurial culture at UIC that would ensure greater financial stability for the campus. During my tenure, we exceeded a fundraising campaign by $25 million, raising a grand total of $676 million. Despite reduced revenue, we were able to renovate almost 100 classrooms, labs, and buildings using reallocation and sharing responsibility with schools, colleges, and UIC administration.

In 2012, approximately 20 years after the Illinois General Assembly approved the expenditure (but neglected to release the funding), UIC's

Academic Chemical and Technology Building (ACTB) was approved by the governor (Rosati, 2012). UIC obtained University Administration approval for the business plan to finance the remainder of costs, and the state of Illinois released $64 million to fund construction. It was a proud moment and the fruit of much labor. The ACTB will house select UIC faculty from chemistry, biology, and physics and will support cutting-edge interdisciplinary research focused on connections between chemistry, physics and biology—tumor growth, HIV/AIDS, immunology, dental services, orthopedics, and environmental science.

Faculty Unionizing

Union history has deep roots in the state of Illinois. Thus, even though I had some experiences with unions prior to leading UIC, and even though faculty unionization had been discussed for decades, the stars aligned during my tenure as UIC chancellor for faculty to unionize on all three campuses. At UIC, both tenured and non-tenured faculties unionized in during the 2012–2013 year, bringing the total number of UIC campus unions to 23. During the 2013–2014 academic year, the tenured faculty unionized at Springfield, and the non-tenured faculty unionized at UIUC.

During the faculty union negotiations—a grueling, complex process, compounded by the timing of my five-year review—and with Board of Trustee support and advice from legal authorities, I attempted to thoughtfully respond to the demands of the two union faculty groups, while preserving the academic culture of merit/performance, and linking merit raises solely to length of employment. The union leadership voices became more pronounced in terms of members on the faculty Senate Executive Committee. During my tenure, we settled two Graduate Employment Organization, and two faculty contracts and actions.

Sibling Rivalry (UIUC/UIC)

Though I served as both faculty and dean at the University of Illinois at Urbana-Champaign, I did not realize the historic tensions that exist between UIC and UIUC. More than a century old, UIUC is Illinois' flagship campus. It brings a rich history, an excellent research tradition, and a global reach to the cornfields of Illinois. At 33 years old, UIC is a young campus; serves a diverse and economically challenged student population (many of whom are first-generation college students); boasts the full complement of health science colleges and schools; and thrives in a uniquely American, but global, city. Each contributed value to the mission of UI. However, evidence of the tension surfaced in the form of duplication and competition, at unexpected—and often difficult—periods.

The UIUC campus proposed to create an engineering-driven College of Medicine, although a College of Medicine existed in Chicago with regional campuses—one at UIUC. At the same time, the new governor, challenged by Illinois' multi-billion-dollar pension liability, announced major reductions in general fund revenue for higher education, cutting the University of Illinois allocation by $209 million. The UIC Senate and others raised serious questions about the cost of a second University of Illinois College of Medicine: A regional college already existed on the UIUC campus, and a new college would duplicate a costly structure despite daunting budget challenges. Yet in 2015 the Board of Trustees and the outgoing and incoming presidents of the University of Illinois approved the creation of a second independent college of medicine at UIUC.

Chancellor's Residence

My contract required that I live in a house bequeathed to UIC. Built in 1882, the house had been vacant for almost two years prior to my tenure. Before I arrived on the campus, the decision was made to bring the property up to city code and make it handicapped accessible since it had become a "public" university space. I was required to finance the furnishing for the second floor.

Some objected to the cost of renovating this historic property; others wondered why more large university events and receptions weren't held there (although the budgetary environment necessitated reduced entertainment and faculty were furloughed). So, the UIC team and I decided to use the house strategically. Despite use-limiting circumstances, including—but certainly not limited to—vandalism and logistics difficulties, we leveraged our hosting efforts, welcoming donors, friends of the university, and student organizations while avoiding duplication of on-campus events.

Lessons Learned

Challenges of the chancellorship aside, I have gleaned a number of lessons along the path of academic administration. These may not be generalizable, but I hope they offer some perspective for other leaders:

1. Organizational success in the social sector cannot be measured by the same standard as success in the for-profit sector. A great organization is one that delivers, superior performance and makes a distinctive

impact over long periods of time. For a business, financial returns are a perfectly legitimate measure of performance. For a social sector organization, (a university); however, performance must be assessed relative to mission, not financial returns. In the social sectors, the critical question is not, "How much money do we make per dollar of invested capital?" but "How effectively do we deliver on our mission and make a distinctive impact, relative to our resources?" (Collins, 2001, p. 5).

2. The organizational frames I learned at Harvard are important—humanistic, symbolic, political, and structural. But more often than not, they are difficult to apply singularly and often require integration in a fluid setting.

3. Some individuals whom you mentor and to whom you provide opportunity for professional advancement forget the support that you offered along the way. Don't be disappointed.

4. Committee creation is both an art and science. Creating committees—developing the charge; composing the membership; managing the politics of who is on, who is not, and why—requires significant consideration.

5. There is usually a "want to be" dean, department chair, or president/chancellor, in the organization who can add value because he or she is anxious to learn from you and to acquire skills for advancement. However, his/her presence and aspiration could undermine or misrepresent you.

6. Some individuals want the title—dean, department head, president, chancellor—but not necessarily the "work duties" associated with these titles. Being a chancellor is a 24/7 responsibility.

7. If you define a vision for the institution too prematurely, without even a moderate "listening and learning tour of stakeholders," you run the risk of being characterized as misinformed. However, early in the interview process for the position, you will be asked to state a "vision" for the institution. It's a balancing act.

8. Even though the demographics of our nation are changing, higher education leadership remains—for large research public, but also for private, institutions—majority dominated. However, it would appear that majority females have prospered from conversations about affirmative action.

9. The "good old boy" and "good old girl" networks are alive and well. They are more subtle than in previous eras, but they appear to be entrenched in the culture of American higher education. Ethnic/

racial minorities in academic leadership roles often do not have access to these networks, or they have limited networks to draw upon.

10. When several members of the university leadership team who hired you, vacate their positions, consider other employment options.

Conclusion

In conclusion, I would like to cite Voltaire (2011), the great French philosopher. "The right of commanding is no longer an advantage transmitted by nature: like an inheritance it is the fruit of labors the price of courage". The second quote that summarizes this chapter is by Eugene B. Habecker (1987), "The true leader serves. Serves people. Serves their best interests, and in doing so will not always be popular, may not always impress. But because true leaders are motivated by loving concern than a desire for personal glory, they are willing to pay the price".

References

Bolman, L., & Deal, T. (2008). *Reframing organizations: Artistry, choice, and leadership* (4th ed.). San Francisco, CA: Jossey-Bass.

Collins, J. (2001). *Good to great: Why some companies make the leap ... and others don't.* New York, NY: HarperBusiness.

Dey, E., Gurin, P., Gurin, G., & Hurtado, S. (2004). The educational value of diversity. In P. Gurin, J. Lehman, & E. Lewis (Eds.), *Defending diversity: Affirmative action at the University of Michigan* (pp. 98–188). Ann Arbor, MI: University of Michigan Press.

Habecker, E. (1987). *The other side of leadership: Coming to terms with the responsibilities that accompany God-given authority.* Wheaton, IL: Victor Books.

Rosati, M. (2012, September 6). Governor announces new advanced science building at UIC. *UIC News.*

Smith, D. P. (2015). Top View: UIC Chancellor Paula Allen-Meares reflects on expanding research opportunities, dealing with Chicago-style politics and celebrating the University's growing academic stature. *UIC Alumni Magazine.*

University of Michigan (1999). *The Compelling Need for Diversity in Higher Education: Gratz, et al. v. Bollinger, et al. No. 97-75231; Grutter, et al. v. Bollinger, et al. No. 97-75928* (E. D. Mich.). Ann Arbor, MI: University of Michigan. Available from http://diversity.umich.edu/admissions/legal/expert/

Voltaire, F. (2011). QuotesEverlasting.com. Zinterra Media Corporation. Retrieved from http://quoteseverlasting.com/author.php?a=Francois%20Voltaire

6. Reflections about African American Female Leadership in the Academy

MENAH PRATT-CLARKE AND JASMINE PARKER

Editors' Note:

    Dr. Jasmine D. Parker is the owner and founder of Parker Educational Consulting, LLC, a college preparation and readiness company with a mission to provide students with the social capital needed to maximize postsecondary opportunity and encourage economic empowerment. She has a research affiliation with Texas Tech University. Over the past decade, Dr. Parker has focused much of her research in the assessment of systemic discrimination and marginalization against people of color and those residing in underserved communities. Her work is rooted in civil, human, and legal rights issues related to educational access and opportunity. She specializes in the educational and legal journey of African Americans, with a specific focus on the American Civil Rights Movement. An interdisciplinary researcher by training, her work intersects the fields of history, education, law, and sociology.

    Dr. Parker obtained her Bachelor of Arts in History with a minor in Sociology at Prairie View A&M University, Master of Arts in Educational Policy from the University of Illinois at Urbana-Champaign, and Ph.D. in Education Policy, Organization & Leadership with concentrations in Educational Administration & Leadership from the University of Illinois at Urbana-Champaign.

Introduction

This chapter examines African American female leadership in the academy. It reviews the scholarship and literature about African American female presidents and key themes from their experiences. The key themes are then used to analyze the journey and experiences of Dr. Paula Allen-Meares as discussed in the prior chapter and in public documents. Given the small percentage of Black women who have served at four-year research-intensive, doctoral institutions, Dr. Allen-Meares' experience provides an important contribution to scholarship about African American female presidents.

There are very few African American female presidents in the academy (American Council on Education, 2012; Lloyd-Jones, 2011; Waring, 2004). According to the American Council on Education (2012), women, regardless of racial identification, represent 26% of presidents and minorities represent 13%. Although the percentage of women increased by 3% since 2006, the number of minorities decreased by 1% (American Council on Education, 2012, p. ix). If minority-serving institutions are not considered in the percentage of minority presidents, then the percentage of minority presidents is only 9% (American Council on Education, 2012, p. x). Looking specifically at African Americans, the data shows that they represent 5.9% of all presidents, compared to 1986 when they represented 5% (American Council on Education, 1986; American Council on Education, 2012). This is less than a one percent change over a time span of nearly 30 years. As of 2012, African American women only represented 2.2% of all college presidents (M. Pratt-Clarke, personal communication, 2015). Britton (2013) noted that the small representation of African American women is also due to the power of the "good ol boys" network which results in the exclusion of African American women from leadership roles and the perpetuation of leadership that is White and male (p. 37). As Dr. Allen-Meares (2016) noted, the "good old boy" and "good old girl" networks are "alive and well," and often work to advance White females, since many "majority females have prospered from conversations about affirmative action" (Allen-Meares, 2016).

Women generally tend to be presidents at community colleges, and are least likely to be presidents at doctoral-granting institutions (American Council on Education, 2012). This has been attributed to the reality that "fewer academic positions and promotions are provided to female faculty in most research and doctoral-granting universities" (Wei, 2007, p. 7). Similarly, minority presidents also have a higher representation at public master's and bachelor's institutions (American Council on Education, 2012). African American female presidents are generally at community colleges, satellite state university campuses, or historically Black colleges and universities (Waring, 2004).

Despite the barriers and against significant obstacles, African American women have persevered and served as pioneers. They recognized that the importance of education and obtaining literacy was "worth every violent act, every oppressive campaign, and every discriminatory law" in order to help the race advance (Bates, 2007, pp. 373–374). One of the first pioneers was Mary McLeod Bethune. She started her school, Daytona Normal and Industrial Institute for Negro Girls, in 1904 (Gaston, 2015, para. 6). She merged her school with Cookman Institute to create Bethune-Cookman College in 1923 and served as the institution's first president (Gaston, 2015, para. 6).

Other notable early African American women presidents were Anna Julia Cooper and Mary Frances Berry. Anna Julia Cooper, the fourth African American woman in United States history to earn a Doctor of Philosophy degree, was the president of Frelinghuysen University in Washington, DC in 1930 (Williams, 2012). Mary Frances Berry was the first African American woman president of a predominantly White research-intensive institution (Taylor, 2008). In 1976, at the age of 38, she was selected as president of the University of Colorado Boulder (Taylor, 2008).

Other well-known African American women presidents include Dr. Johnnetta B. Cole who served as the first female president of both Spelman College and Bennett College—two historically Black colleges for women; Dr. Julianne Malveaux who succeeded Dr. Cole as president of Bennett College; Dr. Charlene Drew Jarvis who served as president of Southeastern University; Dr. Thelma B. Thompson, president of the University of Maryland Eastern Shores; Dr. Jewel Plummer Cobb of the University of California-Fullerton; and Dr. Shirley Jackson of Rensselaer Polytechnic Institute (Gaston, 2015; Journal of Blacks in Higher Education, 2016; Latimore, 2009; NovaSkegee, 2009). Dr. Marguerite Ross Barnett was the first African American woman to lead a major American university as president of the University of Houston; and Dr. Ruth J. Simmons was the first African American women to lead both a predominately White all-female liberal arts school, Smith College, as well as one of America's ivy league institutions, Brown University (Gaston, 2015; Journal of Blacks in Higher Education, 2016; Latimore, 2009; NovaSkegee, 2009).

Despite these successes, the barriers and obstacles continue to impact the number of African American women leaders, as well as the amount of scholarship about them. Much of the research on African American women presidents is in the form of dissertations. The dissertations also tend to focus on community college presidents, which is consistent with the data on the types of institutions where women typically serve as presidents (American Council on Education, 2012). These dissertations primarily use African American Feminism and Critical Race Theory for their theoretical framework and they also use a qualitative methodological approach involving interviews and narrative analysis (Choates, 2012; Humphrey, 2012; Latimore, 2009). Their research, though, provides a general overview of the broad issues and challenges faced by African American women presidents.

Despite the barriers that exist to their advancement in the Academy, including "racism, sexism, double-outsider status, exclusion from formal and informal networks, ineffective diversity programs, and unwelcoming institutional environments or climates" (Latimore, 2009, pp. 31–32), the journeys of African American women presidents can be defined by the themes of preparation, performance, and perseverance (Choates, 2012; Humphrey, 2012; Latimore, 2009). African American women must be exceedingly qualified; they must perform at an even higher level; and they must persevere in spite of the obstacles they and their institutions face. They also have a strong commitment to social justice and diversity and serving as change agents (Bates, 2007).

Literature Review

One of the earliest dissertations on African American women presidents was by Latimore (2009). Latimore's (2009) dissertation explored career preparation and career paths of eight African American women presidents of two year colleges from the southern, northern, eastern, and western United States. She identified five key themes. The first key theme was "striving and succeeding through extensive preparation" (Latimore, 2009, p. 110). This theme recognized the challenge of the "Black Tax." The "Black Tax" is a term that involves African Americans paying extra in terms of double duty, double work, and extensive career preparation and training (Latimore, 2009). Because of higher and differential standards, African American women community college presidents had extensive preparation, volunteered for special projects, participated in formal leadership training programs, and earned advanced degrees and certifications (Latimore, 2009). Mentors were also critical in African American women community college presidents' preparation. The mentors shared important information, assisted in avoiding pitfalls, and provided guidance (Latimore, 2009).

The second key theme was "constructing a well-developed professional image" (Latimore, 2009, p. 126). Image construction involved creating a presidential persona as reflected by personal appearance and interpersonal skills, including "confidence, credibility, integrity, trustworthiness, and ethics" (Latimore, 2009, p. 126). Since African American women executives are always on stage (Latimore, 2009, p. 131), they are generally conscious of their professional experience and credentials and recognize the importance of exemplifying a positive professional image.

A third finding was "taking risks for learning and professional advancement" (Latimore, 2009, p. 135). This involved risks at the personal level for career advancement and risks at the institutional level for the advancement of the organization. The fourth theme was "race and gender discrimination—a double plenty" (Latimore, 2009, p. 139). As one president stated:

> I think the greatest challenge for me all through my career is having people
> to accept me for my abilities and who I am rather than looking at me and

immediately deciding that because of who I am that there is nothing to learn from this person. But when you're an African-American woman you're going to have to deal from both angles with race and gender. It's a double plenty and you have to deal with it. Sometimes you must respond to it and other times you just let it go. ... (Latimore, 2009, p. 144)

Women often compensate for discrimination by working harder and being more competent—consistent with the Black Tax (Latimore, 2009, p. 146). The importance of performance was reflected by the 1996 survey of 1700 minority women executives and CEOs of Fortune 1000 companies by the American Council of Education that found "the primary strategy used [by African American women] to address barriers and obstacles in the workplace was exceeding performance expectations" (Jackson & Harris, 2007, p. 132).

The final theme in Latimore's (2009, p. 146) work was "supported by their village community." This theme recognized the importance of community and family support for the overall wellbeing and success of the African American higher education administrator and leader. The five themes illustrate the importance of preparation and support, including the role of mentors, to counter the racism and sexism that exists in the Academy. The reality is that African American women face racism and sexism, must work harder to be accepted, and must meet a higher standard of expectation (Choates, 2012; Latimore, 2009). These findings are consistent across the dissertations of Ausmer (2009), Smith-Ligon (2011), Humphrey (2012), and Britton (2013).

Ausmer (2009) found in her interviews of four African American female presidents that they draw from multiple leadership styles, including transformational and transactional. They also have a strong commitment to the African American community. Though they faced racial and gender oppression, they remained tenacious (Ausmer, 2009). Smith-Ligon (2011) also interviewed four African American women presidents and examined their journeys to the presidency. Key findings were the importance of a strong family foundation, as well as formal and informal mentoring.

Humphrey (2012) examined the experiences of ten African American women community college presidents who rose to the presidency through student affairs pathways. Using an interpretative phenomenological paradigm, her research revealed that the women's decisions to aspire to a presidency were influenced by their faith, the support of family, and a strong commitment to the importance of education (Humphrey, 2012). All of the women studied were willing to take risks while also being motivated by the desire to leave a legacy. The women worked to ensure that they were prepared and had the necessary skill set and credentials to be successful. A majority of them participated in a leadership institute which enabled them to network with one another and also expanded the scope of their leadership styles. In addition, personal and professional mentors provided guidance and advice to the women (Humphrey, 2012). Key challenges were inequality with respect to salary and promotional opportunities, racism, sexism, and balancing family and career (Humphrey, 2012). Likewise, Britton (2013) interviewed four college presidents and found that key themes were preparation for leadership through academic achievement and administrative experience; the importance of mentoring; ability to lead in times of adversity and change; and the role of racism and sexism.

Similar themes are evident in Choates' (2012) dissertation. Although Choates' (2012) work does not include African American women presidents, she does examine the experiences of five African American women administrators through a Black Feminist Theory lens to explore the role of race and gender in influencing their career paths. Using a life story approach, Choates (2012) gathered the stories from five women with the titles of vice president, vice provost, senior associate vice provost, campus director, and dean. One key theme that emerged throughout this study was the need to "knock on the door for opportunities," by ensuring appropriate preparation in skills and experience (Choates, 2012, pp. 78–84). For example, many of the women interviewed sought to take on extra assignments and also shadow colleagues (Choates, 2012). They also developed nontraditional mentoring relationships through family, friends, and co-workers. These relationships were important to fight being "hidden behind the veil" and being invisible and overlooked (Choates, 2012, p. 78).

Jackson and Harris (2007) found related results in their work on the experiences of 43 African American female presidents. Although the barriers for women were multiple and varied, they often involved issues of race and gender discrimination (Jackson & Harris, 2007). They included experiencing stereotypes and being excluded from informal networks. Strategies used to obtain a presidency included exceeding job expectations, holding positions with visibility, developing leadership skills outside of education through leadership training programs, and finding mentors (Jackson & Harris, 2007, pp. 129–132).

Bower and Wolverton (2009) also examined African American women leaders. Their work includes the reflections of seven African American women leaders who have been successful in the midst of racism and sexism. The presidents profiled were Debra Austin, Florida State University; Marvalene Hughes, Dillard University; Yolanda Moses, University of Southern California; Beverly Daniel Tatum, Spelman College; and Jerry Sue Thornton, Cuyahoga Community College. Lois Carson from the Riverside County Department of

Community Action and Belle S. Wheelan from the Southern Association of Colleges and Schools were also highlighted as leaders of state and national policy organizations. The work examined the leadership attributes of African American leaders. Key qualities were caring, confidence, competence, communication, credibility, and calling (Bower & Wolverton, 2009).

These are important qualities because African American women must often master the bi-cultural lifestyle (Bell, 1990). The lifestyle recognizes the importance of adapting to organizational and workplace cultures that are often "large, hierarchical, White, and male ... [and] dominated by norms, traditions, and values that represent the White Anglo-Saxon Protestant Ethic" (Bell, 1990, pp. 464–465). Adaptation requires that Black women develop a "dynamic, fluid life structure that shapes the patterns of her social interactions, relationships, and mobility, both within and between the two cultural contexts" (Bell, 1990, p. 463). It allows them to retain their connection to the African American community while participating in the dominant White culture (Bell, 1990). Navigating the bi-cultural lifestyle often means that African American women in higher education are constantly proving their worth in order to compensate for their race and gender. They often have to "stay one step ahead" and "be ten times better than them [Whites] just to be respected" (Bell, 1990, p. 474). Staying ahead and being better often means the adoption of a unique leadership style that includes "divergent thinking, creativity, risk-taking, and boundary spanning as adaptive responses to biculturalism" (Parker & ogilvie, 1996, p. 203).

When considering the multifaceted elements that help to comprise the African American woman's lived experiences in the ivory tower, African American women must often lead from a social justice framework:

> Social justice leaders strive for critique rather than conformity, compassion rather than competition, democracy rather than bureaucracy, polyphony rather than silencing, inclusion rather than exclusion, liberation rather than domination, action for change rather than inaction that preserves inequity. (Jean-Marie, 2006, p. 91; Lee & McKerrow, 2005, pp. 1–2)

As such, African American women presidents must be change agents and "revolutionize the thinking" prevalent in White male centered higher education administration (Bates, 2007, p. 373).

The scholarship on African American female presidents reflects that the barriers to ascending to the chancellor's helm are significant. Black women must overcome barriers related to their race and gender and they must learn to succeed in the midst of tremendous challenges. Dr. Paula Allen-Meares' journey to the chancellorship at UIC illustrates many of the key themes from the research. The defining characteristics of her journey include preparation, performance, perseverance, and a commitment to social justice.

Preparation and Performance

In 2008, University of Michigan Norma Radin Collegiate Professor Emerita of Social Work, Professor Emerita of Education, and Dean Emerita Paula Allen-Meares accepted the position of Chancellor and Vice President at University of Illinois at Chicago (American Association for Access, Equity, and Diversity, 2008). Upon beginning her tenure in UIC's chancellorship helm, Dr. Paula Allen-Meares became the first Black woman to lead Chicago's largest research university (University of Illinois at Chicago, 2013). She was well prepared for this senior leadership position.

An important component to her preparation was parental influence and overcoming obstacles, even as a child. Written in a memoir excerpt documented by the University of Michigan, Paula Allen-Meares dreamed of becoming a physician (The University of Michigan Faculty Memoir Project, n.d.). In fact, Allen-Meares noted that her desire to become a physician was so strong that she shared her dream with her high school counselor. Expecting to be supported and encouraged, Allen-Meares was flabbergasted when her counselor attempted to dissuade her: "My counselor bluntly told me there was no way an African American woman could become a doctor and advised me to pursue the more 'realistic' vocation of teaching, considered at the time the professional pinnacle for women" (The University of Michigan Faculty Memoir Project, n.d.). Her parents, however, were deeply involved in her education, believing it to be the "great equalizer" (Allen-Meares, 2016).

Their influence was able to counter the guidance counselor's advice. Her parents' guidance was complemented in her career by mentors. She refers to a teacher who was a mentor to her as a child, as well as mentors from different organizational sectors (Allen-Meares, 2016). As the literature reflects (Britton, 2013; Latimore, 2009; Smith-Ligon, 2011), mentoring is often a critical component of preparation for the presidency. Seeking out mentors was critical to Dr. Allen-Meares' success in fundraising. Reflecting on how she was successful, she noted that she "read a lot of books, but talking with people who had done an outstanding job of raising money was the most helpful" (Materka, 2008). Key mentors for her included Michigan colleagues President James Duderstadt, Provost Gil Whitaker, School of Business Dean Joseph White, Associate Vice President for Development Chacona Johnson, Provost Nancy Cantor, and members of University of Michigan's Central Development Office (Materka, 2008).

Another important component of her preparation was the quality of her academic and scholarly work. A social worker by training, Dr. Allen-Meares gained substantive leadership expertise by first mastering her craft as a school social worker in Urbana, Illinois (Allen-Meares, 2013). Recognized for her dedication to the field, she was invited to both supervise social work interns and teach in the School of Social Work at the University of Illinois at Urbana-Champaign (Allen-Meares, 2013). This was the beginning of Dr. Allen-Meares' academic career. In the years following her arrival to campus, Dr. Paula Allen-Meares rose through the ranks by becoming a full Professor of Social Work, Acting Dean and thereafter, Dean of the School of Social Work at the University of Illinois at Urbana-Champaign (Allen-Meares, 2013). She remained committed to her scholarship even while serving as dean. She published numerous articles, book chapters, co-edited books, and other thought pieces during her tenure at the University of Illinois at Urbana-Champaign.

She left the University of Illinois at Urbana-Champaign to serve as Dean of the School of Social Work at the University of Michigan for fifteen years, a tenure that well-prepared her for the chancellorship at UIC. As dean, she continued her scholarship. She said,

> I wanted to be a role model. If I am asking the faculty to publish, to secure grants, and to work with doctoral students, I believe I should engage in those activities as well on a smaller scale. I wanted to have a respectable record so that as I step down from the deanship, the faculty will want me as part of their community. (Materka, 2008)

Thus, during her tenure as dean, she published twenty-five journal articles, eight books, and ten book chapters. She also secured major grants and served on editorial boards and national professional societies and organizations. Her excellence as a scholar is reflected in her achievements. She has received external funding for over 24 consecutive years and is the author or co-author of more than 160 publications—including journal articles, books, and book chapters (The University of Michigan Faculty Memoir Project, n.d.).

In addition to her academic and scholarly work, she also was a vision leader as dean. Under her leadership, the University of Michigan School of Social Work transcended into a world-renowned program of study that garnered an excess of $140 million dollars, and the rating as the top school of social work in the nation (The University of Michigan Faculty Memoir Project, n.d.). This was due to the innovation, collaboration between faculty, staff, and administrators, a clear vision for success, and her willingness to create cross-campus partnerships and endowed professoriate chairs. Her accomplishments at Michigan were impressive: an endowment that increased from $1 million to $42.3 million;

externally funded interdisciplinary research awards of $94 million; increasing the diversity of the student body to 26% students of color; diversifying the faculty; and securing a new modern building for the school (Materka, 2008).

She arrived at Michigan with goals related to a focus on interdisciplinary research and she achieved those goals and more. Her accomplishments at Michigan as dean provided a solid foundation for her chancellorship at UIC. Yet, she was not satisfied with her preparation. She sought out additional training opportunities (Allen-Meares, 2016). These included programs with the CIC (Committee on Institutional Cooperation), Harvard University Graduate School of Management Program, University of Michigan's business school, and Northwestern University (Allen-Meares, 2016). She recognized the importance of understanding higher education finance, compensation, legal issues in higher education, the makeup and framing of organization structures, and how communities impact university systems. The leadership training at Harvard informed her chancellorship. Her discussion of the organizational frames (Bolman & Deal, 1984) illustrates the important role that the experience at Harvard played in her preparation and training for the leadership role (Allen-Meares, 2016). She notes that the four frames—structural, human resource, political, and symbolic/cultural—provided a resource for her as part of her leadership role (Allen-Meares, 2016).

Dr. Allen-Meares was exceptionally prepared for the chancellorship. She had a record of scholarly productivity; she had leadership experience; and she had a strong record of significant accomplishments. She had also developed a reputation for her work ethic. She said,

> My years at Michigan were defined by rewarding hard work. I kept a tape recorder by my bed so that I could make a note to myself in case some idea occurred to me in the middle of the night. Although my work ethic was passionate, I tried never to ask more from others than I asked of myself. As a personal goal, I wanted to be a role model. (University of Michigan Faculty Memoir Project, n.d.)

As President White said of her appointment at UIC, "When it comes to hard work, I've never met anyone who sets a pace like Paula Allen-Meares" (Center Publication, n.d.). Although most presidents typically serve as provosts, her stellar accomplishments at Michigan enabled her to assume the chancellorship at the University of Illinois at Chicago.

Perseverance

This fierce commitment to the mission of higher education and to excellence enabled her to be persistent and persevere, despite many challenges. The state's budget, faculty unionization, a sibling rivalry with University of Illinois at Urbana-Champaign (UIUC), and the university's governance structure were land mines that she had to navigate. The instability of the university's leadership meant that she had four different presidents and four different board chairs during her six-year tenure required requiring constant recalibration and adjustment (Allen-Meares, 2016).

The financial landmines required her to focus on fundraising. She was tenacious in her efforts. Through her advancement work, UIC exceeded the campus fundraising goal by $25 million. She renovated almost 100 classrooms, labs, and buildings through reallocation and shared partnerships with colleges (Allen-Meares, 2016). In addition to the financial situation, the faculty unionization effort which created a total of 23 unions on campus was another difficult dynamic during her tenure involving months of negotiation to ensure a positive outcome for UIC. Finally, additional instability was caused by the exacerbation of long-standing tensions between UIC and UIUC (Allen-Meares, 2016). A proposal for a college of medicine at the Urbana campus increased the tension between the two campuses in light of the existing regional UIC College of Medicine campus in Urbana. Again, during months of engagement and negotiation, she sought to protect UIC's best interest.

In addition to these campus challenges, another challenge seemed more personal. It related to criticism she received for renovating the Chancellor's residence. She was required by her contract to live in the residence built in 1882. It had been vacant for almost two years and required substantial renovation. Media outlets constantly reported the spending costs and renovation fees associated with the home's upkeep (Zekman, 2011). Other entities, including the University's faculty senate, discussed the residence and determined that it was financially excessive (Zekman, 2011). Given the role of identity, one must speculate about whether the housing issue reflects the role of race and gender, and whether the same concerns would have been raised if a White male was Chancellor and renovating the house. In fact, one may argue that it is customary to assume that a University's president or chancellor will live in a university's presidential home until their professional appointment has expired and that the residence would be consistent with the quality warranted by the stature of the position.

Dr. Allen-Meares was very conscious of her identity as a Black woman and was aware of her persona in the Academy and the challenges she would face. She noted that her "physical profile" was not typical for those in higher education leadership positions and was such that she "could go unnoticed and/or ignored" (Allen-Meares, 2016). She acknowledged the contrast between the typical profile of a Chancellor as a "majority male, at least six feet tall, and graying or balding," compared to her background as a "short African American female with a softer voice" (Allen-Meares, 2016). Consistent with the scholarship on the professional persona that African American women must exemplify (Latimore, 2009), her physicality was another challenge and obstacle that she had to be aware of in her leadership role.

The theme of perseverance is most evident in the lessons learned section at the end of her reflection. Succeeding in the academy requires understanding people and personalities. Sometimes those who are mentored forget who mentored them. Sometimes individuals with leadership aspirations might seek to undermine or misrepresent the existing leader (Allen-Meares, 2016). Some individuals seek the title and prestige that come with the title, but not the work associated with the title (Allen-Meares, 2016).

Succeeding in the midst of challenges requires an unwavering commitment to the mission of higher education and a recognition of the costs and sacrifice of leadership. Unpopular decisions for the long-term greatness of an institution can come with significant professional and personal risk. Yet, she was willing to take risks to help advance her institution, particularly in light of her commitment to social justice.

A Commitment to Social Justice

Dr. Paula Allen-Meares' journey reflects a strong commitment to social justice. As a scholar of social work, she has focused on mental health of poor children, adolescent pregnancy, and African American parents and communities (Center Publication, n.d.). This commitment to traditionally marginalized groups was evident in her diversity efforts at UIC and her commitment to access. As her narrative and the media release (University of Illinois at Chicago, 2013) recognized, she was a champion for diversity. Dr. Allen-Meares was a strong advocate for the participation of women and students of color in the science, technology, engineering, and math (STEM) fields. She recognized that "much of the responsibility for making progress rests with individual colleges and universities, as our mission [as higher education administrators and faculty members] includes recruiting, educating and graduating the STEM professionals of the future" (Allen-Meares & Rao, 2011). To further her commitment to diversity at UIC, she created an Office of Diversity to help coordinate the work of UIC's Centers for Understanding and Social Change (African American, Asian American and Latino cultural centers; Disability Resource Center; Women's Leadership and Resource Center; and Gender and Sexuality Center). She started the UIC Dialogues

Initiative to promote diversity discussions and engagement among students (University of Illinois, 2013).

The Chancellor's Cluster Initiative to Increase Diversity and Interdisciplinary Culture at UIC helped promote the recruitment of underrepresented minorities whose scholarship involved issues of diversity (University of Illinois at Chicago, 2013). The goal was to recruit senior faculty who could then help facilitate the recruitment of a cluster of junior faculty with related research interests. In addition, she sought to advance diversity through an unwavering commitment to the importance of structural and representational diversity, classroom and curricular diversity, and interactional diversity (Allen-Meares, 2016).

Her social justice commitment is reflected in a blog she wrote about the imperative for access to higher education, health care, and economic opportunity (Allen-Meares, 2011). She wrote about realizing how many students work multiple jobs to attend college and feeling a significant responsibility as chancellor to ensure that even during the recession of the 21st century, students would be able to pursue their goals at UIC, regardless of background (Allen-Meares, 2011). Although an educated workforce is vital in addressing human suffering and supporting a healthy economy, a healthy environment, and healthy population, the ability of higher education to meet the needs of humanity is being compromised by a lack of resources and lack of state support (Allen-Meares, 2011). With higher tuition being used to fill in the gap from state support, the door to education is closing for many or resulting in significant debt, longer graduation rates, and changing career paths (Allen-Meares, 2011).

Just as the Morrill Act of 1862 helped uplift citizens of often rural areas through agriculture and mechanics, other public institutions, such as UIC, continue that mission in urban and inner city communities as part of the Coalition of Urban-Serving Universities, producing educators, doctors, dentists, and scientists, focusing on first generation students and recent immigrants (Allen-Meares, 2011). She recognized that higher education is about shaping the future:

> One of the great rewards of running a college or university is that every day I see countless faculty, staff and students working to bring about change—transmitting knowledge, making new discoveries, serving communities, caring for the sick. It is our responsibility to ensure that current and future generations of students have the same opportunities, in ways large or small, to help shape history. (Allen-Meares, 2011)

This is truly a commitment to service and social change.

Conclusion

It is clear, then, that presidential leadership by African American women requires a high level of preparation, performance, and perseverance in the midst of sacrifices and challenges. Thus, when reflecting upon the lived experiences of Dr. Paula Allen-Meares, it is evident that she is a woman of dedication, determination, and relentless pursuit in the name of excellence. At all levels of the academy, Dr. Allen-Meares has been an exemplar of excellence. In recognition of her achievements at UIC, she was named among the 100 Influential Women in Chicago, Who's Who in Chicago Business, a 2013 Business Leader of Color by Chicago United, and the 2015 Educator of the Year by the Chicago chapter of the National Association of Black Social Workers (Chicago Chapter of the National Association of Black Social Workers, 2015; Flood, 2013; Gambini, 2012; University of Illinois at Chicago, 2013).

As she noted when she accepted the appointment at Chicago, "At the end of the day, it is all about excellence, relevance and collaborative spirit" (Center Publications, n.d.). Her leadership journey to the helm reflects her commitment to these values. She exemplified them and sought to be a role model for others. A passion for excellence, a strong work ethic, a commitment to social justice, and sheer determination, regardless of the amount of adversity, define Chancellor Paula Allen-Meares' legacy in higher education.

References

Allen-Meares, P. (2011, August 9). Why it's imperative that everyone have access to higher education. *HuffPost Black Voices*. Retrieved from http://www.huffingtonpost.com/paula-allenmeares/higher-education-access_b_922752.html

Allen-Meares, P. (2013, July). Curriculum vitae of Paula Allen-Meares, Ph.D. Retrieved from http://www.lib.umich.edu/faculty-memoir/sites/www.lib.umich.edu.faculty-memoir/files/cv/cwitte/Paula_Allen-Meares_CV_July_2013_UPDATED_0.pdf

Allen-Meares, P. (2016). A view from the helm: A Black woman's reflection on her chancellorship. In M. Pratt-Clarke & J. Maes (Eds.), *Journeys of social justice: Women of color presidents in the Academy*. New York, NY: Peter Lang.

Allen-Meares, P., & Rao, M. C. (2011, October 27). *More focus on math, science education vital to economic progress*. Retrieved from HuffPost Education at http://www.huffingtonpost.com/paula-allenmeares/stem-education-gap_b_1019768.html

American Association for Access, Equity, and Diversity. (2008, June 23). *African-American woman, Paula Allen-Meares, selected to lead University of Illinois at Chicago*. Retrieved from http://affirmact.blogspot.com/2008/06/african-american-woman-paula-allen.html

American Council on Education. (1986). *American College President Study: 2012 edition.* American Council on Education: Center for Policy Analysis. Washington, DC.

American Council on Education. (2012). *American College President Study: 2012 edition.* American Council on Education, Center for Policy Analysis. Washington, DC.

Ausmer, N. M. (2009). *Redefining leadership: Examination of African-American women serving as presidents in institutions of higher education* (Doctoral dissertation). Retrieved from https://etd.ohiolink.edu/rws_etd/document/get/ucin 1243164670/inline

Bates, G. (2007). These hallowed halls: African-American women college and university presidents. *The Journal of Negro Education, 76*(3), 373–390.

Bell, E. L. (1990). The bicultural life experience of career-oriented black women. *Journal of Organizational Behavior, 11*(6), 459–477.

Bolman, L. G., & Deal, T. (1984). *Modern approaches to understanding and managing organizations.* San Francisco, CA: Jossey-Bass.

Bower, B. L., & Wolverton, M. (Eds.). (2009). *Answering the call: African-American women in higher education leadership.* Sterling, VA: Stylus Publishing.

Britton, L. M. (2013). *African-American women in higher education: Challenges endured and strategies employed to secure a community college presidency* (Doctoral dissertation Paper 68). Retrieved from National Louis University Digital Commons http://digitalcommons.nl.edu/cgi/viewcontent.cgi?article=1069&context=diss

Center Publications (n.d.)). New Chancellor at UIC. *Illinois Issues.* Retrieved from http://illinoisissues.uis.edu/UICChancellor.html

Chicago Chapter of the National Association of Black Social Workers. (2015, March 25). *Paula Allen-Meares, Educator of the year NABSW awardee.* Chicago Chapter of the National Association of Black Social Workers Facebook page. Retrieved from https://www.facebook.com/Chicago-Chapter-of-the-National-Association-of-Black-Social-Workers-176769317753/timeline/

Choates, R. (2012). *In their own words: African-American women narrate their experiences to leadership* (Doctoral dissertation). Retrieved from ProQuest Dissertations & Theses (Order No. 3516385).

Crain's Chicago Business. (2013). 2014 who's who in Chicago business. *Chicago Business.* Retrieved from http://www.chicagobusiness.com/section/whos-who-2014

Flood, B. (2013, July 22). *Allen-Meares makes list of 100 influential Chicago women.* Retrieved from http://news.uic.edu/allen-meares-makes-list-of-100-influential-chicago-women

Gambini, B. (2012, April 5). *Two to receive SUNY honorary degrees at UB commencement.* Retrieved from http://www.buffalo.edu/news/releases/2012/04/13329.html

Gaston, A. (2015, February 4). *A celebration of African-American women college presidents.* Retrieved from http://www.forharriet.com/2015/02/a-celebration-of-african-american-women.html#ixzz3mHor541q

Humphrey, M. (2012). *Experiences of African-American community college presidents using a student affairs pathway: A phenomenological study* (Doctoral dissertation). Retrieved from https://dspace.library.colostate.edu/bitstream/handle/10217/71567/Hum-phrey_colostate_0053A_11430.pdf?sequence=1&isAllowed=y (Order No. 3551624)

Jackson, S., & Harris, S. (2007). African-American female college and university presidents: Experiences and perceptions of barriers to the presidency. *Journal of Women in Educational Leadership*, 5(2), 119–137.

Jean-Marie, G. (2006). Welcoming the unwelcomed: A social justice imperative of African-American female leaders at Historically Black Colleges and Universities. *Educational Foundations*, 20(1–2), 85–104.

Journal of Blacks in Higher Education. (2016). *Key Events in Black Higher Education: JBHE Chronology of Major Landmarks in the Progress of African American in Higher Education*. Retrieved from http://www.jbhe.com/chronology/

Latimore, R. S. (2009). *Rising to the top: A nation study of Black women community college presidents* (Doctoral dissertation). Retrieved from https://getd.libs.uga.edu/pdfs/latimore_robbie_s_200905_edd/latimore_robbie_s_200905_edd.pdf

Lee, S. S., & McKerrow, K. (2005). Advancing social justice: Women's work. *Advancing Women in Leadership Online Journal*, 19, 1–2. Retrieved from http://www.advanc-ingwomen. com/awl/fall2005/preface.html

Lloyd-Jones, B. (2011). Diversification in higher education administration: Leadership paradigms reconsidered. In: G. Jean-Marie & B. Lloyd-Jones (Eds.), *Women of color in higher education: Changing directions and new perspectives* (pp. 3–18). Bingley: Emerald Group Publishing Limited.

Materka, P. (2008, January 9). A tenure marked by growth, diversity, and collaboration. *University of Michigan School of Social Work News*. Retrieved from http://ssw.umich.edu/stories/48989-a-tenure-marked-by-growth-diversity-and-collaboration

NovaSkegee (2009, May 19). *African-American presidents and chancellors at non-HB-CUs over time [Post 17028]*. Retrieved from http://onnidan1.com/forum/index.php?PHPSESSID=f58213b93cf0993d743500622a928be1&topic=27463.0

Parker, P. S., & ogilvie, d. (1996). Gender, culture, and leadership: Toward a culturally distinct model of African-American women executives' leadership strategies. *Leadership Quarterly*, 7(2), 189–214.

Smith-Ligon, P. (2011). *An examination of African-American female college presidents' professional ascendancy and mentoring experiences* (Doctoral dissertation). Retrieved from http://search.proquest.com/docview/1015210784 (Order No. 3506921).

Taylor, C. (2008, October 17). Mary Frances Berry: CU's first black chancellor. *Colorado-Daily.com*. Retrieved from http://www.coloradodaily.com/ci_13104849

The University of Michigan Faculty Memoir Project (n.d.). Paula Allen-Meares, Dean Emerita of Social Work, Professor Emerita of Social Work and Education: Biography and Memoirs. Retrieved from http://www.lib.umich.edu/faculty-memoir/sites/www.lib.umich.edu.faculty-memoir/files/cv/cwitte/Paula_Allen-Meares_CV_July_2013_UPDATED_0.pdf

University of Illinois at Chicago. (2013, November 14). *Chancellor Paula Allen-Meares: Background and achievements*. University Relations. Retrieved from http://uofi.uilli-nois.edu/emailer/newsletter/44111.html

Waring, A. L. (2004). Road to the presidency: Women of color assuming leadership roles in the academy. In: C. Y. Battle & C. M. Doswell (Eds.), *Building bridges for women of color in higher education* (pp. 4–17). Lanham, MD: University Press of America.

Wei, F. (2007, Summer). Cross-cultural teaching apprehension: A coidentity approach toward minority teachers. *New Directions for Teaching and Learning, 2007*(110): 5–14.

Williams, P. K. (2012, February 18). Anna Julia Cooper & Frelinghuysen University. *The house history man.* Retrieved from http://househistoryman.blogspot.com/2012/02/anna-julia-cooper-frelinghuysen.html

Zekman, P. (2011, October 19). UIC spends $625k on chancellor's home. *CBS Chicago.* Retrieved from http://chicago.cbslocal.com/2011/10/19/uic-spends-625k-on-chancellors-home/

7. Re-envisioning the Academy for Women of Color

PHYLLIS M. WISE

Editors' Note:

Dr. Phyllis Wise is the CEO of the Colorado Longitudinal Study, a new study with the goal of establishing the largest biobank in the world. She served as Chancellor and Professor of Molecular and Integrative Physiology, Animal Sciences, and Obstetrics and Gynecology in the School of Molecular and Cell Biology at the University of Illinois at Urbana-Champaign. She was interim President of the University of Washington from 2010 to 2011, where she had served as Provost and Executive Vice President for five years. Previous academic roles included serving as Dean of the College of Biological Sciences at University of California-Davis, also holding the rank of Distinguished Professor of Neurobiology, Physiology and Behavior in the College of Biological Sciences, and of Professor Physiology and Membrane Biology in the School of Medicine.

Prior to her appointment at Davis, she was professor and chair of the Department of Physiology at the University of Kentucky in Lexington for eight years. Wise began her academic career at the University of Maryland, Baltimore as an assistant professor and was promoted through the ranks to full professor of physiology. She holds a BA degree from Swarthmore College in biology and a Ph.D. in zoology from the University of Michigan. Dr. Wise also holds honorary doctorates from Swarthmore College and the University of Birmingham (England).

Introduction

Let me start with a story. More than sixty years ago a young girl sat with her parents who were both educators in higher education. They were having one of innumerable discussions about the need to study hard, the need to compete, the need to overcome the stigma of being a minority and a female, and the need to never quit. The father was a physician-scientist and the mother was a nurse-educator. Both had immigrated to the United States from China to finish their educations. Both were classic first generation immigrants; they were willing to sacrifice anything to make the lives of their children better. But they also had high expectations for their children; both parents expected their young daughter to excel in school at all levels and then enter the field of education. Both expected their daughter to rise through the ranks and get farther than they had. They firmly implanted these expectations in their daughter's mind from the time she was very young. I was that child.

I'm a first generation American daughter of parents who immigrated to the United States from China. Why did I start here? Because with all this parental encouragement, my journey has still been challenging and bumpy. Indeed, it has been rewarding and stimulating. But it has not been without frustration; sometimes facing seemingly insurmountable hurdles. I have experienced the demands; sometimes different than the demands made of men, personally and professionally. I am here because of some fortunate choices; some that I made and some that were made for me along the way. I am where I am because of some acts of fate and because I found people ahead of me who were willing to share their advice, offer their guidance, and open some opportunities for me.

Leadership

Since I come from a family of educators, being in higher education was like falling off a rock—it was the natural, expected thing to do. I am a neuroscientist by training. I went to Swarthmore College, a small private undergraduate college in the 1960's. It was the time when Martin Luther King and John F. Kennedy dominated our country's hopes and dreams for a better world. It became a decade of great conflict with the Vietnam War dominating all of our lives. It was a time when there were very few women who went on to graduate school. There were no women on the Biology Department faculty and only one woman on the faculty of the Zoology Department at the University of Michigan where I went to get my doctoral training. I remember very clearly when I asked a professor whether I could do my doctoral research in his lab and his response was, "I don't take women graduate students because they get married and have children and never use their educations."

After being turned down by the first professor who I asked to work with, I found another male professor, Dr. B. E. Frye, who was my graduate student mentor. He was more than any graduate student should expect to have. I was equally fortunate to find a post-doctoral mentor who was a woman, Dr. Anita Payne, who mentored me professionally and personally in ways that I never expected. Both of them urged me to seek balance in my career and to not be ashamed of wanting to have a family. As I began my career as a researcher in endocrinology and brain chemistry, they urged me to accommodate and adapt the experience so I could do both the last parts of my thesis research and my post-doctoral work while I had my first child.

I was the rare woman—much less an Asian one—in a field largely dominated by men. And my father, who had a long and noteworthy career in neurological research, was disappointed that I "only" earned my Ph.D. He strongly believed that I, as a woman, needed to earn an M.D. so that I would be more easily employed and make it easier to follow the career of a husband. I have consciously attempted to strike a healthy balance in my career and personal life throughout the years, especially in every endeavor I undertook. But I have not always been successful. I remember the struggle to perform the research while mothering an infant. It wasn't easy, but I would have never given up being a mother and I would have never given up my career in biomedical research.

I started out at the University of Maryland, Baltimore, as an Assistant Professor and rose through the ranks. At Maryland, I was the only woman in the department, and in fact, I headed the committee that hired the second one. After becoming a full professor, a colleague told me that he had been watching me in various committees that he and I had served on and he thought that I would become bored if I did not explore academic leadership. He nominated me for several positions and I accepted the offer to be the Chair of the Department of Physiology at the University of Kentucky, College of Medicine. When I got my first invitation to the annual national meeting of physiology department leaders, I was asked about scheduling a tee time. I realized that I was among a different group of people. When I got to that first meeting, I found out that I was one of two women "chairmen" among 126 departments. At that time, the association was known as the Association of Chairmen of Departments of Physiology. In my second year attending, I tried to change the name of the association from the "Chairmen of Physiology" to the "Chairs of Physiology," and I was told that chairs were pieces of furniture. Just for the record, I would like to note that this organization is now known as the Association of Chairs of Departments of Physiology.

I left Kentucky to be the dean of the College of Biological Sciences at University of California, Davis and then the Provost and Executive Vice President at the University of Washington. When I got to the University of Washington and was the Provost, one of the things I realized on my listening and learning tour was that there were incredible strengths in the broad areas of the environment. However, they were spread out and were not leveraging each other's strengths. There were no synergies being created. So, I started talking about creating a new College of the Environment. This road took a little bit longer than I ever expected. To maximize learning and impact opportunities, I was trying to combine the College of Forestry with the College of Ocean and Fishery Sciences. The state of Washington's claim to fame is their license plate that says "The Evergreen State." Fifty percent of their land is covered by forest. I actually got threats from the forest industry saying that I did not have any understanding of the environment. The forest industry even tried to pass a law in the legislature to prevent the University of Washington from being able to reconfigure. But we got it done, and the University of Washington now has a College of Environment that is probably one of the most powerful in the country. The institution now attracts students, faculty, and research dollars that it was not able to do successfully before.

As Provost, I learned that leadership involves taking some calculated risks and actions that sometimes do not work out as well. Another initiative involved my belief that the College of Arts and Sciences would be more effective if it were two colleges: one that focused on the humanities, social sciences, and arts, and the other that focused on math and the sciences. The idea failed because I did not take time to listen and learn or consult broadly enough about the history and culture at the University of Washington to understand how much the faculty felt that such a change would be damaging. This experience showed me that in order to make important decisions you have to take time to hear the many voices and perspectives on the campus. It really does matter. It does not mean everyone has to be on the train of change. It does mean that you have at least heard and considered the comments of the really respected people before you make any kind of big decision.

The balance between listening to many voices and willingness to take action is always a difficult one and one that differs based upon the specific situation that is being considered. Sometimes I had good ideas, but sometimes the decisions I made were not the best ones. Over time I learned that what really begins to set you apart in your career is how you move on from mistakes and how you manage the consequences of them in the moment. I also know that with these challenges comes an enormous opportunity to make it easier for the next generation to enter the Academy and to lead it forward.

After serving as Provost, I served as the Interim President for one year at the University of Washington and then came to Illinois and served as Chancellor. These experiences have given me a perspective on higher education. Some of the opportunities I had and some of the challenges that I faced were colored by the fact that I am a woman and I am a woman of color. When I became chancellor at the University of Illinois at Urbana-Champaign, I became the first Asian American woman to lead a major public research university. I know exactly what it is like to be the one who stands out in a department, a college, or a field.

Those of us in the Academy who are reaching the point where we will be stepping aside and leaving many of the oncoming challenges to others have a responsibility to share the lessons we have learned along the way. There is too much work to be done and there is no time to be reinventing wheels and going down non-productive paths that have already been explored. I really began shaping my ideas around leadership and impact as my own laboratory got larger and larger. When I became a Chair of the Department of Physiology, I realized that leadership was all about recognizing and mentoring other people. It was no longer a matter of whether or not I could get my name on another paper or give another talk at a meeting. My newfound role was about pushing forward young faculty. I realized that we turn very quickly into becoming a mentor as we rise in rank.

In some ways I feel that I was an accidental chancellor because I did not plan my career the way it has turned out. But, I have been mentored and advised all my life in many ways and by countless people. And I have to say, when people ask me to please tell them how I got here and what I did to plan it, I have to admit that in many ways my career decisions were not concretely planned but were fluid. Nonetheless, I feel like I have been a very fortunate woman in my profession.

When I think about what has been most important for me and allowed me to succeed in academic leadership, it was seeking great mentors. I was fortunate sometimes to get advice from people who cared about me, before I even knew that I needed their advice. I learned that it is important to watch others and emulate those who have achieved similar goals in ways that could be adopted. It is also important to actively ask questions. It was very, very rare that someone would tell me that they did not have time to talk to me. In my experience, people are more than happy to give advice. They are more than happy to share their stories. They are more than happy to be mentors.

I learned that we will never be able to accept all the advice from people who offer it. There are times when their advice does not fit the occasion. Sometimes the advice from one person will contradict what another person suggests. Sometimes the advice is not appropriate for one decision, but may be appropriate for the next decision. Sometimes the advice will urge us to take actions that are just not who we are. What we must understand is that first and foremost is that we have to be able to live in our own skin. We have to be able to stay true to ourselves. However, by seeking advice from a variety of people at a variety of stages in their own careers, we will be able to get a repertoire from which we can pick and choose. It is always good to have many, many people around and many avenues of advice. But seeking advice is critical—we benefit from others' experiences, both successful and unfortunate.

Each step of the way I learned a little bit more about planning and thinking about the long term. As graduate students we tend to think about the next six months, the next experiment, or the next paper. When we are faced with our first faculty position or our first instructional position, we tend to begin to think more about the next two, or three, or five years and what we would really like to achieve. For our own unique careers, planning is important to the success we hope to have.

Women and Minorities in STEM

Looking back, I realize just how fragile that path through a science career in the academy was for me. The challenges of bringing women and other underrepresented minorities into a pathway that ultimately leads to a career in a STEM field is no secret. A complex and overlapping system—and I mean that in a biological sense—of educational, governmental, social, and cultural agencies all combine or contrast in ways that impact every age and every level of transition. The numbers recruited on to this path and persevering on it are shaped by different forces at play. In 2010, according to the National Science Foundation (NSF) (2010), about 25,000 doctorates were awarded nationally in the sciences: about 46% of these went to women, 7% went to minority candidates, and 4% went to minority women. In that same year, specifically within engineering disciplines, about 7,500 doctoral degrees were awarded nationally (NSF, 2010). Only 23% of these were to women and less than 5% were to minority candidates; and in a discipline like physics, the news is worse; of the 1,570 doctorates, 52 went to minority candidates—about 3% (NSF, 2010).

These numbers certainly tell a story about women and minority participation in STEM programs in our nation's university system. Statistics are good for giving trends and broad pictures at high levels. But sometimes they make it easy to forget that each of these numbers represents a personal experience and those experiences—good or bad—have lifelong implications. These numbers are very personal to me. They are a reminder that while we've made progress over the years, there are still too many who will have similar experiences and challenges to those I faced 40 years ago. I have a vested interest, personally and professionally, in making sure that keeping women on the STEM path isn't a matter of luck, but one that is grounded in an institutional commitment to fostering an environment where everyone has the same opportunity to excel.

For a doctoral student, there is effectively a five-year window in a lifelong continuum to recruit a student, prepare her academically, and to provide her with a comprehensive experience that keeps her on the STEM path. Out of professional self-interest, this means a STEM path that leads into the professoriate. A critical mass of women and minorities on campus and leading programs is the fundamental key to creating that environment and experience that will let all students persevere and thrive. Until we have that critical mass, and until we have it in a way that is institutionally stable and sustainable, we are locked in an annual cycle of competitive recruiting that focuses more on getting a bigger share of a scarce pool of human potential rather than making real progress in broadening and deepening that pool for everyone in the nation.

The route to enhancing this population involves partnerships. Many efforts around partnerships have been too focused externally. Over the years there has been an abundance of external initiatives—notably from NSF and the National Institutes of Health—to both explore the basis for this gender and race gap and to close it. Obviously, there is some evidence of success—we have seen the participation numbers trending upwards—particularly in the biological sciences. But, we haven't seen a tipping point or a real fundamentally sustainable reaction.

What happens when these programs end? What happens when the external funding that offers a boost to recruitment packages concludes? Where are we when federal or state political priorities shift and fiscal concentration moves to another issue? Have we just been using these opportunities to do more of what our standard practices have been—and as they conclude, do we trend back down to our baseline levels? In too many cases, the answer is yes. I am not suggesting that these external partnerships and initiatives aren't critical investments and aren't drivers of change. But I think that we as universities haven't aligned our programs, our financial priorities, our administrative practices, our governance philosophies, and our long-term academic visions in ways that use these external funds and opportunities to their full potential.

We need to begin work within our universities. As a university with a historic and current global reputation for accomplishments in the sciences and engineering—one of our own great challenges is how we can enhance our doctoral, postdoctoral, and faculty communities, both in the sciences and comprehensively on a campus. We need to expand both the number of women and minorities coming into our STEM programs and the number who remain in them for a career. The University of Illinois at Urbana-Champaign ranks third nationally in Science and Engineering doctorates to men between 2006 and 2010 and 14th in Ph.D.'s to women in that time. Illinois is a big provider of STEM human capital. If it can increase that capacity and productivity, and do so in a way that sustains constant growth over time, one university really can make a measurable impact on the STEM field.

Illinois should be a national role model for how a research university can organize itself and create a graduate, post-graduate, and faculty experience where a diverse population isn't the result of add-ons—but comes about through a sustained, strategic, and collectively-shared commitment. This means integrating the idea of diversity as a foundation for excellence into every part of our operation—from financial planning to how our colleges and departments interact and to how we as administrators establish policies.

Illinois is organizing itself to more efficiently work with external partners. We are putting ourselves in a position where external funding from these opportunities with NSF, other agencies, or corporations will have a greater, longer, and more measurable impact. We are positioning ourselves to ensure that when these external opportunities end or diminish, the programs they augment do not simply fade away and that we are better prepared to take advantage of these partnerships when they appear. We have already see this in action with our Graduate College being chosen to coordinate a $1.75 million, NSF-funded Alliances for Graduate Education and the Professoriate (AGEP) initiative that we believe will double the number of underrepresented STEM faculty members hired among the twelve university members of the Committee on Institutional Cooperation (CIC).

The Professorial Advancement Initiative will establish 85 new postdoctoral positions and bring together more than 250 faculty mentors across this 12 university network in the next 4 years. The project goal is to boost annual hiring of among CIC members from about 24 minority candidates to about 50 each year. This partnership between a network of public and private research universities and the NSF is going to have a 30 to 50-year impact on the STEM disciplines. It is a direct result of our ability to foster lasting, collaborative and institutional-wide internal partnerships to build our excellence around our diversity.

As a nation, we've spent a lot of time, money, and effort to expand the STEM pathway for more women and minority candidates. While there has been undeniable progress, at least in higher education, we have yet to see a model that is sustaining and scalable. I think it is time to stop looking outside for solutions and to begin investing from the inside. I can tell you from my experience, this isn't an easy path nor necessarily a fast one. But I am convinced that it is the one we must take. The idea of this being a long-haul proposition is one that is important to remember. These are enormously complex societal and practical issues. Many of the issues around them are rooted in practices and policies that have been in place for generations. Even looking at the educational pathways—we know that experiences in the first year or two of elementary school can and do shape the lifelong educational opportunities of our students. So, right there, we are talking about changes that might take a decade or more to see positive outcomes.

The key for us is to carve out new ways to pool these unique viewpoints and to put them into the collaborative, constructive debate that is going to shape how we teach, who we teach, and how we make sure our universities of this 21st century offer experiences that are relevant to the society around us. We have a record, unfortunately, of leaving some of our best and brightest minds out of our conversations in this nation—and that extends into the higher educational arena as well. That must change quickly and permanently. The challenges our society faces are too complex with consequences for failure too high for us to face without every talent at our disposal. We are on the edge of a new kind of Academy—one that is going to need to learn to incorporate every viewpoint and to find ways to bring every potential partner to the table. Women of color in the academy are going to determine how we make that ideal a reality.

Diversity

When I came to Illinois in 2011, my first public remarks made it clear that enhancing diversity and building inclusivity would be my priority. I promised from my first comments that one of my key objectives and areas of focus would be a firm and unwavering commitment to diversity and inclusion. As a pre-eminent public research university, one of the nation's original land-grant universities and an institution with a global reach, creating a community of diverse voices, perspectives, experiences, and identities is essential to excellence. I made this a point of relentless emphasis. With my leadership team, we made sure that beyond talking, we had accountability. That accountability started with me.

Although I couldn't mandate diversity happens any more than I could declare our state budget woes should disappear, I could use my position to lead the campus community in developing a framework and vision, and investing the resources to position the University of Illinois at Urbana-Champaign to develop the robust, broad, inclusive, and comprehensive community we must have. I had a responsibility as both a faculty member and as a university leader to spark discussions on these issues and to put into place structures, strategies, and resources to foster diverse environments on my own campus.

Aspiring to increase the diversity in our students, our faculty, and our staff is not a new idea. Many universities have tried for many years to do this. Many people as well-intentioned as I have worked hard to increase the numbers of under-represented people on our campuses. And we have made some progress. The trend lines are, in general, going in the right direction.

So why do I think that we need to work even harder and smarter? Why do I believe that we must accelerate the rate of change and increase the slope of the curve to greater diversity? It is because I believe this is not a matter of making our campus just look more like the world around simply by the numbers and percentages. This is a matter of excellence which is tied inextricably to diversity. When it comes to meeting complex societal challenges, the conversation is richer and the solutions are better when the people are around the table are more diverse.

We do not have the luxury of placing any sort of limit on potential new approaches to the complex issues we all face. Whether it is energy and sustainability or social equity and democracy—the age of simple problems with easy solutions is over. The solutions to the issues that we must resolve in the future will stem from non-traditional partnerships that cross disciplines. They will ignore geographical and political boundaries and require simultaneous analysis from multiple perspectives. Simply put, the solutions to complex problems require a diverse approach. Part of that approach means embracing a very broad and flexible definition of what we even mean by "diversity."

In many respects we've seen the word "diversity" narrow and become synonymous with racial diversity—African-American, Native American, Latino/a, or Caucasian. But when we speak of a diverse community on a university campus—that definition falls short of what we need it cover. It must encompass not only how we look, but how we think, where we come from, and what we believe. If we are going to be comprehensive universities or a comprehensive higher educational system, we need a comprehensive definition of diversity. We need to think of it in terms of ethnicity, language, gender, national origin, sexual orientation, religion, cultural perspectives and intellectual approaches. In short, we need to view diversity as not about just how you look, but how you think and where your story began.

The power of universities comes from our ability to engender new ways of thinking and to open up new perspectives. If we have a "product"—it must surely be the creation of ideas and ideas aren't limited by skin color or by the language you speak or where your parents came from. They are born out of life and educational experiences. They grow in environments where robust and respectful debate is encouraged.

I'm not an academic historian, so I'm not speaking as an authority, but from my perspective and from my own experiences in the professoriate. I think it is unlikely that there has ever been a period in American higher education where we have seen so many forces for change converging on us all at the same time. Traditional funding sources are diminishing; global competition for intellectual capital is intense and unrelenting; we are in the midst of a societal redefining of the priority of college and education; and demographically, technology is shredding the traditional limits of the learning environment we all know. In addition, the national identity of our country is shifting rapidly away from a White majority. Any one of these issues could send shockwaves through our profession. But we are at the conjunction of all of them. These forces are going to reshape us as educational institutions in the next 20 to 50 years. There is going to be a vastly different landscape in American higher education. We have an obligation right now to lay the foundations that will see us through this period and let us emerge on the other side as the world model for educational opportunity and success.

Beyond a shared, broad idea of diversity, we as a university need to reframe the context in which we are considering the issue. When we talk institutionally about diversity, on this campus and across the nation, the discussions seem to be based primarily around fairness and equity. We are pushing for a more diverse representation because it is the "fair" or the "right" thing to do. This may have made sense in the past—and for my own university, given our land-grant heritage, the concept is rooted in our institutional and personal values. What is fair and right should always be the foundational compass for our decisions at any level as educators. But, diversity no longer hinges solely on social justice, fairness, and equity. We live in a time when we must move the basis for the debate beyond fairness and equity and equate diversity as an essential part of excellence. When we make this the starting point and basic assumption in our conversations around diversity—that's when we'll really open the door to sustained change.

This is a critical point—diversity has to go from a mandated exercise to an instinctive way of operating. The unfortunate truth is that while fairness is an important social value, it is not always a necessary factor in achieving success in competitive endeavors. Until we make it one, there will always be a pressure to ignore or minimize it. In business, for example, it is possible to act unfairly but to be very successful. It is far more difficult to be mediocre and to be successful. Enhanced diversity is the only viable route to excellence and success in the competitive environments we're entering. It isn't a path; it is the path. We need to institutionally internalize the idea that diversity is a competitive and economic advantage. We are sitting in a perfect time and place to initiate that change.

It is complex work—building diversity *in practice* on a campus, not simply in statistics. It isn't enough to have representatives of every race or nation or belief. That isn't diversity—that's just math and geography coming together. As an example, at Illinois, we have more than 5,000 Chinese students on campus. But, if they only spend their time and create their Illinois experience with other students from China—we haven't achieved anything of any real value. We may be diverse on a spreadsheet, but no one in our community gains anything in terms of educational opportunities or world-views or cross-pollination of ideas.

We thrive on the crossing of boundaries when it comes to academics and research. We talk constantly of multidisciplinarity and collaboration in our work and teaching. It is ingrained and unconscious in our daily experiences as university scholars. That's where we need to be when it comes to the issue of diversity. That intersection of numbers and life is where we find the payoff that we all promise when we talk about diversity.

Building a campus and local community that doesn't just bring these perspectives to campus, but brings them together requires a sustained and unrelenting collective commitment from the president, chancellor or dean's chair to the classrooms, to the sidewalks of our campuses, and out into our local neighbors. Diversity for those of us in universities cannot be simply about increasing numbers. We must be prepared and able to offer everyone who comes to us a campus that they can call home. We have to continue to think about our organizational and administrative structures.

At Illinois, there is a campus-level coordinating Office of Diversity, Equity and Access that is charged with developing strategies and identifying opportunities for enhancing and fostering an inclusive community. What is important about this office is that they are charged with identifying and implementing methods to diffuse diversity efforts throughout the entire campus organization. This ranges from student activities to training our new department heads and executives in best practices for minority recruitment at the student and faculty level. Just having a central office does not mean we are really providing services that translate to a more diverse campus.

We also have an initiative called Illinois EDGE (Enhancing Diversity, Guiding Excellence) that is designed to comprehensively embed the goal of fostering a diverse community of students and scholars in every part of the university—from faculty hiring to student recruitment to budgeting to fundraising. This isn't an administrative body, or an executive edict. It is a bottom-up, comprehensive organizing paradigm. It is one driven and governed by faculty—not by the Chancellor, provost, or dean. This program's goal—to make a truly Inclusive Illinois experience—is based on establishing transparent, consistent, and trusting relationships between departments, among our respective colleges, and across our leadership team. It is faculty-guided and it is driven not by administrative decree, but by a shared vision of Illinois as a pre-eminent public research university with a land-grant mission.

We are seeing results. Between December 2013 and August 2014, 46 new faculty members joined Engineering's ranks and 23 of them were women. This is the first time—at least in modern memory—when half of this college's faculty class was comprised of women. At the recommendation of the senior faculty leadership committee organized under EDGE, we committed $1.4 million of recurring funds for investment in campus programs and initiatives outside of hiring and scholarships to establish a stronger culture of respect and academic welcome. In addition, we annually host a national conference on Faculty Women in the Academy beginning almost four years ago. A standing Gender Equity Council guides our policy-making in everything from salary to childcare to ensure women are fully represented in every part of the campus. Additionally, there are other standing campus diversity committees (also consisting of faculty and students) addressing disability, race, sexual orientation, and climate that are charged (and funded and empowered) with implementing actions and policies that enhance our community. Another initiative involves faculty hiring. Illinois committed to 500 new tenure and tenure track hires in the coming five to seven years across the campus in strategic areas. Within that 500 goal, we put in place programs to build our diversity just as strategically as we build our expertise.

For the first time, the faculty hiring proposals submitted by college deans include short and long term plans for enhancing the diversity of their programs. This does two things: it makes diversity consideration a routine part of the process rather than an afterthought and it lets departments plan and hire strategically to enhance their excellence. As an institution, we committed to increasing investments to help these departments make those hires. The Targets of Opportunity hiring program provides permanent funding up to $85,000 a year towards the hiring of a faculty member from an underrepresented population. These are intended to be career-long incentives—again, committing not just to getting candidates in the door, but keeping them here. In addition, we contribute $60,000 annually to the salary line if a search yields a second diverse candidate who would be an outstanding hire.

As the campus considers gearing up for a substantial capital fundraising campaign, the goal is to double our annual cash donations in the next three years. This campaign will be one focused on faculty endowments and student fellowships—again with diversity plans incorporated into how we will invest these new resources. A specific example of the impact from this action is the College of Engineering. The freshman class is 22% women, compared to 16.5% in the previous couple of years—a 27% increase. That's attributable, at least in some significant part, to additional scholarship support offered to incoming students from money raised as part of the Engineering Visionary Scholarship Initiative—a $100 million scholarship campaign. The intent is very specifically to establish a pool for recurring, major scholarships for undergraduates.

I realize these examples are scattered throughout the campus organization, but the one thing they have in common is this: they are all investments from existing, traditional sources of funds. We have skin in the game and that "skin" is in the form of permanent investments that are unwaveringly aimed at creating a university that is a premiere destination for scholars and students from underrepresented populations. We are reprioritizing how we spend state, tuition, and private gift funds and directing them into programs and policies that are laying a permanent foundation for human growth in the sciences certainly, but across the entire organization.

There is the need for constant vigilance and determination when it comes to creating diverse and inclusive campuses. There is no finish line for us—no point where we get to say "We did it! We won." The line is always going to be ahead of us—and what defines success is going to be one that requires constant adjustment based on the world around us. We cannot let up and we cannot let our commitments become hollow formalities. The reality of our position in the world of higher education is one where excellence and pre-eminence come with significant costs. But, as we are seeing, the capacity and interest from private and corporate sources for these investments is there and available to institutions with reputations like Illinois.

These are all components of a comprehensive approach to organizing ourselves to be a university that isn't simply chasing after this year's top women or minority candidates to boost our numbers. We are striving to be a university that operates on all fronts to really, fundamentally transform our business and academic practices to create a self-sustaining incubator of diverse graduates who we hope will be new members of the professoriate. No matter how intensely we individually try to change the institutions that we live in, or higher education in general, or even more broadly our entire society around the importance of diversity and inclusion and its connections to excellence, we will not make real progress unless there is institutional commitment to this goal.

Conclusion

How do we attract and retain a greater number of women, particularly women of color, into careers in higher education? How do we get ourselves to the place where our recruitment is not unusual, does not require heroic investments of resources and efforts, and does not wax and wane in what seems like arbitrary waves? How do we reorganize our institutional organizational and governance structures and rethink some entrenched processes and traditions so that we do not just increase the numbers, but fundamentally integrate diverse perspectives and ideas into the identity of higher education? I am not just talking about creating platforms that give women of color a louder voice in the faculty of the Academy. But rather I am talking about creating an Academy that listens and learns from the broadest spectrum of voices so that it grows in strength and excellence from those voices and perspectives.

If we are going to increase the number of women of color in the academy, and if we are going to ensure their success and progress, and if we are going to ensure that they are compensated and rewarded fairly, and that they are fulfilled, we have to work personally but we also have to act institutionally. I see an inevitable transition in the makeup of the Academy on the horizon in the coming decades. But I know right now we need to lay the ground-work to ready our universities to embrace these changes. We also need to realize the full intellectual potential of this next great influx of new ideas, new cultural identities, and new approaches to education.

As faculty members, our primary responsibilities are to educate students to be ready for the global world that they will be entering, to expand the universe of knowledge through our research and our scholarship, and to engage with the community (local, state, national, and the global) around us to so that there are no boundaries between the institutions of higher education in which we work and the world around us. Only by fulfilling all three missions can we extend access and opportunity for everyone in the world. Reaching that goal does not have to be limited to our teaching, research, or discovery. Who we are—women, women of color—also gives us the ability to influence our environment and the future of our universities, through our mentoring of each other.

As women of color in the Academy, the key is to be persistent, to be resilient, and to thrive. We should do this by carving out new ways within our communities. Together we should pool these unique viewpoints and to put them into the collaborative, constructive debate that is going to shape how we teach and who we teach. As women of color faculty and administrators, we are taxed with the responsibility of monitoring what and how we create, maintain, and ensure opportunities. It is our collective responsibility to guarantee that our universities of this twenty-first century offer experiences that are relevant to the society around us.

This is, of course, on top of the traditional scholarly and teaching demands institutions and disciplinary fields place on the shoulders of women of color faculty. We ask that you be leaders in your academic careers—in publishing, exploring, educating, and serving. But we also ask that you advise and mentor people—women and minorities who are following your path so that their journeys are easier than yours or mine. In short, we expect you to be modern pioneers in pushing the boundaries of race and culture within a higher educational system that in some ways still holds onto traditions established centuries ago. In so many ways, we expect women, particularly women of color, among our ranks to be role models and to break new ground not just in research, but in personal potential. We dually request that you be light-bearers for future generations of powerful and thought provoking women.

When it comes to a group of people to lead the way, when it comes to integrating unique or different viewpoints into the shared governance of our profession—how could we find any better-prepared or equipped to do than women of color in our faculties? For many of us, this is already an ingrained part of our identity and an inseparable component of our life experiences. We may be in the minority, whether culturally or academically or both, but when it comes to leading this particular effort, we are going to be the experts the rest of the Academy looks to for guidance. Because it is through discussion, debate and the exchange of viewpoints where we, together, are going to move the needle when it comes to building truly diverse communities of students, staff, and faculty who will be generating the solutions to the grand challenges of our times.

Reference

National Science Foundation. (2010). *National Center for Science and Engineering Statistics.* Survey of Earned Doctorates.

8. Reflections about Asian American Female Leadership in the Academy

MENAH PRATT-CLARKE

Introduction

I met Dr. Phyllis Wise when she arrived at the University of Illinois at Urbana-Champaign Illinois in October 2011. At that time, I was the Associate Chancellor for Strategic Affairs and Diversity. Although I had been offered another position at the University of Illinois as Secretary of the University, the interim chancellor shared that the new incoming chancellor would probably be someone I would enjoy working with and suggested I might want to wait for the individual's arrival. Because of the secrecy of presidential searches, no details could be disclosed to me. I decided to decline the offer to serve as Secretary and waited expectantly for the new chancellor. When Chancellor Phyllis Wise was introduced as the new chancellor, I was excited and surprised. She asked me to serve as her chief of staff as she began her tenure and I served in that role for her first year.

Although the chief of staff position can have many different manifestations, I saw my role as one of education and protection. Since the learning curve for a new chancellor is steep, I felt a responsibility to help her learn the politics, the people, the culture, and the history of Illinois. I also felt a responsibility to share as much as I knew, to help her be prepared for meetings, and to help advance her agenda and vision for the institution. It was a relationship of trust and loyalty.

As Dr. Wise's chief of staff, I was asked to help her fill key vacancies. I served as the staff support for three vice-chancellors' searches. Although all the hires were males, I learned several lessons about the importance of leadership programs in developing women leaders and preparing them for the interview process. I learned that women have an additional burden of having to sell themselves aggressively and promote their accomplishments. The humility of many women often undermines a committee's perception of her as a strong visionary leader. In addition, the role of unconscious or implicit bias in higher education and its effect on women and minorities has been well documented (Equality Challenge Unit, 2013). These challenges based on gender are compounded for women of color.

I worked with Dr. Wise for four years. During that time, I was able to support and participate in many of her strategic initiatives. I also witnessed the difficulty she faced as an Asian American female leader in higher education. As the literature reflects, Asian American women leaders in higher education face unique challenges based on their intersectional identities of race, gender, and culture (Li, 2014; Li & Beckett, 2006). At the same time, their identities and backgrounds enable them offer unique perspectives, approaches, and contributions to the academy. This was true for Dr. Wise. The next section explores these issues.

Literature Review

While Asian Americans is a broad category encompassing multiple social, cultural, and geographical identities, Chinese Americans, Filipino Americans, Korean Americans, and Japanese Americans tend to be the larger Asian American groups studied in education scholarship due to the similarity of cultural values (Somer, 2007). As a group, Asian Americans have been referred to as "arguably one of the most marginalized and misunderstood populations in higher education" (Museus & Chang, 2009, p. 104). They are frequently treated simultaneously as the "forgotten minority," but also subjected to stereotypes associated with the "model minority" (American Council on Education, 2013). Despite their citizenship status, they are often seen as the "perpetual" or "forever foreigner" (Li, 2014, p. 153; Ng, Lee, & Pak, 2007). This "othering" of Asian Americans perpetuates discrimination and marginalization (Ng et al., p. 122).

Sue, Bucceri, Lin, Nadal, and Torino (2007) document racial microaggressions experienced by Asian Americans, including being treated as an alien in their own land, being invisible, being subject to second-class citizenship, and being impacted by the pathologizing of cultural values and communication styles. Sue et al. (2007, p. 76) also noted that Asian Americans experience the denial of interethnic differences and the denial of their racial reality. In addition, Asian American women are frequent victims of "exoticization" (Sue et al., 2007, p. 76). Similarly, Cho (2003) noted the particular susceptibility of Asian American women to "racialized sexual harassment" which occurs when "sexualized racial stereotypes combine with racialized gender stereotypes" (p. 35). The intersection of these stereotypes with the model minority myth and associated traits of passivity and submissiveness can perpetuate the belief that there are no consequences for harassing Asian American women (Cho, 2003).

The challenges for Asian American women in higher education are compounded by their low representation in senior leadership positions, including presidencies. Asian Americans, including men and women, represent only 1.5% of college and university presidents (American Council of Education, 2013). Asian American women presidents, then, constitute an even smaller percentage and often serve at two year institutions (Mella, 2012). As a result, they have been called the "invisible minority in higher education" (Mella, 2012, p. 71). Their invisibility has impacted scholarship on their experience because it is difficult to provide the anonymity often requested for narrative inquiry given their deeply personal and often identifying information. As a result, there is very little scholarly work on Asian American women presidents.

A majority of the scholarship on Asian American women leaders in higher education has been found in dissertations written by Asian American female scholars (Chung, 2008; Ideta, 1996; Mella, 2012; Somer, 2007; Torne, 2013; Wilking, 2001). Their scholarship, along with the work of Chen and Hune (2011) and Kobayashi (2009), reveals common themes and challenges related to the experiences of Asian American female leaders. Although they often experience discrimination, the bamboo ceiling, and stereotypes, they are also resilient, innovative, entrepreneurial, and willing to take risks to advance their institutions (Hyun, 2005; Li, 2014).

One of the earliest works on Asian American women administrators was by Ideta (1996). Ideta (1996) utilized narrative inquiry to interview ten Asian American female senior level administrators in higher education, including three community college presidents. The key themes that emerged from her research were finding strength through adversity, attributing success to good fortune, and pursuing excellence (Ideta, 1996, p. 40). Ideta (1996) noted that these themes appear to be aspects of Asian culture. The women experienced challenges based on their race and gender identities in traditional White male environments (Ideta, 1996).

Wilking's (2001) findings were similar to Ideta's (1996) based on a narrative inquiry of five Asian American women college presidents and provosts, four of whom were at community colleges. She (Wilking, 2001) found that the challenges faced by these women administrators included balancing work and home, dealing with stereotypes about women and Asians, and enduring phases of self-doubt. Positive influences in these women's lives included a willingness to take on new challenges, family support, the continual development of leadership skills, a "servant" leadership style, a strong work ethic, feeling lucky/fortunate, having a positive attitude, and feeling different from the typical Asian American (Wilking, 2001).

Somer (2007) also explored the experiences of five Asian American female senior leaders in community colleges who were seeking either the vice presidency or the presidency. She (Somer, 2007) found that barriers to advancement included Asian physicality and invisibility. Somer (2007, p. 133) noted that many Asian American females are described as "petite" and that Asian Americans "tend to be slight and diminutive in stature." Their stature, as well as a "youthful appearance," caused them to be invisible, ignored, and being perceived as unable to be leaders (Somer, 2007, p. 135). The women also experienced discrimination, stereotyping, and "very hurtful statements and actions by non-Asian Americans" (Somer, 2007, p. 137). Despite the challenges, a positive attitude, a strong work ethic, and having good mentors and role models were important components in their success, especially in light of their accidental leadership path (Somer, 2007).

Chung (2008) also found similar themes. Chung interviewed twelve senior administrators, eleven of whom were in student affairs at four year universities and colleges. She explored challenges, leadership styles, networks, ethgender, and cultural identity. She (Chung, 2008) found that women leaders had to fight the challenge of breaking stereotype myths, and being the only one. The issues of intersectionality based upon race, gender, age, and physical stature were clearly illustrated in the comments by some of the administrators. Chung found that there were common stereotypes about Asian women as either being the "wallflower" and quiet, submissive, and obedient, or the "dragon lady" and mean and vicious (Chung, 2008, p. 194). Some administrators referenced their experience with racism and sexism:

> Someone said to me and I can quote him, "I don't mind at all that you're oriental, or you're younger than me, or you're a woman." The fact that he is saying this is total racism and sexism. ... We get minimized every day. We need to be incredibly self-assured with some thick skin. That is why I think access and equity are critical with our institutions—not just for Asians but in multiculturalism and diversity. (Chung 2008, p. 187)

Another comment is also illustrative of the challenge of not fitting the package because of their physical stature and not being perceived as a leader:

I've always had to work against people's stereotypical expectations about a very petite Asian American woman who takes charge and is in a leadership role. Problem is when your behavior doesn't match the stereotype and people have negative reactions (negative consequences usually). I always had to work harder, faster, more and smarter to gain the credibility. I was never given the things automatically. (Chung, 2008, p. 189)

Despite these challenges, mentors and networks played an important role in the women's success.

Kobayashi (2009, p. 80) also mentioned the importance of being connected to the Asian American network, and being "plugged in" as a key finding from his research on five deans and six vice presidents, including five women and six men. While there were some common themes across gender, including becoming an accidental administrator, there were also unique findings for female administrators. Key themes for women included having an entrepreneurial spirit, taking risks and initiative to advance the institution, and working on projects that were "outside of the box" (Kobayashi, 2009, p. 82). Kobayashi (2009, p. 85) noted that the entrepreneurial spirit involved "the organizing and reorganizing of social and economic mechanisms to turn resources and situations to practical account" and the "acceptance of risk or failure."

Unlike men, female administrators' challenges involved issues of intersectionality related to their race, gender, age, and physical stature:

You know I could never tell if I was being mistreated because of my age, my gender or my race. I couldn't tell. But there are some people that feel very free to totally thrash me and put me down, either one-on-one or publicly. And I don't know what gives them permission to think they can do that. And they don't do that to all people. Is it because I'm student services? Is it because I'm a woman? Is it because maybe I might say something bad? Is it the stand that I take on issues, so I'm a target, mark or what? You know, I don't know because it's all mixed in there together. (Kobayashi, 2009, p. 86)

Another shared a similar comment related to her identities:

When I came here, whenever I felt less than or felt overlooked or discriminated against, I didn't really know whether it was because I was female, I was young, I was more quiet, because I was really part of the good-old boys arena. Whether it was female, whether it was because I was Asian or whether it was because I was young and I was always questioning myself, "Why was I overlooked?" (Kobayashi, 2009, p. 87)

The physical stature of Asian American women was also mentioned: "we don't have the stature, the physical stature, that's imposing, that seems to indicate that person can be, 'strong,' quote/unquote, in situations" (Kobayashi,

2009, p. 95). These examples illustrate the impact of intersecting identities in Asian American females' experiences in higher education.

Mella's (2012) work confirmed these findings. Her work was one of the few dissertations that focused on Asian American women presidents. At the time of her dissertation, Mella (2012) found that there were only eleven Asian American women presidents. She interviewed eight female presidents, six of whom were from two-year public colleges, one from a two-year private college, and one from a four-year public university (Mella, 2012). She examined the impact of the model minority stereotype on the representation of Asian American women in university presidencies. She found that typical words used to describe the model minority stereotype associated with women were "successful," "hard working," "submissive," "quiet," "docile," "never complaining," "subservient," and "meek"—thus, creating "the perfect unassuming, non-threatening minority group for the dominant culture" (Mella, 2012, p. 179). This stereotype about Asian American women, when combined with a shorter physical stature, creates a perception that is inconsistent with the dominant culture's expectations of leaders and leadership: "You think about leaders as being tall people. It might not be a good thing to think about … but many Asian women are short. And many people don't look at them as leaders because they're short" (Mella, 2012, pp. 147–148).

Another participant acknowledged that the stereotypes actually described her perception of herself:

> As an Asian woman, I think the barriers I face is the stereotype of what Asians are like, and many of the stereotypes—I actually fit those stereotypes. Well, I'm a soft-spoken person; my voice doesn't get excited or very loud. I've always been like that … I like to smile a lot. I'm not particularly tall and muscular. You know, I'm the traditional Asian woman. So, and the stereotypes, the descriptors I got all the time was, "You're so nice. You're so friendly." Those are words that don't describe a good leader. (Mella, 2012, p. 110)

In addition to perceptions about leadership ability based on identity, the women also experienced discrimination and bias based on their identities: "I really feel that I was the victim of racism, sexism and ageism, with the older White faculty who were so entrenched in the academic senate and the union. More so the academic senate than the union" (Mella, 2012, p. 117). Often accidental administrators, the women worked hard to overcome the barriers and stereotypes; they focused on making transformational difference and relied on mentors for support and guidance (Mella, 2012).

These themes were also present in the work of Torne (2013). Torne (2013) studied the career and leadership experiences of five Asian American female presidents at two-year colleges in the Pacific Coast region. Her dissertation revealed the continuing role of race and gender discrimination and gender inequality. Another finding was the need to manage the stereotype that "Asians are too soft, passive, quiet," and avoid conflict (Torne, 2013, p. 110). The strategies for success included extensive preparation through ensuring academic credibility, documented accomplishments, making contributions in other leadership roles in local and national organizations, having strong people skills, and relying on cultural values about leadership (Torne, 2013). Other factors in their success include having mentors, networks, and social support groups (Torne, 2013).

Her findings are consistent with those of Neilson and Suyemoto (2009). Based on a survey of Asian American leaders, including five men and five women serving in senior administrative positions at community colleges and four year institutions, they (Neilson & Suyemoto, 2009) found that cultural values play an important role in influencing success. The key values were hard work as honor, legacy, and moral obligation; collaboration as interconnection; and risk taking as sacrifice for future generations (Neilson & Suyemoto, 2009, pp. 90–91). Khator (2010), however, noted that other common Asian values, such as "deference to authority figures, respect for elders, self-effacement, restraint, avoidance of family shame, and placing others' needs ahead of one's own" can also be seen as incompatible with leadership roles.

The scholarship, then, about Asian American women in higher education leadership reflects that they do experience challenges from their intersectionality identities of race, gender, culture, physical stature, and youthful appearance (Hune, 2006). These realities often result in experiences of the "Plexiglas" ceiling: "We call it Plexiglas, because it gives you an illusion you can break through it and you get bounced back" (Kobayashi, 2009, p. 94). Chen and Hune (2011) also discuss the reality of a Plexiglas ceiling for Asian American women. They (Chen & Hune, 2011) analyzed the pipeline and noted that despite gains in the number of doctoral degrees compared to Asian American men, Asian American women lag behind men in obtaining faculty positons, being tenured, and being promoted to full professor. They also lag behind White male and female peers (Chen & Hune, 2011).

The leaky pipeline is often the result of a "chilly" campus climate based on racial and gender stereotyping, accent biases, and the "privileging of white and male values, norms, and interests" (Chen & Hune, 2011, p. 179). Asian American women are often "punished" regardless of whether they conform to "male-defined and Eurocentric notions of leadership" or defy "racialized gendered stereotypes" (Hune, 2006, p. 32). Chen and Hune (2011, p. 183) also mention the "glass cliffs" and the concern that women of color are often set up for failure with high–risk opportunities, compared to "glass elevators" for White men that promote their ascendancy through the pipeline.

Although Asian American women face unique challenges in the Academy based on their identities, they also make unique contributions to the Academy. Asian American women are resilient, innovative, and have an entrepreneurial spirit. They are hard workers and willing to take risks. Several of these themes and experiences are reflected in Chancellor Phyllis Wise's journey. Based on her own narrative in Chapter 6, as well as the public record, there was extensive preparation for the presidency, including influential mentors; an entrepreneurial spirit guided her leadership style; she had an unwavering commitment to diversity; and her intersectional identities of race, gender, and culture impacted her experiences in significant ways. The section below explores these themes.

Foundation and Preparation

In her narrative, Chancellor Wise shares that her parents, both educators, had high expectations for her and were very influential in her life. Her father had a medical degree and a doctorate, and her mother had a nursing degree and a teaching nursing education degree (Tajika, 2010). As a child, Dr. Wise would often go to her father's lab on the weekend and watch experiments (Tajika, 2010). She noted that her mother taught her "manners, etiquette, courtesy, compassion, humility. She taught me to strive for the highest goals, but, most importantly, she taught me generosity. She did this through her life story" (Wood, 2011b). These values of her mother were reflected in Dr. Wise's own "modest demeanor" (Long, 2010). As Dr. Wise's cousin noted, Phyllis "never boasts about her success. In our culture, we were taught not to do that" (Wood, 2011b).

Dr. Wise's parents had high expectations for her. She (Wise, 2016) noted that her parents emphasized through "innumerable discussions" the "need to study hard, the need to compete, the need to overcome the stigma of being a minority and a female, and the need to never quit." The four mantras influenced her journey as a scientist and as a leader. Despite obtaining a bachelor's degree in biology from Swarthmore College, a master's degree, and then a doctorate in 1972 in zoology from the University of Michigan, she notes that her father was "disappointed" that she had "only" earned her PhD, rather than a medical degree (Wise, 2016). It is important to note that when she obtained her doctorate in 1972, she was the "the rare woman—much less an Asian one—in a field largely dominated by men" (Wise, 2016).

Another important component of her preparation was the influence of mentors. She (Wise, 2016) mentions the role of mentors at several stages in her career, while as a graduate student, post-doctoral fellow, assistant professor, associate professor, and full professor. A mentor was instrumental in encouraging her to purse the administrative path beginning with a department chair position. As a self-described "accidental chancellor," she recognized the she had been "mentored and advised" all her life "in many ways and by countless people" (Wise, 2016). She had a tremendous respect and appreciation for the role of mentors. As she told the Swarthmore graduating class in 2008 when she was awarded an honorary doctorate, "My humble words of advice for you: take note of the people you encounter who inspire you, who energize you, who live the way you aspire to. Watch how they work, learn from them. Never stop observing" (Swarthmore Commencement, 2008; Wood, 2011b).

Though the guidance of mentors and through her hard work and commitment to excellence, Dr. Wise was well-prepared for leadership in the Academy. In addition to her experience as department head and dean, she had exceptional scholarly credentials. She served on multiple scientific advisory boards and received two MERIT (Method to Extend Research in Time) awards from National Institute of Health from 1986 to 1996, and from 2001 to 2010, a sign of her "superior competence and outstanding productivity" (Roseth, 2005). She was featured in a Parade Magazine cover story on "The Quiet Heroes," which profiled individuals engaged in lifesaving research (Roseth, 2005).

When her appointment as Provost was announced at Washington, the president said, "She brings all the requisite skills and values needed to be the provost of one of America's top research universities: an eminent scientist, a brilliant educator, a talented leader" (Roseth, 2005). When she was announced as the interim president, she was the first woman and first Asian American woman to serve as UW President (Roseth, 2010). The Board noted that she brought "exceptional strengths" to the role (Roseth, 2010). One of those strengths included her indomitable work ethic. As a colleague at the University of Washington remarked when she was appointed interim President, "she is well known for sending emails in the wee hours of the morning, a sign that she never stopped working and thinking about university business" (Long, 2011).

When her appointment was announced at the University of Illinois, the press release noted that, "she has a remarkable record of scientific accomplishment that includes more than 200 scientific publications and an impressive record of over 30 years of continuous funding for her research" (University of Illinois Alumni Network, n.d.). The president at the time of her appointment noted that her "research and teaching credentials provided her with a high degree of credibility" with faculty and deans (Illinois Public Media News, 2011). Dr. Wise's preparation for the chancellorship of the University of Illinois was grounded in an entire career as both a scholar and administrator. When she assumed the chancellorship at Illinois, she had over 40 years of experience in the academy (Wood, 2011a). Her understanding of the academy enabled her to be a creative and innovative leader.

Entrepreneurial Spirit

Consistent with scholarship on Asian Americans that recognizes their entrepreneurial spirit and willingness to take risks (Kobayashi, 2009), Dr. Wise's initiatives in her higher education leadership roles involved efforts with significant risks, but also high potential rewards. In her narrative, she acknowledged that "leadership also involves taking some calculated risks and actions" that are sometimes successful and sometimes unsuccessful (Wise, 2016). At Washington, despite significant opposition, she successfully created a new College of Environment, by combining the College of Forestry with the College of Ocean and Fishery Sciences (Long, 2010). As the chairman of the board of regents at UW noted, "Very seldom do you ever see a provost take on a challenge like this" (Long, 2010). Dr. Wise also mentioned a less successful effort involving an attempt to separate the College of Arts and Sciences into two colleges. The proposal was to have one college focused on the humanities, social sciences, and arts, and another college focused on math and the sciences. Though the idea failed, it remains an example of her entrepreneurial spirit.

Her most significant entrepreneurial efforts at the University of Illinois began as a result of a new visioning process she undertook when she arrived. "Visioning Future Excellence" involved answering two questions: what are the challenges the world will face in the next 20–50 years and what role should Illinois play in addressing them? (University of Illinois, July 2013). Six areas emerged from that exercise: economic development, education, energy and the environment, health and wellness, information and technology, and social equality and cultural understanding (University of Illinois, 2013). In response, she developed two critical areas of focus: a diversity effort under the umbrella of EDGE (Enhancing Diversity and Guiding Excellence) and an economic development and health/wellness effort based upon developing a College of Medicine.

The College of Medicine was a significant goal for Dr. Wise. She recognized early on that Illinois' competitiveness as an institution hinged on its ability to have a distinct college of medicine. While there was a college of medicine on campus, it was the University of Illinois at Chicago's College of Medicine with an Urbana campus. As the Chicago Tribune (Cohen, 2015a, 2015b) reported, the effort to create a new medical school was a year-long process. It was a courageous initiative to differentiate the institution and to help ensure its continued relevance. She felt it was necessary for the university to remain competitive. She saw it as a "game-changer" for the university and an opportunity to "truly redesign medicine" (Cohen, 2015a, 2015b). The College of Medicine is an important legacy for Dr. Wise's tenure at Illinois. In the face of opposition, she tireless worked to position Illinois for a lasting future. It is truly an example of her entrepreneurial spirit and her willingness to undertake significant risk to advance the institution.

Commitment to Diversity

As is evident in her chapter, diversity was another key priority for her. She emphasized from her first public remarks that one of her "key objectives and areas of focus here would be a firm and unwavering commitment to diversity and inclusion" (Wise, 2016). She recognized that accountability started with her. She realized that as a leader, she could use her position to effect change. She focused on developing a clear framework and vision and then investing resources to support the vision. She understood that it would be critical to integrate diversity as a foundation for excellence into every element of the university's operations, from financial planning to campus policies.

As the Associate Chancellor for Strategic Affairs and Diversity, I was able to see first-hand the extent of her commitment to diversity. She spoke about it relentlessly; she sought to institutionalize the commitment through operational structures; and she worked to advance it through significant financial investments. She helped to resource the campus' diversity committees by providing them a budget; she increased investments to graduate fellowships and undergraduate scholarships; and she aggressively supported a faculty diversity hiring initiative. She was instrumental in the founding of the Faculty Women of Color in the Academy conference at Illinois, and she provided extensive support to the Office of Diversity, Equity, and Access.

The issue of diversity was very personal for her as a woman in STEM and as a woman of color leader in the academy. Her narrative reflects that she recognized the importance of increasing the number of women in STEM fields. She knew first-hand the challenges women face balancing careers and families as scientists. She knew first-hand the challenges of sexism for women scientists. She recognized that women of color bear multiple burdens: burdens related to personal success and also responsibility for the larger community of women of color to serve as role models and resources. Dr. Wise's experiences at Illinois with racism and sexism reveal that she herself would be tested as a woman of color in the academy.

Experiencing Racism and Sexism

The literature reflects that Asian American women's experiences are influenced by their race, gender, culture, and physical status (Chung, 2008; Kobayashi, 2009). As a petite woman, as an Asian American woman in the neurosciences, and as an Asian American female senior administrator, Dr. Wise was subjected to many of the stereotypes and biases that are mentioned in the literature. She (Wise, 2016) acknowledges that her experiences have been influenced by the fact that she is a woman and a woman of color. She acknowledged the reality she faced as the only woman chair of physiology at the annual association meeting. She mentions the initial refusal of the "Association of Chairmen of Departments of Physiology" to change their name to "Chairs of Physiology" and being told that "chairs were pieces of furniture" (Wise, 2016).

Although Dr. Wise choose not to address two very public experiences related to her identity in her narrative, they are discussed here given the critical importance of illustrating the complicated nature of presidencies for women of color. The first episode was at the University of Illinois in January 2014 when Dr. Wise publicly announced that classes would not be cancelled for a snow day. In response to her email that the campus would remain open, there was a social media storm. Buzz Feed captured the racist, sexist, offensive, personal, violent, and misogynistic nature of the tweets, including the hashtag that was selected (Buzzfeed, 2014):

> "It's going to be –27 without wind chill tomorrow morning and I have class at 8 #FuckPhyllis #Cunt #Bitch #Whore";

> "phyllis can go shove tomorrow's weather up her wideset vagina. #fuckphyllis";

> "In a room with Phyllis Wise, Adolf Hitler, and a gun with one bullet. Who do I shoot? #fuckphyllis";

> "Asians and women aren't responsible for their actions FuckPhyllis"

> "@ChanPhyllisWise #fuckphyllis";

> "Communist China no stop by cold #FuckPhyllis";

> "Phyllis Wise is the Kim Jong Un of chancellors #fuckphyllis"

As the Chronicle of Higher Education noted, "a flurry of comments focused either on Wise's status as a woman, as an Asian American, or both. The hashtag of choice: #fuckphyllis" (Jaschik, 2014). The article acknowledged the reality that if Dr. Wise was a White male, "the texts with the violent sexualized tones would have been absent or presented in a different manner" (Jaschik, 2014). The tweets also reflected the common "dragon lady" stereotype of Asian American women with them portrayed as cold and heartless (Jaschik, 2014).

Dr. Wise chose to address this issues in an article published in Inside Higher Education entitled, "Moving Past Digital Hate" (Wise, 2014). In her (Wise, 2014) response, she acknowledged that "vitriolic attacks on an individual ... can be discouraging and damaging—personally and institutionally." She (Wise, 2014) noted that the attacks on her were "vulgar, crude and in some instances racist and sexist." She discussed the tension between protected speech and expectations for civil discourse from students in higher education, noting that "racist, intimidating or culturally derogatory epithets have no place in any debate in any circumstance" (Wise, 2014). In reaffirming her commitment to diversity, she emphasized the importance of an "an unwavering and unrelenting commitment to building truly diverse communities of students and scholars," such that there is a true appreciation and value for different ideas, values, and perspectives (Wise, 2014).

What is clear from her response is her recognition of the critical responsibility that universities have for educating students on issues of diversity. She also continues to connect diversity to excellence. She recognizes the complicated issues of freedom of speech, though many could argue that some of the statements, including threats of violence, were outside the bounds of freedom of speech. This incident, however, is illustrative of the challenges that Asian American women leaders can face in the academy by virtue of their race, gender, and culture.

This first incident, however, almost foreshadowed the second public incident. Although the second public incident does not explicitly reference her identity, it is clear that her experience related to her resignation was very different than many other chancellors and presidents (Meisel, 2015c). Like many men, her resignation was a negotiated agreement with the University in which she would return to the faculty and receive a $400,000 bonus, based upon the retention agreement in her contract which provided that she would earn $100,000 a year for five years (Bossert, 2015; Cohen, 2015c; Illinois Public Media News, 2011; Meisel, 2015b). Her resignation was announced on August 6, 2015, to be effective on August 12 (Wurth, 2015a). In announcing her resignation, Wise stated that "external issues have arisen over the past year that have distracted us from the important tasks at hand.

I have concluded that these issues are diverting much needed energy and attention from our goals. I therefore believe the time is right for me to step aside" (Cohen, 2015c; Wurth, 2015a).

The issues to which she refers involved a lawsuit by Steven Salaita, the resulting boycott of the University of Illinois by the academic community, and the subsequent censure by the AAUP (Meisel, 2015c). They also involved lawsuits and concerns raised from student athletes (Cohen, 2015c). In announcing her resignation, the president of Illinois commended Wise, noting that "In addition to other accomplishments too numerous to list, her vision and advocacy for a new College of Medicine represents a major contribution and provides for a lasting legacy" (Wurth, 2015a). One of the trustees noted that she was a "tremendous chancellor" (Bossert, 2015).

After she submitted her resignation, it was revealed that an ethics investigation discovered that emails from personal email accounts had not been reported and released as part of Freedom of Information Act requests (Meisel, 2015c). Legal counsel, public affairs officers, and other senior officials, including Board members, were aware of the use of the personal accounts to discuss campus strategy around personnel matters and the new college of medicine (Abunimah, 2015). Many of them, in fact, were copied on the emails (Abunimah, 2015). The use of private email accounts reflects the reality of public higher education leadership and the challenge of communicating, strategizing, and risk-taking to advance a critical university initiative in the face of opposition. Though the strategy was successful and necessary in order to get the College of Medicine approved by the Board, the institution's failure to disclose the personal emails ultimately resulted in difficult consequences for Dr. Wise.

The Board, at its meeting on August 12, 2015, voted not to accept her resignation, not to pay her the $400,000 retention bonus, to reassign her as an advisor to the President, and to begin formal dismissal proceedings under Illinois' statues (Meisel, 2015a). Dr. Wise, however, chose to fight the Board's unprecedented decision. On August 14, she submitted her resignation a second time, accompanied by a public statement. In her statement in which she acknowledged the use of personal email accounts for university business, she noted,

> some reports suggested I did so with illegal intentions or personal motivations. This is simply false. I acted at all times in what I believed to be the best interests of the University. In fact, many of these same communications included campus counsel, board members, and other campus leaders. (Meisel, 2015b)

She also indicated that in response to the Board and the president's request for her resignation, the university agreed to provide the compensation and benefits to which I was entitled, including $400,000 in deferred compensation that was part of my 2011 employment contract. The $400,000 was not a bonus nor a golden parachute; it was a retention incentive that I earned on a yearly basis. (Meisel, 2015b)

She noted that it was her intention to make a substantial donation from her deferred compensation to support the College of Medicine (Meisel, 2015b).

In a decision she felt was "apparently motivated more by politics than the interests of the university," she said that the "board reneged on the promises in our negotiated agreement and initiated termination proceedings. This action was unprecedented, unwarranted and completely contrary to the spirit of our negotiations last week" (Meisel, 2015b). In tendering her resignation for a second time, she concludes her public statement by stating:

These recent events have saddened me deeply. I had intended to finish my career at this university, overseeing the fulfillment of groundbreaking initiatives we had just begun. Instead, I find myself consulting with lawyers and considering options to protect my reputation in the face of the board's position. I continue to wish the best for this great institution, its marvelous faculty, its committed staff and its talented students. (Meisel, 2015b)

In response, her second resignation was accepted and the university decided not to pursue dismissal proceedings. This turn of events and scenario was viewed as unprecedented in the national media. One headline from the Chronicle said, "Stage is set for uncommon ugliness in Illinois Chancellor's exit" (Stripling, 2015). Dan L. King, president of the American Association of University Administrators, that represents presidents and other administrators, expressed his surprise at the university's actions, saying, "This really surprised me. ... I can't remember one, and I've kind of been a student of higher ed for 30 years" (Mercer, 2015).

Despite this very public experience, which many believe was the result of her race and gender, the Champaign-Urbana community recognized the value of her tenure. A public letter of support signed by more than 250 campus and community members praised her tenure and her vision related to the College of Medicine (Wurth, 2015b). The letter, submitted to the Board, acknowledged that Dr. Wise

worked tirelessly for the advancement of the University of Illinois. No chancellor in recent history accomplished in such a short time what Dr. Wise has in her limited tenure. Perhaps, the new medical school will be the tangible, ongoing salute in honor of Dr. Phyllis Wise, University of Illinois Chancellor 2011–2015. (Wurth, 2015b)

Conclusion

What are the lessons learned from the experiences of Dr. Phyllis Wise, one of few Asian American women to head a major research university? As the literature suggests, Asian American women's experiences in higher education leadership roles are impacted and influenced by intersectional identities of race, national origin, and gender (Chung, 2008; Mella, 2012). Despite these barriers, Asian American women can bring a unique perspective and lens to the presidency which can help an institution advance in creative and transformational ways. Dr. Wise's leadership at UW helped create the College of the Environment and her leadership at the University of Illinois helped start the College of Medicine. She demonstrated a strong work ethic; a willingness to take on new challenges; and the ability think outside of the box. She also exhibited resiliency and strength through adversity (Ideta, 1996; Kobayashi, 2009; Somer, 2007; Wilking, 2001).

As we see from Dr. Wise's journey, being prepared, focusing on excellence, and having role models and mentors can help prepare Asian American women for higher education leadership. At the same time, her experience illustrates that the academy must be more intentional in supporting the careers and aspirations of Asian American women, women in STEM, and women of color in the academy. The important contributions that Asian American women can make to the academy can only be made through a recognition and commitment to their success by faculty, deans, presidents, and governance boards.

References

Abunimah, A. (2015, August 12). Is Univ. of Illinois scapegoating Phyllis Wise to maintain Salaita coverup? *The electronic Antifada: Rights and accountability*. Retrieved from https://electronicintifada.net/blogs/ali-abunimah/univ-illinois-scapegoating-phyllis-wise-maintain-salaita-coverup

American Council on Education. (2013, May 1). *ACE brief examines scarcity of Asian Pacific Islander American leaders in higher education*. Retrieved from http://www.acenet.edu/news-room/Pages/ACE-Brief-Examines-Scarcity-of-Asian-Pacific-Islander-American-Leaders-in-Higher-Education.aspx

Bossert, J. (2015, August 6). University of Illinois Urbana Chancellor Wise to resign effective next week. *Illinois Public Media News*. Retrieved from http://will.illinois.edu/news/story/university-of-illinois-urbana-chancellor-wise-to-resign-effective-next-week

BuzzFeed. (2014, January 27). *After being denied a snow day, University of Illinois students respond with racism and sexism*. Retrieved from https://www.buzzfeed.com/regajha/after-being-denied-a-snow-day-university-of-illinois-student#.tqO8JzNn0

Chen, E., & Hune, S. (2011). Asian American Pacific Islander women from Ph.D. to campus president: Gains and leaks in the pipeline. In G. Jean-Marie & B. Lloyd-Jones (Eds.), *Women of color in higher education: Changing directions and new perspectives* (Diversity in Higher Education, Vol. 10, pp. 163–190). Bingley: Emerald Publishing.

Cho, S. (2003). Converging stereotypes in racialized sexual harassment. In A. Wing (Ed.), *Critical race feminism: A reader* (pp. 349–366). New York, NY: NYU Press.

Chung, J. (2008). *The journey: Asian American females in higher education administration* (Order No. 3311039). Available from ProQuest Dissertations & Theses Full Text (193487327). Retrieved from http://search.proquest.com.proxy2.library.illinois.edu/docview/193487327?accountid=14553

Cohen, J. (2015a, March 12). U. of I. president endorses new medical school at Urbana-Champaign. *Chicago Tribune.* Retrieved from http://www.chicagotribune.com/news/local/breaking/ct-u-of-i-medical-school-0313-20150312-story.htmtl

Cohen, J. (2015b, March 12). U. of I. trustees approve new medical school. Chicago Tribune. Retrieved from http://www.chicagotribune.com/news/local/breaking/ct-u-of-i-medical-school-0313-20150312-story.html

Cohen, J. (2015c, August 6). After tumultuous year, U. of I. chancellor abruptly steps down. Chicago Tribune. Retrieved from http://www.chicagotribune.com/news/local/breaking/ct-university-of-illinois-chancellor-resigns-20150806-story.html

Equality Challenge Unit. (2013). *Unconscious bias in higher education: Literature review.* Retrieved from http://www.ecu.ac.uk/publications/unconscious-bias-in-higher-education/

Hune, S. (2006). Asian Pacific American women and men in higher education: The contested spaces of their participation, persistence, and challenges as students, faculty and administrators. In G. Li & G. H. Beckett (Eds.), *"Strangers" of the academy: Asian women scholars in higher education* (pp. 15–36). Sterling, VA: Stylus Publishing.

Hyun, J. (2005). *Breaking the bamboo ceiling: Career strategies for Asians.* New York, NY: HarperCollins.

Ideta, L. M. (1996). *Asian women leaders of higher education: Tales of self-discovery from the ivory tower* (Order No. 9713953). Available from ProQuest Dissertations & Theses Full Text (304303112). Retrieved from http://search.proquest.com.proxy2.library.illinois.edu/docview/304303112?accountid=14553

Illinois Public Media News. (2011, August 3). *University of Washington's Phyllis Wise named UI vice-president, UIUC chancellor.* Retrieved from http://will.illinois.edu/news/story/u.-of-washingtons-phyllis-wise-named-new-ui-vice-president-uiuc-chancellor

Jaschik, S. (2014, January 28). Snow hate. *Inside higher education.* Retrieved from https://www.insidehighered.com/news/2014/01/28/u-illinois-decision-keep-classes-going-leads-racist-and-sexist-twitter-attacks

Khator, R. (2010). Breaking the bamboo ceiling. *Back to the presidency, diversity in leadership.* Retrieved from http://www.uh.edu/president/about/articles/pdf-files/Khator_ACE_bambooceiling.pdf

Kobayashi, H. F. (2009). *Moving up in California community college administration, the perspectives of Asian American deans and vice presidents* (Order No. 3375208). Available from ProQuest Dissertations & Theses Full Text (304837357). Retrieved from http://search.proquest.com.proxy2.library.illinois.edu/docview/304837357?accountid=14553.

Li, G., & Beckett, G. H. (Eds). (2006). *"Strangers" of the academy: Asian women scholars in higher education.* Sterling, VA: Stylus Publishing.

Li, P. (2014). Recent developments hitting the ceiling: An examination of barriers to success for Asian American women. *Berkeley Journal of Gender, Law & Justice, 29*(1), 140–167.

Long, K. (2011, August 3). UW's Phyllis Wise leaving for University of Illinois. *The Seattle Times.* Retrieved from http://www.seattletimes.com/seattle-news/uws-phyllis-wise-leaving-for-university-of-illinois/

Long, K. (2010, October 1). Phyllis Wise takes over as interim president at the UW. *The Seattle Times.* Retrieved from http://www.seattletimes.com/seattle-news/phyllis-wise-takes-over-as-interim-president-at-the-uw/

Meisel, H. (2015a, August 13). Phyllis Wise out with no $400k bonus. *Illinois Public Media News.* Retrieved from http://will.illinois.edu/news/story/phyllis-wise-out-with-no-400k-bonus

Meisel, H. (2015b, August 14). Phyllis Wise resubmits resignation, calls Board's move politically motivated. *Illinois Public Media News.* Retrieved from http://will.illinois.edu/news/story/phyllis-wise-resubmits-resignation-calls-boards-move-politically-motivated

Meisel, H. (2015c, August 18). The path to Phyllis Wise's resignation. *Illinois Public News Media.* Retrieved from http://wuis.org/post/path-phyllis-wises-resignation#stream/0

Mella, H. R. (2012). *Exploratory study of Asian Pacific American female leaders in higher education* (Order No. 3505800). Available from ProQuest Dissertations & Theses Full Text (1013836891). Retrieved from http://search.proquest.com.proxy2.library.illinois.edu/docview/1013836891?accountid=14553.

Mercer, D. (2015, August 14). Outgoing Chancellor Phyllis Wise declines new U of I job, again tries to resign. *The State Journal Register.* http://www.sj-r.com/article/20150814/NEWS/150819742#

Museus, S. D., & Chang, M. J. (2009). Rising to the challenge of conducting research on Asian Americans in higher education. *New Directions for Institutional Research, 142,* 95–105.

Neilson, P. A., & Suyemoto, K. (2009). Using culturally sensitive frameworks to study Asian American leaders in higher education. *New Directions for Institutional Research, 142,* 83–93.

Ng, J. C., Lee, S. S., & Pak, Y. K. (2007). Contesting the model minority and perpetual foreigner stereotypes: A critical review of literature on Asian Americans in education. *Review of Research in Education, 31,* 95–130. Retrieved from http://www.jstor.org.proxy2.library.illinois.edu/stable/20185103

Roseth, B. (2005, June 6). Phyllis Wise selected as University of Washington provost. *University of Washington News Archives.* Retrieved from http://www.washington.edu/news/archive/id/10539

Roseth, B. (2010, July 8). UW Board of Regents names Provost Phyllis Wise as interim president. *UW Today.* Retrieved from http://www.washington.edu/news/2010/07/08/uw-board-of-regents-names-provost-phyllis-wise-as-interim-president-2/

Somer, M. G. (2007). *The experiences of Asian American females seeking vice president and president positions in community colleges: A view of the barriers and facilitators* (Order No. 3295650). Available from ProQuest Dissertations & Theses Full Text (304820270). Retrieved from http://search.proquest.com.proxy2.library.illinois.edu/docview/304820270?accountid=14553.

Stripling, J. (2015, August 13). Stage is set for uncommon ugliness. *Chronicle of Higher Education.* Retrieved from http://chronicle.com/article/Stage-Is-Set-for-Uncommon/232379/

Sue, D. W., Bucceri, J. M., Lin, A. I., Nadal, K. L., & Torino, G. C. (2007). Racial microaggressions and the Asian American experience. *Cultural Diversity & Ethnic Minority Psychology, 13,* 72–81.

Swarthmore Commencements. (2008). *Phyllis Wise, 1967.* Retrieved from http://www.swarthmore.edu/past-commencements/phyllis-wise-67

Tajika, C. (2010, September 2). Phyllis Wise, first Asian American president of the UW, maintains a passion for science. *Northwest Asian Weekly.* Retrieved from http://nwasianweekly.com/2010/09/phyllis-wise-first-asian-american-president-of-the-uw-maintains-a-passion-for-science/

Torne, J. (2013). *Asian American women leaders in the pacific coast: Their pathway to presidency in two-year institutions* (Order No. 3591112). Available from ProQuest Dissertations & Theses Full Text (1433827151). Retrieved from http://search.proquest.com.proxy2.library.illinois.edu/docview/1433827151?accountid=14553.

University of Illinois. (2013, July). *Visioning Future Excellence at Illinois outcomes report.* Retrieved from http://oc.illinois.edu/visioning/reports/VFE_outcomesreport.pdf

University of Illinois Alumni Network. (n.d.). *Dr. Phyllis Wise named new UI vice president and Urbana chancellor.* Retrieved from http://www.uialumninetwork.org/article.html?aid=221

Wilking, K. A. (2001). *Asian Pacific American female chief executive officers in higher education: Their challenges and strategies to the top* (Order No. 3008665). Available from ProQuest Dissertations & Theses Full Text (304702365). Retrieved from http://search.proquest.com.proxy2.library.illinois.edu/docview/304702365?accountid=14553

Wise, P. (2014, January 30). Moving past digital hate. *Inside Higher Education.* Retrieved from https://www.insidehighered.com/views/2014/01/30/chancellor-u-illinois-responds-twitter-incident

Wise, P. (2016). Re-envisioning the academy for women of color. In M. Pratt-Clarke & J. Maes (Eds.), *Journeys of social justice: Women of color presidents in the academy.* New York, NY: Peter Lang Publishing.

Wood, P. (2011a, August 3). New UI chancellor named. *News Gazette*. Retrieved from http://www.news-gazette.com/news/local/2011-08-03/new-ui-chancellor-named.html

Wood, P. (2011b, October 16). New chancellor took her own path. *News Gazette*. Retrieved from http://www.news-gazette.com/news/local/2011-10-16/new-chancellor-took-her-own-path.html

Wurth, J. (2015a, August 6). Updated: Phyllis Wise to resign as UI chancellor, effective next week. *News Gazette*. Retrieved from http://www.news-gazette.com/news/local/2015-08-06/updated-phyllis-wise-resign-ui-chancellor-effective-next-week.html

Wurth, J. (2015b, October 10). 250-plus sign letter in support of Wise. *News Gazette*. Retrieved from http://www.news-gazette.com/news/local/2015-10-10/250-plus-sign-letter-support-wise.html

9. My Climb to the Highest Rung

CASSANDRA MANUELITO-KERKVLIET (DINÉ)

Editors' Note:
Dr. Cassandra Manuelito-Kerkvliet is President Emerita of Antioch University Seattle. Appointed in July 2007, Dr. Manuelito-Kerkvliet became the first Native American woman to ascend to the presidency of an accredited university outside the tribal college system. She retired in 2013. Prior to her appointment in Seattle, she served as first woman president of Diné College, the first tribally-controlled community college, located on the Navajo reservation in Tsaile, Arizona from 2000 to 2003. She founded and directed the Indian Education Office at Oregon State University and has worked in various student service and counseling positions at Oregon State University, University of Oregon, University of New Mexico and University of Wyoming.

Dr. Manuelito-Kerkvliet is the great, great granddaughter of Navajo Chief Manuelito of the Diné tribe. She received a Bachelor of Arts degree in Social Work, a Master's degree in Counselor Education, and a doctorate in Educational Policy and Management, with a specialization in higher education administration from the University of Oregon.

My Navajo Foundation

Throughout my thirty years in higher education, I have been guided by my upbringing. The Navajo (Diné) philosophy and traditions have taught me to reach beyond my reservation and origins to influence mainstream higher education. My scholarship as an education policy and management researcher has guided my work with Native students while also increasing my capacity to lead as an administrative leader. Some tenets that brought me success in my roles are based on the importance of rituals and beliefs that are handed down in our Navajo Creation stories and ceremonies.

I have learned that women can and do take leadership roles because of the matrilineal society of our Diné people. Navajos strive for harmony and balance of our physical, emotional, intellectual and spiritual aspects of our lives and with the natural world. We approach life as a process of Thinking, Planning, Living and Assuring called *Sa'ah Naaghai Bik'eh Hózhóón*. Our cultural traditions are grounded in four cardinal directions (east, south, west, north; the four seasons; the cycles of the day and night) that provide a protection from the imperfections in life and for the development of one's well-being. We believe that we all benefit as a community when we share a fundamental respect for everyone and all living things as influenced by our actions, words and decisions. These fundamental understandings and philosophy represent the essence of our Navajo outlook on life and my outlook as a university president.

From Humble Beginnings

I was born and raised in Laramie, Wyoming during the Indian Relocation era in the early 1950s. My mother has an eleventh grade education and my father an eighth grade education. They secured manual labor work in a small town where no other Native American families existed, other than our own. I conjure up memories of discrimination and childhood challenges of being "different" and simply wanting respect for a Diné family making a living in a small, predominately White community.

My parents wanted their offspring to grow up with a deep understanding and preference for the Diné culture. So, we participated in several traditions, Navajo ceremonies and spoke the language. They shared their boarding school experiences, which were laced with recollections of physical abuse. According to my parents, students were harshly reprimanded or ridiculed for speaking Navajo. As a result, every weekend, weather permitting, our family of eight drove 550 miles south on Highway 287 through the Colorado mountains to our family hogan in New Mexico so we could maintain connections to our Navajo roots and visit with grandparents and extended family. My parents encouraged us to never give up on education and promised they would support us with prayers and ceremonies.

I treasure fond memories of being taught the traditional ways of my Diné culture as a young child by my maternal grandparents, who are now deceased. I experienced my first "jolt" of feeling "different" when I entered kindergarten in a public school setting in Laramie, Wyoming. I recognize that my parents did the very best they could with what they knew in order to nurture and raise me and my siblings. I am a product of a strong traditional Diné foundation and a supportive family who laid the course to my corn pollen path that emphasizes achieving balance in aspects of our physical, emotional, intellectual and spiritual aspects of life.

My parents shared oral stories of my great-great-grandfather Chief Manuelito, who had the keen foresight to see the importance of education. When he signed the Navajo Treaty of 1868, he made a statement of belief that "Education is the ladder to success. Tell my grandchildren to climb that ladder." As his descendant, my grandfather's legacy is mine to move my people forward. This connection to my ancestors guides me in life and there is no chance for failure.

I have had unique opportunities open up for me with scholarships, academic resources and financial support for my education when I most needed it. Indispensable advisors/mentors/teachers would come into my life when I needed them. For example, when I commuted to graduate school at the University of Oregon, I found shared living accommodations to reduce commuting costs. I also received support and assistance from helpful individuals in higher institutions and foundations in the Washington, DC area when I began the arduous task of writing my dissertation. Two individuals who come to mind are Dr. Meg Weekes, of American University, who gave me access to several university libraries for my research and Dr. Sally O'Connor, of the National Science Foundation, who facilitated an NSF-sponsored grant to support my travels to gather fifteen interviews. These sister-friend connections continue to support and propel me to greater things and opportunities.

As a student, I also possessed a keen sense of perseverance—to never give up nor become a dropout school statistic. The formal education I achieved was solely my own. It was the education my parents expected from me. My father once expressed the significance of attaining an education as something that could never be taken from me. Education was my modern-day weapon to combat racial discrimination and off-handed comments I experienced, such as "Go back to your reservation and collect welfare." Education was the "ladder to my success" as I broke through glass ceilings and made a successful career in higher education, first in student services advocating for Native American students and subsequently ascending to the ultimate position of college president.

I advocate for Natives to advance their education and become future leaders of our sovereign nations, as my great-great grandfather envisioned. Nearly 150 years ago my ancestors were forcibly marched on the 325-mile Long Walk to *Hwéeldi* or Fort Sumner in eastern New Mexico in 1864. To end the four-year suffering, Chief Manuelito and other leaders signed the 1868 Treaty of Bosque Redondo. Among the treaty terms was a guarantee to education, as my grandfather had proclaimed that education would be the ladder to our people's future. Today, there exists a college scholarship program in his name that was established by the Navajo Nation.

Lastly, I am indebted to the sacrifices my spouse and immediate family members made while I built my career and pursued my dreams. My parents, grandparents, siblings, and extended family and friends have supported me with prayers and good wishes. My father died before I earned my Ph.D. while my younger brother died before I secured presidential appointments. Therefore, I dedicate my efforts, in part, to them.

Ascending to the Top

On July 15, 2007, I became president of Antioch University Seattle and the first Native American woman to ascend to the presidency of an accredited university outside the tribal college system. How I found my way to Antioch is a rich story enhanced by my leadership that is steeped in Diné principles and my understanding and appreciation of inclusiveness.

Through learning, collaborating, networking and being mentored, I became connected in the higher education community. The majority of my career was spent in mainstream higher education working in minority student affairs programs at institutions in the states of Wyoming, New Mexico, Oregon, Montana and Washington. I served as the first woman president of Diné College on the Navajo reservation in Arizona and New Mexico prior to earning my doctorate at the University of Oregon. At each institution I served, I helped achieve positive results with the help of an executive team. We increased student enrollment, established equitable faculty and staff salaries, increased program offerings, and garnered greater financial resources including scholarship dollars to attract students and faculty. With the growth of our college, each institution outgrew its physical facilities. Therefore, capital projects brought forth new buildings or renovated space to accommodate the increased student populations.

In November 2006, a national search firm invited me to apply for the Antioch University Seattle presidential post at the recommendation of a colleague. After visiting the university's website, I envisioned a place of employment there. The Antioch University's mission and values of a progressive education, diversity, inclusiveness, and social justice were founding principles from its inception in 1852 in Ohio. Antioch's forward-thinking early beginnings had African Americans and women among its first student body; women hired to faculty positions at the same salary as their male counterparts; and a woman appointed to the first board of trustees.

Antioch's values and its philosophical principle of giving back to the community are consistent with my Diné values of serving one's community. I saw a match to move through the interview process. It is uncanny that before arriving at Diné College and Antioch University Seattle to become their "first female" or "first Native woman" president, I privately held onto a notion that it was a matter of "when"—not "if"—I would lead Diné College and Antioch University Seattle.

My beliefs in higher education access and inclusiveness motivated me to apply. I wanted to create access for diverse students who may never have believed they could be part of a private non-profit school. Antioch Seattle's enrollment and attention to diversity and access for all students, faculty, staff, and administrators from all walks of life was attractive because I was effective at opening doors to access.

I assessed Antioch University Seattle as very do-able due to its size of student enrollment, its talented faculty and staff, its notable mission and values, and sharp focus on four solid academic disciplines in applied psychology, leadership, education, and liberal arts. I decided Antioch was a progressive school worthy of my skills, expertise and experiences, if they would have me as their next leader.

I was chosen as Antioch Seattle's fourth president in May and began serving in July 2007. One of my initial goals was to increase our institution's presence in Seattle and with tribal communities in the Puget Sound region. Antioch University has a special niche in the city, and with further outreach, we were well-positioned for growth in a competitive market. Scholars have amazing stories about their college experiences. Alumni describe their education as transformational and the best investment they ever made. I promoted our story and our successes to a wider audience of cultivated donors who understood the importance of philanthropy and the merits of what their contributions could provide for our students.

I encouraged a review of admissions processes to reduce redundancies and decrease the application period to ensure that student applications were handled in a timely manner. The more we reviewed and improved upon our recruiting practices, the more we increased our responsiveness to potential students who applied to Antioch Seattle.

In my initial interviews, I addressed low morale issues I recognized in constituent groups I was meeting with. I fit those early perceptions of diminished morale into exercises in community-building and community-trusting to turn the institution around using a nurturing leadership approach.

The following accounts illustrate my ability to cultivate relationships and garner contributions. At Oregon State University, while serving as the director of the Indian Education Office in the early 1990s, an elderly woman sent my office the equivalent of a dollar a day or $365 to support an Indian student with an annual scholarship. Each year I would send her a photo of the student who benefited from her gift, and included a thank you letter from that student. Three years later, the university president inquired about my connection with this individual before informing me that she had passed away and bequeathed nearly one million dollars to Oregon State University. He summoned me to meet with his executive team and college deans—all were White males. Eventually, those "grey suits" became my mentors and encouraged me to pursue a terminal degree.

Then as president of Diné College, I met the internationally renowned Navajo artist, R. C. Gorman. We quickly developed a warm and nurturing friendship that later resulted in Mr. Gorman donating his personal library collection and several original sculptures, the largest gift ever received by Diné College. In addition, he created a new artwork entitled *New Horizons* for our college fundraising event. We remodeled our college library to house his book collection and art work. Before his untimely death in 2006 he presented me with a beautifully framed lithograph he created entitled *Cassandra*.

Tapping Traditional Wisdom

I stand firm in my Diné values and integrity. It is important to me to walk my talk, because it is how I operate. I approach my leadership and decision-making like weaving a Navajo tapestry, where we work across disciplines and from the bottom up as well as from the administration down to the student. I draw attention to individuals who have never been acknowledged or appreciated before. I encourage people who have been on the sidelines to get involved, because I consider everyone invaluable to our higher education communities.

A large share of who I am and how I nurture my personal and professional relationships are what Navajos refer to as *k'é*, a *relationship*—not just between people, but with our natural environment and the world around us. Those relational connections mean a great deal to me. I have deep appreciation and genuine respect for the people who work with and for me. Often I ask people to consider the philosophy of *k'é*, a concept that captures the relational manner in which I engage in respectful relationships while envisioning our institution's future.

One example of demonstrating this care and support for my employees came from my idea to establish a *Heartship Fund*, playing off the word *hardship*. At the sole discretion of the president and with assistance of the human resource director, this special reserve of funds was established to help staff and faculty with personal financial emergencies. A one-time monetary "gift" could be provided upon completion of a confidential request form to access these reserves. Every honorarium dollar I received, and an annual tax-deductible contribution I made, subsidized this account. Eventually, employees made voluntary contributions to maintain a positive balance in this account so others could access funds in times of need.

I asked constituents to also consider the Navajo word *hózhó* as concepts of *beauty* and *balance*, to envision a brighter future that is stable and balanced in all aspects of our professional and personal lives. I encouraged my team to often work together to create a balanced future for our graduates. What emerged were faculty, staff, administrators, and students who supported a healthier balance of institutional realities and professional and personal responsibilities. The expression "it takes a village" is a time-honored concept endorsed by Native peoples long before it became a catch-phrase. "It takes a village" conveys our institutional support in our collective efforts and embraces *hózhó*.

One simple illustration of group unity came about with a cup of latte. Our small, private graduate school was a hallmark of excellence in progressive education, yet Antioch's enrollment was declining. Faculty members were passionate about the courses they taught and the lives they transformed in our students. This paralleled the staff and administration's fervent support and expertise in accommodating and assisting students. Knowing that Seattle was home to Starbucks coffee and that a coffee shop was on the premises, I instituted the *LATTE* Initiative: *Let's All Take Time for Enrollment*. The Office of the President purchased every coffee or beverage ordered by faculty, staff, students, alumni, administrators, and board members as they shared their personal Antioch stories with potential students. It became everybody's business to help recruit new students, not just my own personal priority. Early skepticism that people would take advantage of the freebies proved to be unwarranted and recruiting chats over a cup of coffee became the norm.

I built *communities* at my institutions and disclosed the manner in which I personally use Diné values. I shared aspects of my personal life to bring me closer to people and to expose my vulnerabilities. I brought Navajo teachings and traditions to Antioch for events such as convocations, graduations, and appreciation luncheons. For example, having genuine respect for all individuals working with me, I was interested in the faculty and staff's backgrounds and professional work. I was able to turn around a dysfunctional and distrustful working atmosphere at both institutions I served. On many occasions, I politely called out unacceptable behaviors and communication and defined "respect" from my Diné culture as a deeply held practice for all members of a community.

It was indeed a grave risk on my part when I introduced Navajo ceremonies to my "mainstream" constituents and shared the source of this silent strength to support my leadership. In fact, some witnessed firsthand the prayers and chants I recited in the presence of my executive leadership team and my Board of Trustees. On rare occasions, I would "loan" my little eagle feather to my supervisor at decisive moments in her administration.

I frequently turn to my ceremonial practices and traditions to gain insights into my leadership. With a small eagle feather I keep in my portfolio, it prompts me to appeal to the Holy People for guidance and spiritual support. My feather also serves to remind me to have respect for others and to interact fairly and justly with those who work with and for me.

I am grateful for the lasting gift my constituents afforded me by embracing Diné leadership prayers, songs, or offerings of mountain tobacco or sage for my presidencies. Specifically, I am grateful to those who contemplated on *hózhó* for all aspects of my professional and personal life. I would like to think my appeals to the Holy People kept me and my community grounded and focused on *hózhó* and to "walk and work in *Beauty*."

On two special occasions at my inaugurations, the Navajo "Journey Song" was chanted during processionals and recessionals. Other times I returned to Dinétah and sat through late night prayer and quiet consultation with my medicine man around a simple altar and fireplace with complex significances while mountain tobacco was firmly packed into the stone pipe I offered to the Holy People on behalf of my students, employees, and executive leaders.

A personal ordeal for me was to maintain *hózhó*, a *balance* or *harmony* among the emotional, physical, intellectual and spiritual dimensions of my professional and personal life so I could be at my best as a leader. I could not avoid nor anticipate barriers, obstacles, or challenges that came my way as president, but I firmly believe life, in general, puts these "bumps" in my corn pollen path so I can learn and grow from such experiences.

My spiritual practice is to offer traditional mountain tobacco, cedar or sage, songs, or sacred corn pollen to the Holy People during times of stress and when my life feels out of balance to restore *hózhó*. This ritual sustains me. Whenever I encounter challenges I might also smudge sweet grass or sage to de-clutter my mind and to reestablish confidence. My position had its fair share of challenges, but I navigated through rocky times by first tapping into my Diné rituals and practices.

I remember one very wearisome period when I felt most defeated and knocked off balance and recall a vivid dream about my deceased father. He appeared in my dream and spoke to me in Navajo, "*Shiyázhi, nidii'nééh, niká'iishyeed*—My baby, get up, let me help you." I felt his strong grip as he pulled me to my feet. When I awoke, I felt his presence and acknowledged that while my father had departed from our physical world, he will reassure me from the spirit world. I evoke this special dream whenever I want to feel my father's support.

Melding a Distinctive Leadership Style

When I was a graduate student years ago at the University of Wyoming, my academic advisor shook her finger at me and severely asserted that I would never be successful because my leadership style was so nonconforming. That pivotal memory of being misunderstood for using my traditional teachings to guide my leadership style only strengthened my resolve to interact with people in a caring and empathic manner. Perhaps my former training and work experience in counseling and social work helped me become a compassionate leader. I am adept at working and interacting effectively with almost everyone, particularly students. People can approach me and feel comfortable in my presence. Yet, it has been my zest for original leadership strategies that have been my greatest asset.

I relate to faculty, staff and administrators with genuine sincerity and in a caring manner. I learned of the trials and tribulations of leading a tribal college and a private, liberal arts, graduate school. I provided a strong and forward-thinking leadership approach necessary to deal with all the issues, and give thoughtful attention to process and a gentle nudge in implementation. One example to illustrate positive results from this approach was the time I insisted that administrators establish a collaborative environment for Antioch faculty to deliberate. My insistence that administrators also reach a unanimous agreement to pilot a nine month, three-year rolling contract ultimately led to the redefinition of faculty workload issues. The program also provided the distribution of reasonable compensation, system-wide, for the remaining four Antioch campuses.

Prior to the appointment of president, my supervisor defined my leadership style as embodying a reflective nature within my day-to-day management of a "mainstream" higher educational setting through the practice of my Diné culture. Often, individuals could sit at my conference table and learn something meaningful and helpful to the organization and about their own leadership styles.

As president, I became excited about new ideas and program initiatives because they motivated me to inspire stakeholders to consider possibilities and to instill a broader vision of what we could all achieve. I listened intently to the dialogue and observed non-verbal behaviors before taking any action on a new academic program initiative and its development or the implementation of any new institutional policy or procedure. I did this because I believe a series of transparent checks and balances are required. I selected short and long range goals with university stakeholders and became motivated by positive results due to a transparent approach. I approached my institution as a community, as a village, and as a family.

I subscribe to a personal philosophy that everyone is a leader, whether that someone is an employee, a student, or at the simplest level, oneself. Therefore, I am not solely responsible for the successes of my institutions, nor our challenges. But rather, my executive team plays a critical role in leading our institution. Antioch University Seattle's achievements reflect a remarkable team spirit, representative of skillful administrators and colleagues.

In my role as leader, I practiced a customary ritual of acknowledging key individuals by draping them in Pendleton blankets to signify respect, honor and gratitude for accomplishments, major milestones, or distinguished service. Dating back to 1896, Pendleton Woolen Mills began designing and weaving legendary trade blankets inspired by legends, beliefs, ceremonies, heroes, art, and symbols of American Indian tribes that soon became objects of prestige among Native people. I took this symbol of appreciation and prestige to honor key individuals throughout my presidency.

Release, Respite, and Breathing Space

With retirement comes the greatest gift of time and contemplation: to sit, think and reminisce on the events and experiences that defined my career journey. Prior to this "pause," I led a very busy life and seldom took time to reflect on my career and accomplishments. There were frequent demands to attend to and time constraints that kept quiet reflections at bay. Will I revel in retirement and soak up the down-time or simply take a break long enough to catch my breath, but not let the fragrant sagebrush sprout beneath my moccasins? I will rejuvenate and move back to Oregon to restore our home with renovation projects and delve into consulting work, conceivably with tribal colleges. In the short term, I yearn to be taught the fine art of Navajo weaving from my 82-year-old mother. This creative and artistic expression will indeed give me the opportunity to use a new set of brain synapses and perhaps take me into a new direction altogether.

I have been able to gauge my ability to succeed in leadership by successfully finishing my terms of appointment on high and positive notes as my constituents were saddened to see me leave. I reflect back to my first class in Oregon, when asked why I wanted to pursue my doctorate in education administration, I eagerly responded that "One day, I want to be a college president!" and remained steadfast in reaching my dreams.

I am thankful for the vast experiences that have shaped and defined my journey. I am grateful, too, for the strength of character, my perseverance, determination, stubbornness, and tenacity. These traits allowed me to dream possibilities and achieve my goals. They reaffirm me and I have deep appreciation for maturing from these efforts and achievements. I am filled with immense joy and gratitude for the foundations of traditional Navajo philosophy that my parents instilled in me. Now it is finished in *Beauty*.

10. Reflections about Native American Female Leadership in the Academy

MENAH PRATT-CLARKE, JOHANNA B. MAES, MELISSA LEAL, AND TANAYA WINDER

Editors' Note:

Dr. Melissa Leal is Esselen and Ohlone and grew up in Sacramento, CA. She earned her Ph.D. in Native American Studies from the University of California, Davis in 2012. She was the Lead Researcher and Advisory Board Coordinator for Rebel Music: Native America, an MTV World documentary. In addition, she is a Production Contributor for Little Thunder Films where she has worked on several documentaries and short films. She has taught Native American Film and Cinema at California State University, Sonoma and currently teaches Ethnic Images in Film at Sierra College.

Melissa has more than 15 years of experience working with American Indian youth at Indian Education Programs throughout the Sacramento Region. Her research includes the reciprocal relationship between Hip Hop culture and indigenous communities with an emphasis on performance, activism, and visual sovereignty. She believes in the power and necessity of revitalizing indigenous languages. Melissa is currently the Executive Director of Education for the Wilton Rancheria Tribe of Miwok Indians. She teaches culture, language, and dance for various tribal communities in Northern California.

Tanaya Winder is a poet, writer, artist and educator who was raised on the Southern Ute reservation in Ignacio, CO. An enrolled member of the Duckwater Shoshone Tribe, her background includes Southern Ute, Pyramid Lake Paiute, Navajo, and Black heritages. A winner of the 2010 A Room Of Her Own Foundation's Orlando prize in poetry, her work has appeared or is forthcoming in Cutthroat magazine, Adobe Walls, Superstition Review, Drunkenboat and Kweli, among others. Her poems from her manuscript, "Love in a Time of Blood Quantum," were produced and performed by the Poetic Theater Productions Presents Company in New York. Her debut poetry collection, "Words Like Love," was published in September 2015 by West End Press.

She has a BA in English from Stanford University and a MFA in creative writing from University of New Mexico. She is a co-founder and editor-in-chief

of As/Us: A Space for Women of the World. She lectures and teaches courses and creative writing workshops about different expressions of love (self-love, intimate love, social love, community love, and universal love) at high schools and universities internationally. She is the Director of the University of Colorado Boulder's Upward Bound Program and also founder of Dream Warriors Management, a management company for indigenous artists.

Introduction

This chapter provides a reflection on the narrative of Dr. Cassandra Manuelito-Kerkvliet through the lens of research on Native women and leadership. The literature demonstrates that Native women interweave their cultural beliefs and traditions into their leadership practices (Ressler, 2008). Additionally, Native women lead with a sense of obligation to expand the legacy of those within their communities who come after them (Barkdull, 2009). Finally, Native women lead with resistance, resilience, and reconciliation while recognizing that their positions within their respective nations call for them to be co-leaders with men as they use their power to be the voice to the often voiceless within their communities (Lajimodiere, 2011; Leeds & Gunsaulis, 2012).

Literature Review

There is a small but growing body of work on Native American women's leadership (Barkdull, 2009; Fox, Luna-Firebaugh, & Williams, 2015; Jensen, 2013; Lajimodiere, 2011; McCoy, 1992; Portman & Garrett, 2005; Prindeville & Gomez, 1999), and on Native American women's leadership in higher education (Krumm, 1998; Ressler, 2008; Sitting Crow, 2013; Waterman & Lindley, 2013). As more Native women pursue higher education, they are increasingly assuming leadership roles. They now represent more than half of all students at tribal universities and colleges (Sorensen, 2015; Waterman & Lindley, 2013). Women such as Marie Smallface-Marule (Blood) at Red Crow Community College; Verna Fowler (Menominee/Stockbridge-Munsee) at College of Menominee Nation; Olivia Vanegas-Funcheon (Tohono O'odham) at Tohono O'odham Community College; Linda Sue Warner (Comanchee) at Haskell Indian Nations University; and Phyllis Howard (Mandan, Hidatsa, and Arikara) from the Association of North Dakota Tribal Colleges are seen as trailblazers (Archambault & Allen, 2002; Bowman, 2009).

Recent scholarship encourages the examination of the experiences of Native American females through a critical Native lens and a critical indigenous feminist lens that is sensitive to Native feminism, the Native American cultural perspective, and a recognition of "pre-colonial egalitarian gender systems" (Lajimodiere, 2011, p. 64). Tribal Critical Race Theory recognizes the impact of colonization and the role of social structures and institutions in perpetuating oppression and marginalization (Brayboy, 2005; Waterman & Lindley, 2013). It recognizes that research on Native Americans must be grounded in "the values, goals, categories of thought, and models of inquiry that are embedded in the philosophies of knowledge generated by Indian people, rather than ones imposed upon them" (Garoutte, 2003, p. 144). Engaging in research through a Tribal critical race lens facilitates a focus on the concepts of sovereignty, obligation to the community, native resiliency, nation building, language, cultural traditions, cultural practices, and ceremony (Garoutte, 2003). Most importantly, Tribal critical race theory draws upon stories, the importance of storytelling, and the necessity of counterstories (Garoutte, 2003).

Counterstories are particularly important to Native women in order to counter the effects of European colonization that eroded much of the power of women, particularly in nations where Native women were often co-leaders with men and many tribes were matrilineal (Lajimodiere, 2011). Native women have been and continue to be the "backbone and the heartbeats" socially, culturally, politically, economically, and spiritually (Lajimodiere, 2013; Young, n.d.(a,b)). Women have had to fight against the silence, invisibility, and lack of voice: "We never hear their voices and are never told their tales" (Klein & Ackerman, 1995, p. 3). Prindeville (2002) notes that women from tribes where there was a significant influence of Christianity were often left out of conversations or their voices were not heard because the religion suppressed the woman's voice and failed to fully acknowledge their role as a leader.

Green (1990) discusses how Native women need to revisit roles within families, communities, and broader society. Tradition dictates that Native women and men have specific responsibilities in order for balance to be kept (Green, 1990). This is exemplified in Diné culture and heritage, but is also emphasized and understood in thousands of other tribal/indigenous communities. Many Native American tribes are matrilineal with leadership roles and decision making by women (Green, 1990). While that ideology has changed due to an unwelcome influence by western society, Native women have begun to move to the front of not only tribal leadership, but political and educational leadership in the public sphere (Green, 1990).

When discussing the notion of women and power in traditional societies, LaDuke (1999) uses the notion that a womb is the first society for a human being. Every person begins their existence under the leadership of a woman and through her leadership, life is created. The argument here is not that women are intrinsically leaders because they are mothers and are by nature nurturing. But rather the argument is that women are given the responsibility of birthing and caring for something other than themselves. A woman has to make decisions that affect her fetus and later her children. This is not something that she has to convince herself to do but it is something biologically and spiritually interwoven into her existence. "Motherly" responsibilities are not delegated solely to the children that a woman has birthed but to the entire community that she resides in (LaDuke, 1999).

Scholarship on Native American female leadership reveals several common themes, including a commitment to nation building, a commitment to tribal communities, and the incorporation of cultural values and traditions (Barkdull, 2009; Lajimodiere, 2011; Sitting Crow, 2013; Sorensen, 2015; Waterman & Lindley, 2013). Women emphasize the importance of using their voice and speaking out; being a bridge and liaison in relationships; and community service (Fox et al., 2015). Native American women's leadership is under girded by a focus on nation building (Fox et al., 2015) and an awareness of the concepts of resistance, resilience, and reconciliation (Leeds & Gunsaulis, 2012). It has been a fight for visibility, rights, opportunities, and recognition and has involved legal battles in courts, including tribal courts and legislatures (Leeds & Gunsaulis, 2012). Their fights and battles are on behalf of women, but also on behalf of their nations and tribes (Leeds & Gunsaulis, 2012). As McLeod (2002, p. 10) noted, "tribal leadership is the embodiment of a lifestyle, an expression of learned patterns of thought and behaviors, values, and beliefs. Culture is the basis; it formulates the purpose, process, and ultimately, the product." Despite barriers related to their gender, sexual discrimination, and historical socio-cultural barriers, Native women continue to push forward to make change for their communities (Jensen, 2013, p. 82).

There are two films about Native American women as leaders which clearly demonstrate their power and resilience. One is *Where the Spirit Lives* (Pittman & Leckie, 1989) which is a film about a young woman who is kidnapped by an Indian agent and taken to an Indian Residential School in 1937. The main character, Ashtecome (whose name is changed to Amelia once she arrives at the school) is asked by one of the teachers, "what do you want to be when you grow up?" Ashtecome answers, "I would like to be a woman." The teacher thinks that this is a "backward" answer. She looks at Ashtecome as if she has not really understood the question. Within this scene there is an understanding that there is a deep responsibility in being a woman. Throughout the film, Ashtecome resists against the leadership of the school even if it gets her punished. She begins to see how other children are being abused and homesick to the point of running away without any food or water. Ashtecome at times refuses to speak English and continues to sing and practice tradition, even if she is punished. Ashtecome becomes a leader—a leader who just wanted to be a woman.

Another film with a very similar plot is "Rhymes for Young Ghouls" (Barnaby, Chin-yee, & Christou, 2013). Set in 1976 on the Red Crow Mi'gMaq Reservation, the film tells the story of 15-year-old Aila, who was left in the custody of her uncle after her mother commits suicide and her father is sent to prison for admitting to a crime that he did not commit. During this time in many places in the United States and Canada, the law required that every Native child between the ages of five and 16 attend an Indian Residential School. Any child who did not attend the school could be taken into custody by an "Indian Agent" who was allowed to use as much force as the circumstance required. Aila plays a similar role as Ashtecome. In one scene, Aila is taken into the residential school and her hair is cut while she sheds tears for the generations of boys and girls who were forced to mourn those who had not yet died (for many tribes, hair cutting is typically done when someone important has died). Aila is relentless and chooses to fight rather than to run away (Leal, 2015).

Like the films, the scholarship on Native American female leaders reflects these key themes of female strength and power. One of the earliest works on Native American female leadership was Prindeville's (2002) analysis of Native women leaders in 21 Southwestern Indian nations. In order to understand Native women in leadership, it is important to first understand the role that Native American individuals and communities have in state, federal, and tribal political spheres (Prindeville, 2002). Native Americans are not solely an ethnic or minority group, but a political group that includes over 560 nations that each have a domestic and dependent relationship with the United States of America (Prindeville, 2002). Legally, Native American tribal communities are sovereign nations and the federal government has a trust responsibility to them. The Bureau of Indian Affairs describes the federal Indian trust responsibility as "a legal obligation under which the United States has charged itself with moral obligations of the highest responsibility and trust toward Indian tribes (Seminole Nation v. United States, 1942)" (US Department of the Interior, 2016). As one of the most important principles in federal Indian law, the trust doctrine also creates a legally enforceable fiduciary obligation on the part of the United States to protect tribal communities, including their land, rights, and resources (US Department of the Interior, 2016).

Sovereignty and trust responsibility are the framework for Native women to participate in leadership roles within their communities and among other communities. Sovereign nations are able to "elect" their own tribal leaders. Because women have traditionally been decision makers, some tribes are more willing to have a woman leader. One of the biggest roles for women leaders of tribal nations is to ensure that the trust responsibility is upheld and that nations are able to exercise their sovereign rights (Prindeville, 2002):

> American Indian women have a rich history of political involvement in the life of their communities. Their struggles to attain tribal sovereignty, preserve their culture, and manage native lands and natural resources are unique to their status as colonized indigenous peoples. As tribal leaders, Native women have continually challenged federal, state, and tribal authorities to formulate and/or reform policy for the benefit of their communities. (p. 2)

Given the role of Native women in political activism, Prindeville sought to gain a deeper understanding of their roles. In her examination of women leaders, Prindeville (2002) asks these questions:

> what are the characteristics of women in tribal leadership? What role do these leaders play in tribal politics? Why do they participate? What are their political goals? What are their policy priorities? What sorts of constraints to participation do women face? Finally, what institutional or social conditions enable women to hold formal positions of political leadership within their tribes? (p. 3)

She found that Native women chose to participate in leadership positions because of their belief in public service as ethical; they wanted to improve the quality of life for their people; and they felt like it was their civic duty (Prindeville, 2002). As a result, Native American women were very influential in the political and social life of their communities (Prindeville, 2002).

Similar themes were found in the work by Barkdull (2009) in her exploration of four Southern Ute women in leadership roles with tribal agencies. Crucial challenges for Native American tribal communities include self-determination, economic development, and sovereignty (Barkdull, 2009). These challenges have been met with a fierce commitment to resilience and resistance by Native women and the incorporation of culturally based innovations into the community that focus on traditional values, spirituality, and native language (Barkdull, 2009). Additionally, this research suggests that women have played a critical role in their communities based on their sense of obligation to the maintenance of cultural values and traditions. Barkdull (2009) found five key themes that influenced the women's experiences as leaders: self-awareness and self-knowledge, which included awareness of tribal identity and affiliation, spirituality, and a sense of duty; influential turning points in their lives; the awareness of walking in two worlds and being part of a bi-cultural world that included Anglo and Native culture; a call to service; and an understanding of the importance of gender matrilineality and supporting women and families as part of supporting the larger community.

Lajimodiere (2011) also found that the experiences of Native American female leaders included poverty; family support and mentors; valuing tribal culture and spirituality; experiencing gender bias by men and political sabotaging by men and women; and possessing strong survival skills—including self-esteem, resiliency, academic excellence, and the ability to overcome racism. The nine Native American female leaders of the Ogimah Ikwe tribe exhibited determination to overcome stereotypes and low expectations from others, including teachers and counselors, and had strong mentoring from their mothers that supported their self-esteem and resiliency (Lajimodiere, 2011). Key tribal virtues that guided one university president were bravery, loyalty, generosity, and respect (Lajimodiere, 2011).

Women leaders were committed to the tribal traditions, ancestors, spirituality, rituals, ceremonies, and working on and off reservations to promote the advancement of their communities (Lajimodiere, 2011). Though they did not define themselves as feminists, Lajimodiere (2011) concluded that they were feminists based on their commitment to the values and tenets of Indigenous feminism. They were sensitive to the bi-cultural lifestyle and blending traditional and modern roles and expectations as they navigated gender roles, tribal politics, personal and professional aspirations, and the effects of colonialism and racism (Lajimodiere, 2011).

Fox et al. (2015) conducted a quantitative and qualitative survey of 17 Native American female leaders in a variety of positions. Their (Fox et al., 2015) study revealed that cultural values, including respect, trust, humility, and honor, as well as valuing relationships and valuing traditions were important elements to female leadership. Key leadership skills were sharing, communication, a commitment to community, and a commitment to practicing the tribal traditions (Fox et al., 2015). Cultural traditions included using the language, remembering ancestors, leading by example, peace-making, talking circles, the use of silence, appreciating differences, and incorporating humor during dispute resolution (Fox et al., 2015).

Similarly, a study of the experiences of 53 Native American women in higher education reflected that they relied upon community, family, traditions, and cultural integrity in order to survive, be successful, and negotiate their experiences in higher education (Waterman & Lindley, 2013). Women in the tribal communities, particularly their mothers, aunts, grandmothers, and sisters were important role models (Waterman & Lindley, 2013). Education was seen as critical to nation building and strengthening families (Waterman & Lindley, 2013).

One of the earliest works to focus on Native American women presidents looked at four female tribal college presidents (Krumm, 1998). Krumm (1998) examined the experiences of Dr. Janine Pease Pretty-On-Top, president of Little Big Horn College; Dr. Verna Fowler, president of the College of the Menominee Nation; Tanya Ward, president of Cheyenne River Community College; and Margarett Campbell Perez, president of Fort Belknap College. She found that culture played a critical role in women's leadership style, with a focus on the good of the people, the tribe, and the nation (Krumm, 1998).

More recently, Ressler (2008), Sorensen (2015), and Sitting Crow (2013) have examined Native American women college presidents. Ressler (2008) interviewed eight women leaders at five North Dakota tribal colleges. Key findings were the use of servant leadership; the value of family and community; the importance of role models, mentors, and professional development; and the importance of Native traditions, including spirituality, kinship, ceremonies, oral traditions, and storytelling (Ressler, 2008). Sorensen (2015) looked at three tribal college presidents: Verna Fowler, founding president of College of Menominee Nation; Cynthia Lindquist, president of Cankdeska Cikana Community College; and Maggie George, president of Diné College. Sorensen (2015) found that Native American women tribal college presidents have distinct approaches to guiding their institutions. They focused on details and gaining multiple perspectives; navigating the complicated boundary between autonomy as a higher education institution and collaboration with the tribal government; ensuring a connection between tribal values, tribal history, and educational mission; and navigating tensions between cultural roles of women and institutional leadership roles (Sorensen, 2015).

Sitting Crow (2013) is the most comprehensive examination of the experiences of Native American women leaders in higher education. Through the use of talking circles, she (Sitting Crow, 2013) examined the opportunities and challenges that influenced seven Native American women in senior leadership roles at five tribal colleges and universities in one Midwestern state. She also looked at the role of culture and heritage in their leadership roles; their roles in policy and institutional change; and their own perspectives as leaders (Sitting Crow, 2013). Key themes that emerged were the importance of culture and cultural pride, including valuing place, oral tradition, humor, and language; the necessity of self-determination and tribal sovereignty; and the critical role of strong leadership skills to ensure the strength of the community and the institutions (Sitting Crow, 2013, pp. 86–88).

Other challenges related to women's leadership experiences included navigating the relationship between tribal politics and the institution; balancing technology with face to face interactions; maintaining relevant curriculum and native ways of knowing, including connections to land and animals through authentic cultural learning experiences; and helping to develop the next generation of leaders (Sitting Crow, 2013, pp. 97–98). Given the prominence of culture and heritage at tribal colleges and universities, and the importance of perpetuating sovereignty, as well as empowering the communities, Native studies courses in language revitalization, tribal culture, tribal history, literature, archeology, and engaging with external partners and constituencies, were considered essential (Sitting Crow, 2013).

The scholarship, then, on Native women and leadership demonstrates the vital importance of culture, including the role of cultural traditions and values, the use of language, and commitment to community. Dr. Cassandra Manuelito-Kerkvliet's journey to the presidency exemplifies these values. Cassandra is from a long line of Native leaders where Chief Manuelito's father, Cayetano, was known to be a resistor against foreigners. Chief Manuelito influenced many people and is quoted to have told others "just because they capture you and even take your life, it's just you and not all your people who will suffer" (Denetdale, 2007, p. 73). This idea is intrinsic to Indigenous culture and tradition where everything is connected or related. The community and wellbeing of others comes before oneself. There is a lack of individualism and prominence of the collective. Indigenous peoples believe that these are the ways in which tradition has taught us to be human beings. They believe that it is our duty as human beings to think collectively and to act responsibly not for our own sake but for the sake of the whole. These themes are a true reflection of how Cassandra views her life and her role as a Native woman leader. Her social justice journey involves integrating Diné cultural values, traditions, and ceremonies as a critical component of her leadership style.

Leadership and Native American Culture

Hózhó: Beauty and Balance

A distinguishing component to Cassandra's success was her fierce and courageous determination to maintain her cultural traditions and values, even while leading a majority institution. She recognized the "grave risk" of introducing Navajo ceremonies, traditions, prayers, and chants to the Antioch campus (Manuelito-Kerkvliet, 2016). Yet, for her to be an authentic leader and to be able to form authentic relationships with others, she had to be true to her own identity and culture. Her narrative also showcases leadership as service and actions where everyone is a building-block in creating community. Cassandra brought people into her Indigenous worldview by letting them borrow her eagle feather and using Pendleton blankets as a form of honoring service and dedication (Manuelito-Kerkvliet, 2016).

As Cassandra's narrative illustrates, educators and administrators of color often find themselves navigating multiple spaces within bureaucracy, university dynamics, and racial and ethnic identities. Often Indigenous educators and administrators in academia experience the pressures involved in walking in two worlds. It can be rather difficult straddling an existence with one foot grounded in the Native culture, tradition, and community and the other foot struggling to find balance in the "modern" work places. It is an emotional, mental, and spiritual balancing act to move forward to complete an education and succeed in a majority White, male-dominated academy. Cassandra's journey illustrates her mastery of hózhó—beauty and balance.

Brigham Young University Museum of Art (2012) captures the significance of hózhó and beauty:

> In the Navajo language there is no word for religion, nor for art. The only word that could be used to describe both is "hózhó"—a word that defines the essence of Navajo or Diné philosophy. It encompasses beauty, order, and harmony, and expresses the idea of striving for balance. Every aspect of Navajo life, secular and spiritual, is related to hózhó. As humans we straddle the border between health and sickness, good and evil, happiness and sadness. We are always trying to gain harmony in life, preserve beauty, and find order again after balance has been disturbed. According to the Navajo worldview, the purpose of life is to achieve balance, in a continual cycle of gaining and retaining harmony.

Cassandra grounds herself in her Diné heritage by advocating for hózhó and balance for those within her environment, while also working hard to "walk [her] talk" by living a well-balanced lifestyle herself. In a society that seems to place value on the number of hours worked and regards exhaustion as a status symbol, Cassandra's balance is an example of revolutionary self-love. Winder (2015) writes several poems about this topic in her book *Words Like Love*. Her (Winder, 2015) poem "w(hole): self-medication" speaks to this revolutionary act of caring for oneself, in order to be able to continue caring for others. Cassandra exemplifies the necessity of self-love and it is through her teachings and living example of self-love she was not only able to climb the ladder to success, she also taught others how to soar.

Native women leaders cannot take care of others if they do not first care for themselves. In order to serve others from a full-self, leaders must consider the question—what sustains us? Cassandra's commitment to self-care and to maintaining hózhó was reflected in her recognition that she had to balance the multiple aspects of her personal and professional life— emotional, physical, intellectual, and spiritual. Sometimes this sustenance took place through her spiritual practices and rituals and giving offerings to the Holy People and ancestors (Manuelito-Kerkvliet, 2016). The connection to her ancestors and father provided reassurance and strength for her journey (Manuelito-Kerkvliet, 2016).

Cassandra's ability to embrace hózhó is also reflected in her comments about retirement, and the ability to reflect, reminisce, and rejuvenate (Manuelito-Kerkvliet, 2016). The ability to understand the importance of breath, breathing spaces, and pauses reflects a true integration of balance. Her desire to learn weaving from her mother demonstrates the importance of integrating all aspects of Diné culture into her life and the relationship between balance and beauty. Her excitement about learning weaving from her mother exemplifies the role of family, community, and relationships and the role of women in carrying on traditions and passing them down from one generation to another (Manuelito-Kerkvliet, 2016). It also illustrates the important role of relationships in Cassandra's leadership journey.

The Philosophy of K'é and Relationships

One key aspects of Native American culture and leadership is grounded in an emphasis on collectivism, community, and relationships (Portman & Garrett, 2005). Cassandra embodies k'é. K'é is about relationship and kinship between people, family, and community, as well as the land and environment (Manuelito-Kerkvliet, 2016; Vogelbacher, 2013). Her relationship with her family was paramount. She expressed her love, admiration, and respect for her great-great-grandfather Chief Manuelito and acknowledged that her own leadership methods were shaped by his example and commitment to his community and to the education of his people (Manuelito-Kerkvliet, 2016).

Relational leadership was a defining quality of Cassandra's distinctive leadership style. The relational leadership style for Native women involves "leadership skills of patience, listening, contemplating the situation, and developing innovative strategies to accomplish the needed task are characteristic of many American Indian female leaders" (Portman & Garrett, 2005, p. 285). This method of leadership makes it even more effective to sit back and listen to analyze the situation before making a decision. Cassandra spoke of times during her presidency where she would listen intently to dialogue and observe non-verbal cues before taking action (Manuelito-Kerkvliet, 2016). She recognized that she had a unique and distinctive leadership style. She insisted on the importance of collaborative environment for faculty deliberations.

Relational leadership also acknowledges that we are all connected but also that every action or decision affects the whole (Portman & Garrett, 2005). Cassandra's establishment of the *Heartship Fund* helped faculty and staff in financial need. Her selflessness motivated other colleagues to contribute to this "gift" that served the whole community. She was successful in instilling value in everyone's presence and contributions. Cassandra also sought to further relationships through inclusivity and engagement. Her work and successes demonstrate her commitment to involving people in the mission and vision of her institution. For example, the *LATTE* initiative is an excellent example of Cassandra's style of making everyone a stakeholder in the success of the overall organization where everyone is called to serve (Manuelito-Kerkvliet, 2016).

Authenticity is another aspect that Cassandra used in her relationships and building community. She stood by her values even when it may have compromised the way others at her university or constituents may have viewed her. She always incorporated her Navajo language, ceremonies, or values into her work world, rather than attempt to walk in one world. Cassandra made it customary to share aspects of her personal life and become vulnerable in front of people who were supposed to look up to her as a figure of strength. Nonetheless, her vulnerability allowed her constituents and others who work with her to feel more comfortable. It has been a successful tactic in creating an environment that holds people accountable to the whole community. Cassandra combined them to lead with beauty, grace, and balance.

Native women leaders often hear the expression, "It isn't about you. It's about those who came before you who made it possible for you to be where you are now. It's about those who will come after you because of you." As Indigenous women, a part of the tribe, as persons who contribute to the greater good, it is never solely about the individual. One must always remember and act from the belief—that we are a part of a whole. Native women leaders firmly believe that we are all connected.

Cassandra's traits, practices and beliefs both on a personal and professional level are a clear reflection of what a Native woman leader is. She worked with the students within her institution as if they were her own children as she firmly believes that she is responsible for them and their wellness. Her belief that everyone is a leader allows her to focus on empowerment.

She embraced the concept of "it takes a village." As the president of Antioch University in Seattle and the first Native American woman to become president of an accredited institution beyond the scope of tribal colleges, Cassandra values her relational and collectivism traits given that they are ingrained in many forms of Indigenous perspectives. Cassandra saw her institution as a community, a village, and family (Manuelito-Kerkvliet, 2016).

Conclusion

Cassandra's journey in higher education is an example of how a native woman can take her traditional life's ways and mold them into a methodology for being a successful leader in a non-indigenous sphere. Cassandra has been successful at doing this while providing a framework for others to copy and expand upon. Though her ways and distinct leadership style are indeed tailored to her culture, every tribal nation and cultural group has their own epistemologies and teachings that can be used to transform the Academy. Cassandra's use of two Native concepts, k'é and hózhó, reflect her ability to integrate native culture into American higher education institutional leadership. Native women in leadership positions carry with them generations of knowledge in addition to diverse methods and traits that they develop as they move throughout organizations and communities.

Native American women leaders' journeys in higher education are examples of social justice. They have the ability and potential to create change in a revolutionary manner through their leadership. This leadership must be steeped in tradition and accentuate the community and collective over the self and individual. Native women have held leadership positions within their tribes and communities because of their love for their people and their awareness that the decisions they make may affect everybody as a whole. Cassandra is an excellent example of a leader because of her focus on the good of the community and her commitment to integrating her spiritual and cultural teachings. Native women leaders in higher education understand the value of education for the advancement of a community. Consistent with Chief Manuelito's belief of education as the ladder to success and a modern day weapon for the advancement of Native people, Cassandra and other Native women have been important voices for social change.

In "Rhymes for Young Ghouls" (Barnaby et al., 2012), Aila says "my world ends at the border of the reserve, where dirt roads open up to dreams of things you can never be here." There are thousands of young, Native American girls who, like Aila, believe that they will never have the opportunity to become anything more than what they see on their reservation or neighborhood. Dr. Cassandra Manuelito-Kerkvliet and other extraordinary women like Wilma Mankiller (the first modern female Chief of the Cherokee Nation) and Angelique EagleWoman (the first aboriginal woman to be appointed as dean of a Canadian Law School) provide hope and teach us all how to be revolutionaries of change and tradition (Loriggio, 2016). They are examples of the power of women who use the power of their culture to transform society.

References

Archambault, D., & Allen, T. (2002). Politics and the presidency: Tribal college presidents share their thoughts. *Tribal College Journal*, *13*(4), 14–19.

Barnaby, J. (Director), Chin-yee, A., & Christou, J. (Producers). (2013). *Rhymes for young ghouls* [Motion Picture]. Canada. Prospector Films of Montreal.

Barkdull, C. (2009). Exploring intersections of identity with Native American women leaders. *Afflia: Journal of Women and Social Work*, *24*(2), 120–136.

Bowman, N. (2009). Dreamweavers: Tribal college presidents build institutions bridging two worlds. *Tribal College Journal of American Indian Higher Education*, *20*(4), 12–18.

Brayboy, B. M. J. (2005). Toward a tribal critical race theory in education. *The Urban Review*, *37*(5), 425–446.

Brigham Young University Museum of Art. (2012). *Walk in beauty: Hózhó and Navajo Basketry*. Retrieved from http://www.tfaoi.com/aa/3aa/3aa513.htm

Denetdale, J. (2007). *Reclaiming Diné history: The legacies of Navajo Chief Manuelito and Juanita*. Tucson, AZ: University of Arizona Press.

Fox, M. J. T., Luna-Firebaugh, E. M., & Williams, C. (2015). American Indian female leadership. *Wicazo Sa Review*, *30*(1), 82–99.

Garoutte, E. M. (2003). *Real Indians: Identity and the survival of Native America*. Berkeley, CA: University of California Press.

Green, R. (1990). American Indian women; diverse leadership for social change. In L. Albrecht & R. Brewer (Eds.), *Bridges of power: Women's multicultural alliances*. (pp. 61–73). Philadelphia, PA: New Society Publishers.

Jensen, C. (2013). *Native American women leaders' use of information and communication technologies (ICTs) for work-life balance (WLB) and capacity building*. Doctoral dissertation. Retrieved from Proquest (UMI 3588235).

Klein, L. F., & Ackerman, L. A. (1995). Introduction. In L. F. Klein & L. A. Ackerman (Eds.), *Women and power in native North America* (pp. 3–16). Norman, OK: University of Oklahoma Press.

Krumm, B. (1998). Leadership reflections of women tribal college presidents. *Tribal College*, *9*(3), 24–28.

LaDuke, W. (1999). *All our relations: Native struggles for land and life*. Cambridge, MA: South End Press.

Lajimodiere, D. (2011). Ogimah Ikwe Native women and their path to leadership. *Wicazo Sa Review*, *26*(2), 57–82.

Lajimodiere, D. (2013). American Indian females and stereotypes: Warrior, leaders, healers, feminists; not drudges, princesses, prostitutes. *Multicultural Perspectives*, *15*(2), 104–109.

Leal, M. (2015). *Rhymes for Young Ghouls* Media Review. *Comparative Education Review*, *59*(2), 383–384.

Leeds, S., & Gunsaulis, E. (2012). Resistance, resilience, and reconciliation: Reflections on Native American women and the law. *Thomas Jefferson Law Review, 34*(2), 303–324.

Loriggio, P. (2016). *First aboriginal woman appointed as dean of Canadian law school.* Retrieved on July 21, 2016 from http://www.theglobeandmail.com/report-on-business/industry-news/the-law-page/first-aboriginal-woman-appointed-as-dean-of-canadian-law-school/article28142224/

Manuelito-Kerkvliet, C. (2016). My climb to the highest rung. In M. Pratt-Clarke & J. Maes (Eds.), *Journeys of social justice: Women of color presidents in the academy.* New York, NY: Peter Lang Publishing.

McCoy, M. (1992). Gender or ethnicity: What makes a difference? A study of women tribal leaders. *Journal of Women, Politics, and Policy, 12*(3), 57–68.

McLeod, M. (2002, June 30). Keeping the circle strong: Learning about Native American leadership. *Tribal College, 13*(4), 10.

Pittman, B. (Director), & Leckie, K. (Writer). (1989). *Where the spirit lives* [Motion Picture]. United States: Amazing Spirit Productions, LTD.

Portman, T., & Garrett, M. (2005). Beloved women: Nurturing the sacred fire of leadership from an American Indian perspective. *Journal of Counseling & Development, 83*(3), 284–291.

Prindeville, D. (2002). *Women's evolving role in tribal politics: Native women leaders in 21 southwestern Indian nations.* New Mexico State University.

Prindeville, D. M., & Gomez, T. B. (1999). American Indian women leaders, public policy, and the importance of gender and ethnic identity. *Women and Politics, 20*(2), 17–32.

Ressler, K. (2008). *The path to leadership for Native American women at North Dakota Tribal Colleges* (Doctoral dissertation). Retrieved from Proquest (UMI 3297737).

Sitting Crow, K. P. (2013). *Tribal college and universities in the 21st century: Native American female leadership in tribal higher education* (Doctoral dissertation). Retrieved from Proquest (UMI 3599239).

Sorensen, B. (2015). Walking the talk. *Tribal College Journal, 26*(4), 24–27.

US Department of the Interior. (2016). *Indian affairs frequently asked questions.* Retrieved from www.bia.gov/FAQs/

Vogelbacher, J. (2013). *Navajo philosophy and its application.* Retrieved from http://www.se.edu/nas/files/2013/03/navajophilosophy.pdf

Waterman, S., & Lindley, L. (2013). Cultural strengths to persevere: Native American women in higher education. *NASPA Journal About Women in Higher Education, 6*(2), 139–165.

Winder, T. (2015). *Words like love.* Albuquerque, NM: West End Press.

Young, M. (n.d.(a)). *Education is the future for Native leaders.* University of Nebraska, Lincoln. Retrieved July 21, 2016 from http://cojmc.unl.edu/nativedaughters/leaders/education-is-the-future-for-native-leaders

Young, M. (n.d.(b)). *Native women move to the front of tribal leadership.* University of Nebraska, Lincoln. Retrieved July 21, 2016 from http://cojmc.unl.edu/nativedaughters/leaders/native-women-move-to-the-front-of-tribal-leadership

11. Journeys into Leadership: A View from the President's Chair

NANCY "RUSTY" BARCELÓ

Editors' Note:

Dr. Nancy "Rusty" Barceló served as President of Northern New Mexico College from July 2010 to December 2015. Dr. Barceló is also a full professor in Northern's College of Education. Prior to her appointment as President of Northern, Dr. Barceló served as founding Vice President and Vice Provost for Equity and Diversity at the University of Minnesota. From 2001 to 2006, she served as Vice President and Vice Provost for Minority Affairs and Diversity at the University of Washington, and from 1996 to 2001 as Associate Vice President for Multicultural and Academic Affairs at the University of Minnesota. Dr. Barceló held various positions at the University of Iowa from 1975 to 1996 including Assistant Provost and Assistant Dean with the Office of Academic Affairs.

Dr. Barceló received her Bachelor of Arts degree in Social Work from Chico State College, her Master of Arts degree in Recreational Education from the University of Iowa, and her Doctor of Philosophy degree in Higher Education Administration from the University of Iowa. Dr. Barceló has received many awards, including the NACCS 2012 Scholar award (National Association for Chicana and Chicano Studies), the New Mexico Hispano Round Table "Walk the Talk" award, and was named a Distinguished Alumnus of the University of Iowa.

The View

I come with many thoughts (too many, I am afraid) and complex emotions regarding the presence—or rather, the absence—of women of color in leadership positions in the Academy. I recently participated as a presidential advisor in the newly created American Council on Education (ACE) Spectrum Leadership Fellows Program for people of color who aspire to be presidents. What was abundantly clear right from the start was not only how few presidents are women of color, but also how few women of color even aspire to be presidents, as if executive leadership were an unattainable goal. Sadly, for many, it is indeed unattainable, or at least appears to be so—not because they lack the qualifications and the drive, but because too many obstacles remain in their path.

The concerns expressed were all too familiar, reminding me once again how far women of color still must go in the Academy to be more visible and to be taken seriously as scholars and as candidates for institutional leadership. At the end of the day, I promised to take note of those concerns so that we might explore new strategies for claiming our rightful share of space and legitimacy in the Academy. I knew it would be a long while before that space would be ours—probably not in my lifetime—but I also knew we had to keep trying. We needed to recapture and reaffirm, and perhaps rethink and redirect, some of the spirit and momentum of those early years, when we believed absolutely, with the faith and fervor of young activists, that we could do it. *Sí se puede.* If I did not believe that we could, I would not have been a university president today.

I have always been driven by challenges, in part because I am tenacious by nature, but also because I see challenges as opportunities to solve problems. Show me a locked door, and I will search for a key. If I cannot find the key, I will find another way in. I might even break the door down, if it is for a public good, and then cross the threshold to create accessible and inclusive space. But I will never do it alone. I know that my first step is always discussion, negotiation, and community building for change.

When I first set out in my career in higher education, the Academy was largely a closed system—steeped in tradition, resistant to change, and unwelcoming to outsiders. That description rings true to a degree even today. To be sure, the doors have creaked open. Some of us have infiltrated those hallowed academic spaces, and the dominant culture has moved a few feet off center to accommodate us. But this has happened only with great reluctance, in response to our persistent challenges from the margins. Left to its own devices, powered from within, that culture would have remained closed to us and firmly entrenched.

If not for the activists of color who came together to transgress the borders and begin scaling the walls of the ivory tower roughly a half century ago, we would not be here today. It was our collective work—work born out of a mix of grievance, anger, courage, passion, and conviction, as well as solidarity—that has transformed our institutions in ways that faculty and institutional leaders of that time would barely recognize today. Our shared journey of affirmation, reclamation, and transformation has made us in some ways more visible and given us a voice. It has brought into the Academy our

histories and cultures, and has created a place for academic study and pres-
ervation of what we know and who we are as women of color. And yet, even
today, as women of color, we occupy the academic borderlands, straddling
worlds between inside and outside.

I came of age at a time of a great national movement toward social and
economic justice that began in the factories and farmlands and barrios. This
social movement was led by people like Cesar Chavez and Dolores Huerta,
Martin Luther King and Fannie Lou Hamer. When we first began to enter
the Academy, we were inspired by their example, and by their words: *Sí se
puede*. We vowed to replicate in the Academy some of the disruptions they
had wrought in the dominant ethos of the times. For us, those were times
of great risk and struggle, but also of hope and promise, and of bold dreams
and ambitions.

I did not grow up with even the most modest academic ambitions, much
less the audacious ambitions that some would say later fueled my work. In
fact, I cannot recall anyone talking to me about higher education as a legitimate career path. Never in my wildest dreams did I imagine being a college
president one day. Even going to college was a stretch for me. In fact, I was
the first in my family to do so. And when my few Chicana classmates and I
graduated from college, we never so much as considered becoming players
in the White male world of boardroom negotiations, academic competition,
and power plays. We knew as Chicana women that we had to find our own
way. We had to make up a whole new set of rules and draw our own maps as
we embarked on the untraveled road before us. That is, because there *were* no
road maps or guidebooks for young women of color in the Academy. There
were only a few examples of role models in leadership positions, at least in the
formal or conventional sense.

For us, the paths to leadership were blocked, or at least very rocky and
winding. And so, like the journeys of so many other women of color, mine
followed an improvised and sometime meandering route toward an unknown
destination. My professional life as a diversity educator and administrator
more or less grew out of a kind of inner logic as I personally maneuvered my
way around inequities, built supportive communities with others on the margins, and stepped up to advocate and strategize for equity and inclusion. It
was during that time that the deeply personal—our repeated and often bruis-
ing collisions with the systems of exclusion that prevented us from following
our dreams or even having dreams—became political, and also became the
catalyst for charting a new path toward institutional transformation. And so,
too, the "political"—our collective efforts to create an inclusive Academy—
became educational.

It was not an easy path, to be sure. Everywhere I went, I saw a multitude of needs. People like me were struggling to find their way and being held back by forces over which they had little control. Somehow, despite the roadblocks and stop signs, I always kept going and I knew which direction to turn. I understood that in order to turn *toward* my future, I needed to remain bound to my cultural heritage by turning *towards it, instead of,* away from who I was. To borrow Gloria Anzaldúa's concept, I came to understand that I was a turtle, carrying my home and my family on my back. I knew who I was and what moved me. From this, I felt *called* to what we would one day call diversity work—the work of eradicating educational bias and discrimination, and creating inclusive academic and cultural spaces that work to express, support, and serve the needs of diverse communities. I chose this work because, in a way, I had no choice.

At the University of Iowa in 1969, women of color were few and far between. Though low in number, we could feel the stirrings of a new consciousness. The stirrers, of course, were people like us stirring things up on the margins. As the only Chicana graduate student at Iowa, I found myself thrust into a leadership role, which I took on with great passion. My commitment to service was both as a labor of love and as a means of survival. I came to realize that that is what we do, and what we must do, as women of color. We take responsibility for what needs to be done because we know that no one else is going to. In a way, we are pioneers of experiential learning. We learn and grow on the job. As women of color in the Academy, many times we see what needs to be done and then just do it, sometimes by making it up as we go along while enlisting others to step up. That is how a movement is born; and so are careers.

Once the institution began to pay attention to the disturbances my colleagues and I were creating—as it affected challenges to the existing paradigm and disruptions to the status quo—I was invited to be the "Chicana voice" at the table. Admittedly, I was seen as a "token." I was a "token" in the most simplistic, dominant-culture view of multiculturalism. To several individuals, my presence not only served to fulfill the representational void of "my people," but my presence itself was meant to suffice all forms of diversity requested. I could have declined, or argued for broader participation and some real diversity, but I knew I had to take it one step at a time. I accepted my role because I saw it as a strategic opportunity to create much-needed change. At least I was at the boardroom table where so many decisions are made. My tokenism allowed me to advocate for true diversity and inclusion, rather than promote the illusive ideal of what some believe diversity means.

From that day on, I was appointed to committee after committee, on issues from health to enrollment management. I never declined—indeed, I even welcomed the service burden—because Iowa desperately needed diverse voices (albeit a chorus of one). I also saw these appointments as an opportunity to become educated in the ways of the Academy, and to acquire a broader and more nuanced view of institutional and national educational issues. I was never an insider or the key power player. I was, however, an astute observer and critic. In the view of others, my role was to provide the "diversity perspective," which could all too easily be dismissed. I personally believed my purpose was for educational advocacy. I was there to question, critique, and push back, sometimes in ways that raised eyebrows, not to mention hackles. As I learned to navigate this sometimes treacherous ground, I began to see my future as a diversity educator and administrator. I came to see how critical administrative work could be in advancing equity and diversity in the Academy.

I did once imagine that I would become a professor, with a focus on bringing Chicana/o voices and perspectives to the Academy. But I quickly realized that if we wanted to create spaces for our work, we needed outsider voices inside. We needed not only to scale the walls of the Academy but also to join the administrative ranks and define a new kind of leadership. I felt a responsibility to bring to the table of power, privilege, and institutional decision making not only a destabilizing voice but also a constructive voice for inclusion and empowerment. I took up the gauntlet with a true sense of mission, and an authentic passion for educational justice that was firmly rooted in my identity.

Today, as I reflect on my journey through higher education, I think about how vital the work of women of color scholars has been to me. It has been a constant source of inspiration and validation. And as an educational administrator, I do the work that I do in the hope that I can help others do theirs as women of color in the Academy.

In my role as an educational administrator, I have been privileged to witness, participate in, advocate for, and facilitate the work that Women of Color scholars create. My path runs parallel to, and also intersects with, Women of Color scholars and practitioners. We are on a shared journey of intellect and spirit. And the passion and dedication we share keeps us moving in tandem through our shared cultural and academic spaces toward our rightful place in the Academy.

Today, I realize that I have come full circle, back to my earliest aspirations. And I am more aware than ever of the vital connections we share. I think about who we are and where we began. I think the struggles that brought us here, what we have carried with us, what we have left behind, and what we have *contributed*. And I think about where our journey will take us in the years to come. I believe we share *vital connections* as women of color in the Academy. We do our work in shared cultural and academic spaces and in common purpose. And I know that one of my most important responsibilities as a president, and as a diversity educator, is to study, support, and advance our work as scholars in the Academy.

Especially in these times of growing backlash, people in positions of formal institutional leadership—people like me—have a special responsibility to keep our institutions on the right path, the path toward a truly multicultural Academy where academic freedom and educational excellence are grounded in a bedrock commitment to diversity. By supporting diverse faculty, staff, and students in all disciplines and departments, we not only advance important academic priorities but also open new paths to learning and educational enrichment, achievement, and leadership for everybody. And we help advance the social and educational justice work that made it possible for us to be here in the first place. And yet, sadly, the more we accomplish, the more we are caught in the backlash. In the zero-sum game that passes for academic competition in a time of dwindling resources, we are seen as interlopers, even as dangerous.

As women of color in higher education, our very presence has always challenged the status quo in the Academy. And we have paid a price. When we have posed challenges, we have been told our work is subversive and political, not educational. And after all these years, we are still accused of playing race and gender cards and fomenting class wars. We are accused of using ethnic studies to stir up ethnic and racial hatred. We are accused of rewriting history for our own ends. We are accused of being unpatriotic, playing identity politics, and undermining the American way of life. We have even been accused of "feminizing" the Academy. We have been told again and again, in so many words, to behave and go back to the margins—perhaps never more so than now.

Some of this is nothing new—but these days the charges carry the added burden of a nationwide reactionary movement that puts at serious risk decades of work—our positions, our programs, our scholarly work, and our future in the Academy. Even in my Hispano and indigenous-serving college, serving mostly students of color in a state whose Native and Hispano populations are almost the majority, I am constantly being challenged to defend diversity work. I have even been asked to explain why we should have bilingual education. Despite our slowly increasing numbers, we are still viewed not as central to the academic enterprise, but as add-ons. When the fiscal cuts come, we are especially vulnerable.

With all that we are up against, the path of least resistance would for us be to pull back. But what we are really called upon to do is be more vigilant and more committed than ever. And now that there are more of us in the Academy, we need to do some reevaluating and soul searching of our own, and to come up with some new strategies.

One might think the word *president* in front of my name gives me some kind of formal standing in my institution. After all, the buck stops at my desk. But that title does not give me real authority, especially when my resume is all about diversity work and my biography includes words like *lesbian* and *Chicana*. What is more, even if I did think of myself as having institutional power, all I need to do is leave my office for a reality check. There is nothing like testifying before the legislature or meeting with a group of contentious faculty to remind you of how little real power you have, no matter what your formal or institutional position. I may always be at the table, but that does not mean that mine is the most powerful or persuasive voice.

That is why it is so important that we work together in new ways as women of color. We should work together across cultures and generations, across our assigned institutional roles, and across organizational structures and disciplines. No matter where you are on the organizational chart, no assigned formal institutional authority can alone advance equity and diversity. In short, *no one can do this work alone*. It takes critical mass. And it takes broadly collaborative work and shared leadership to create the kinds of *inclusive institutional and cultural spaces* where we can realize our full potential as academicians.

I believe that process begins in deep self-reflection. From the very beginning, our work has been self-reflective and self-interrogating at its core. We have challenged not only traditional academic paradigms and institutional systems of power and privilege, but also ourselves, and our own emerging disciplines. Therefore, one of our most important goals has been, and continues to be, to examine and rethink our own disciplinary and cultural biases and assumptions. As women of color, we must continue to share our deepest truths with each other so we might negotiate our way through our differences and bridge divides.

This kind of community building is not easy. As much as we may occupy some common ground as women of color, we are also very different. We may talk a lot about intersectionality of identities and about the need to be collaborative and interdisciplinary, yet all too often we work in isolation. When we, women of color in the Academy, work in closed groups or disciplinary tunnels our needs and concerns are not intersecting. Our isolation and fragmentation holds us back. When we work against and not with each other, we give power to those who seek to stop us in our tracks and force us to retreat. No need for them to divide and conquer if we are already divided.

Many of us have learned this the hard way. We have learned to work *within* the system, even while the system resisted working *with* us. To survive in that system, we have *had* to work through our differences and work together to change it. That is our great strength as diverse scholars and practitioners—our ability to negotiate the contradictory spaces in which we live and work so that we might *all* move forward. And one source of our strength both individually and collectively is the very thing that both motivates us and keeps us on the margins—our critical edge and our passion for change.

So this is what I say to women who come to me for counsel: If we want an Academy that values us and our work, we cannot just be focused on ourselves, our own disciplines, our own cultural identities, our own institutional transactions, and/or our own career opportunities. We need to find connections amid the disjunctions and be committed *collectively* to institutional transformation. The cost of isolation and infighting is just too great.

I come from a storytelling culture. And I know that stories are what bind us together and make us agents of change. As we brought our stories, our voices, and our ways of knowing and being into the Academy over the years, we began to change the discourse. Our stories—our counter-narratives—rose up from beneath the dominant narrative and began to make, and remake history. We did not rewrite history. We excavated centuries and layers of unexplored terrain. We interrogated the academic and institutional narratives and brought to the surface the living stories—the unspoken truths of millions of people—that had for so long been buried alive.

In short, our stories fundamentally transformed curricula, pedagogies, research methodologies and scholarly work. And yet, contrary to what our detractors believe, we did not politicize the Academy. What we did was to *call attention to the inherently political nature of all that we call knowledge*. And we did that in part through stories that revealed historical and cultural truths by cutting through traditional dualities of subject and object, us and them, insider and outsider. We created a *radically new kind of scholarship* grounded in personal and cultural narratives.

Research and scholarly work began to be relational and human-centered. The work drew on our deep understanding of personal and cultural histories and perspectives. Fortunately, this work also began recognizing the shifting and indeterminate nature of reality, recognizing the truth in the story. But how many of our colleagues really understand the importance of our contributions? How many *really* hear our voices? Not very many, I am afraid.

Fortunately, our stories keep us grounded and connected to our roots. Our stories keep us strong and honest. As long as I am true to the stories that created me, I will never forget who I am, where I came from, how I got here, who helped me along the way, and where I am going. Over the years, majority culture friends and allies often compartmentalized and marginalized my work as a diversity officer, even while they supported it. It made sense to them that I would lead on diversity. It was work of and for "my people," after all. Diversity work was, to them, work I had a personal stake in. But they did not think of me as presidential material. It was my people who believed me worthy of a presidency. And even now that I have achieved that goal, traditional academic circles do not really take me seriously as a president, by and large. Homogenous academic circles continue to see me as "other," especially because my college is a Hispano- and indigenous-serving institution. I am indeed, still and always, "other," and proud to be so. And I must remain "other" if I am to be effective. I also know that if I—if we—want to transform the Academy, we need to work toward change *from* the inside.

But *that does not mean being insiders.* It means living a dual life and playing dual and sometimes contradictory but integrative roles. If we become true insiders, we may as well forget about change. It may be tempting to think that if we just stop focusing on race, ethnicity, gender, and other markers of our outsiderness, we will be better off. We will get the tenure, promotions, and accolades that are so important. Maybe this could happen. But it is not that simple. Assimilation negates us. It denies those parts of ourselves that make us agents of change. *It erases us by silencing our stories.*

I know from long experience that going along to get along is the road to invisibility, silence, dishonesty, and continued inequity and exclusion—and ultimately, the road to a dead end for all of us. Our greatest gains have always been achieved when we have recognized what we are up against. Our achievement is embedded in our sense of mission and sense of self, especially when we stand together against the forces of exclusion and bias. Our history tells us that the only way to transform the Academy and advance real academic freedom is not to succumb to the lure of mainstream acceptance, but to bring our whole selves to the task, and to maintain the critical outsider's edge that keeps us from being swallowed up. We need to be *outsiders working on the inside*, negotiating contradictions, mediating cultures, and joining forces for the greater good with others who identify as, or are allies to, outsiders. Even a president must be an outsider—in fact, she *must*. If she is going to maintain a critical edge and make a real difference from her position of executive leadership, a woman of color president must stay an outsider who is a believer in all facets of diversity.

My Journey: The Backstory

I guess it could be said that my whole life has been a story of moving forward from wherever I am at any given moment, one step at a time. I took advantage of unexpected opportunities, and I gave voice to my own deepest truths. But I did not—and could not—do it alone. If I had traveled that long, winding road alone, I would surely have lost my way.

When I left home, I took with me into the world the support of my Mexican American family and community. These people had instilled in me a fierce pride in my heritage and a deep understanding of who I am at my core. They were my models for persistence and survival, and ultimately, for educational administration. So were many friends and colleagues, teachers, and mentors that I met along the way, people whose support and friendship taught me important lessons about the fundamental importance of community.

I like to think of myself even today as a community builder, not a leader in the usual sense of that term. The word "leader" too often conjures the image of controlling authority figure, managing from the top down. It conveys exclusion, not inclusion, hierarchies of power and privilege, not collaboration. In the final analysis, it is our communities of shared leadership that sustain us and empower us to critique and change the systems that have held us back.

My spirit guides even today are the women of my family who often told their personal narratives in my grandmother's kitchen. I think of that kitchen as a place of communion, a place of women weaving and sharing stories, a place whose sights and sounds—and smells—still sustain me. I often find myself back in that kitchen with my maternal grandmother and her daughters, my mother and my aunts. I remember everyone working and chattering and keeping an eye out for me, and my brothers and sisters. There I sat, watching and listening—watching the strong, agile hands of these women shuck the corn, mix ingredients, and wield those rolling pins. I listened to their stories—stories of grief and loss, stories of struggle and recovery, and most importantly, I listened to their stories of survival.

In that small, enclosed space of the kitchen, these women's stories transcended time and place in ways that I could only wonder at. I did not realize it then, but those stories, passed from generation to generation, were a bridge I would later walk across to find myself. It was there that I learned of their struggles against sexism, racism, poverty, and all manner of hardship. And yet, not once did I hear bitterness in their voices. They spoke from a place of pride and strength about their lives, and the lives of their own aunts and grandmothers. They told of women who had survived the Mexican Revolution who had been sold into White slavery to Texas landowners. They recounted stories of women who had been forced into arranged marriages, and those whom toiled in the fields day after day. And still, they laughed. Regardless of circumstance, the women danced and held their heads high. They never gave up.

These phenomenal women were my first teachers. I learned from them what it was to be Chicana. Their stories would one day be woven into my life narrative. They would become my bridge back to myself when I left home for the larger world.

The day I left home for college at Chico State my mother handed me the $80 that she had saved from her job preparing meals for an airline. "Rusty," she said, "this is all we can give you. Don't forget your family." At the time, I did not understand why she would say such a thing. Of course I would not forget my family.

My moment of truth would come four years later, when I arrived at the University of Iowa. I saw no familiar landmarks, no familiar food. I had never experienced such cold. And when realized that I was the only Chicana graduate student on campus, the isolation felt like a kind of exile. And then one day, as I stared into the abyss that was my new life, the temperature dropped—to *minus 5*. That was it. I called my parents to tell them I would be returning home at the end of the semester. I thought surely they would tell me to pack my bags right then and there and come home. But they did not.

My mother, wise as always, simply said, "Rusty, where there's one Mexican, there's probably another one." Of course, I thought she could not possibly understand how miserable I was. About a week later, she sent me a care package containing some of my favorite Mexican foods and some cultural icons—including Virgen de Guadalupe, and a serape, precious cargo from my culture. The following day, I went on a search for those Mexicans. They were nowhere to be found on campus. I could not find them anywhere in the texts, including on the shelves of the library. But finally, there they were, in the 1960 Census. My mother was right. I was not alone: Iowa had 29,000 Spanish-speaking people. In fact, the second language spoken in Iowa was Spanish! There was a community out there. Yet, beyond the census numbers, they remained invisible.

I set out to find them, inspired by my mother's words and empowered by her gift. Right then, I did not realize the full force or meaning of her message to me, but I would in time. I would make my way only if I remained true to myself. I was that turtle, carrying my home and my people on my back. I vowed to stay in tune with my culture. To do this, I promised myself that I would keep my family with me by telling their stories, and mine. And I would create an extended family in the larger world that would give me strength. As women of color in the Academy, it is imperative that we create an extended family in the larger world to give us abundance and strength. Our stories are transformational. They empower us. They tell us that we are part of a vital community, heirs to the legacy of generations of women who have made history. They tell us that we, too, can make history, each in our own way.

Where We Go from Here

Many of us—scholars, students, and administrators alike—have spent our lives straddling shores, mediating worlds, and learning to tolerate ambiguity and contradictions. As we have become outsiders on the inside, our "hybrid consciousness," to use Gloria Anzaldua's term, has been a powerful survival strategy—and a creative and transformative force.

Ours is not an easy task—all that acrobatic straddling and balancing and juggling. Struggle hurts. And yet it is also a catalyst for connection and liberation and social justice. As I have said so many times: It is by *embracing* the struggle that we do transformative work. Maybe that is why I worry that we will all go back to our corners and resume our conversations in closed groups, or that the spirit of this moment will dissipate. We cannot let that happen.

How do we keep from getting discouraged when we find ourselves once again alone in the room or absent from the leadership table or the highest faculty ranks or even the lunch table? As we move further inside, *how do we maintain the sharp edge of critique?* And how do we continue to bring into the conversation the new generations who will reimagine this work for generations yet to come? How do we *sustain* the new systems we have built, especially against such powerful political crosswinds?

Our work from now on is to reimagine our work for the *next 50 years*, and the *next 50*. That is how we make ourselves and our work sustainable. And we need to lead. The dynamic, collaborative process we lead will *transform the structures of knowledge, the patterns of relationships, and the organizing principles of institutional life.* Translation: no more silos, no more marginalizing of diversity work, no more entrenched systems of exclusion and privilege. The upshot is this: If we do not create the institutional change we want to see, someone else with different priorities will. The reality is we probably will not like the results. So let us create a world where every single day, every single one of us asks: Not only *what can I do to get recognition for my scholarly work*, but *what can I do today, in my interactions with everyone on my campus, to make this a more inclusive multicultural community?* Let us work together to create the kind of Academy where we spend every day making this aspiration happen.

To do that, we all need to be mentors and role models. Perhaps nothing is more critical for our collective future than leadership succession. At this pivotal moment in our history, as we face challenges from every front even while our numbers grow, it is imperative that we bring more junior women of color into the conversations at every level and in every corner of our institutions. And while we mentor them, we also need to listen to them and honor their perspectives when they push back, because push back they will. We need to invite them to revisit, rethink, renew, and build on whatever intellectual, institutional and cultural legacy we leave them.

Let me end by saying that as a Chicana, I am not so sure I will ever feel fully at home in my institutional leadership role. The higher levels of administration can be a very lonely and contradictory place for us. But in the end, I believe that managing the isolation, and also the tensions and contradictions, will make me a better president, just as my Iowa experience made me stronger and taught me how to be an agent of change as an institutional diversity advocate. It also will make me a better teacher.

I know that one of my most sacred responsibilities is to share the leadership that I have earned, and to be a mentor and role model for young women of color. That is a responsibility we all share. Whenever we experience a breakthrough—get promoted, get published, receive a reward, get invited to the leadership table—it is time for every one of us to lift as we climb. Making this work sustainable means clearing the paths for others. That is where all of our journeys begin and end, with the sharing of light and passing of the torch.

12. Thriving as Administrators at America's Land Grant Universities

Waded Cruzado

Editors' Note:
Since January of 2010, Dr. Waded Cruzado has served as the twelfth President of Montana State University (MSU). Prior to coming to MSU, President Cruzado served as Executive Vice President and Provost at New Mexico State University (NMSU), beginning in 2007. Dr. Cruzado also served as NMSU's Interim President from 2008 to 2009, the first woman and second Hispanic in that position. She also served as Dean of the College of Arts and Sciences at NMSU (2003–2007).

A first generation college student, she enrolled at the University of Puerto Rico at Mayagüez and graduated magna cum laude with a bachelor's degree in comparative literature. She earned her master's degree in Spanish language and literature and her PhD in the humanities at the University of Texas at Arlington. Dr. Cruzado began her career as an assistant professor in the Department of Humanities at the University of Puerto Rico at Mayagüez. She was promoted to associate professor and then full professor there. She also served as Assistant Dean for Student Affairs, the Associate Dean for Academic Affairs, and then Dean of the College of Arts and Sciences for five years.

I am encouraged by the fact, that in today's world, perhaps more than any other time and place in modern history women have the capacity and I will say the responsibility to influence events and to transform the lives of countless people. Of course, we cannot be oblivious to the fact that we have experienced trying times and some challenges as well. In fact, I was just thinking that it was a mere seven years ago that I was attending a gathering for women of color in the Academy. When my university president learned that I was attending he asked, "So, all thirty of you will be gathering?" It was so thoughtful of him to consider "all thirty" of us. So let me state that one of the premises of my message is that we have to look to the power of our academic sisters with confidence and optimism. This is not naivety. Looking to our sisters is optimism by choice. Our stories of reflection and success cannot be limited to being narratives of agony and survival. We have the choice of them being a celebration of success. So in order to get us started with telling such important stories I will be sharing some biographical information with my remarks in context. Then, I want to tell you a story. Finally, I want to leave you with some questions.

My accent comes from Puerto Rico where I was born and raised. Specifically, I was born and raised in Mayaguez, which is home to the only land grant university in the Caribbean. The University of Puerto Rico at Mayaguez, is also the only land-grant university in a Spanish-speaking country. Since the turn of the twentieth century, the University of Puerto Rico at Mayaguez has been preparing the engineers, the scientists, and the professionals who have transformed the economic landscape of the island and the Caribbean Basin. Therefore, as a child, I always aspired to attend Puerto Rico's land-grant university.

I was the first person in my family to graduate from college. It still amazes me how many of us there still are. My grandparents were farmers. My father was a coffee merchant and my mother was a homemaker. Both of my parents were endowed with intelligence and drive. When I look back and reflect, I ask myself, "So what was it that made it possible for me to explore a life path different from that of my family?" It was not intelligence; they are very intelligent. It is not talent because my parents were very talented. The answer is striking yet simple: someone opened a door for me. I was given an opportunity to go to college.

As a result, I have the determination to ensure that no other young man or woman is ever deprived of the wonders of a college education. Education truly transforms lives. Higher education has provided us with blessings we could have never envisioned. In my case, it enabled me to start my career back in Puerto Rico, which thereby gave me an opportunity to give back and to pay forward. Education made it possible for me to also work at New Mexico State University, another land-grant institution.

Puerto Rico is known as the "Island of Enchantment," so imagine my surprise when I landed at the El Paso Airport and started driving the forty-five miles to New Mexico where, upon crossing the state line a big yellow sign said "Welcome to New Mexico ... The Land of Enchantment." Thus, I went from the Island of Enchantment to the Land of Enchantment. I was convinced I was crossing the twilight zone. Prior to this, my most recent position allowed me to live and work in the majestic state of Montana and serve the first land-grant university of the state. Upon learning about my appointment as president, a good friend texted me. "Why is it that you only get to work in the most spectacular places on the face of the Earth?" she said. To give a sense of perspective, my native Puerto Rico has a total area of 3,500 square miles. By my hurried calculations, its area could fit into the state of Montana about forty-two times. Keep in mind, however, that there are 4 million people living in Puerto Rico. Juxtaposed to this, we just crossed the mark of one million for the first time in the "Big Sky State."

So, I have known the densely and the sparsely populated, the tropics and the desert, some climate extremes in different latitudes and then the invigorating weather of Montana. When I was first approached to participate in the MSU presidential search, it was an interesting time in my life. I, at the time, was serving as Interim President at New Mexico State University and this is how my story went. As for career planning, I was going to teach and do research there for thirty years and then I was going to retire. That was my plan. When I moved to New Mexico I loved it so much that I decided that I was going to stay there until I retired. One thing led into the next. I started out as Dean of Arts and Sciences then became Provost. Eight months into my appointment of Provost, the president announced that he was leaving the institution. So without much planning, I became Interim President. Ten months into that appointment, I received a phone call that went something like this: "We want you to know that the presidency of Montana State will be open and we would like to have a conversation with you." I responded, "Thank you. I know it's a great university, actually we have added it on the list of peer institutions that we use to evaluate our performance. But you know …," I said. "I'm very happy at New Mexico, and I don't like to move. Thank you." Then I hung up the phone. A month later the same individual called again and said, "We want you to know that you've been nominated for the position."

To that statement I said, "Listen, I have never been to Montana when I think about Montana I think about horses, and snow, and by the way, do you know where I was born? I don't look like … I don't sound like anybody in Montana!" The caller replied, "Well we would like for you to take a look at the email and get back to us." Alright, I thought. I went to the email and I decided to Google the US census data demographic data of Montana. I thought to myself, "Let me take a look at the Hispanic population … two percent." At the time, the census data revealed a mere two percent populace of Hispanic people residing in Montana. So I responded back: "Thank you for the honor of the nomination," I said. Then I continued, "… but this is not a right fit for me." I hit the send button. The phone rang immediately! I remember lowering my head and asking this person what they saw in me that I was not seeing. What I was seeing, what I did not want to tell myself was a long list of demerits in my own mind.

My list paralyzed me into prohibiting myself from seizing many opportunities. This list was the driving force of my life, my beliefs, and my passions, however. On my list was that I am a woman. The other things on my list were that: I had majored in the humanities and comparative literature, that I am five feet tall, that I am a Latina, and that I speak with an accent. "Minus, minus, minus, minus," I keep telling myself. Yet, the individual answering my question went in a very different direction. He said, "Well, we're very interested in you because of your experience working with land grant universities. Your experience working with systems and not only one campus is desirable here. Your experience working with underrepresented minorities is also desirable here." I replied that New Mexico is a minority majority state. Forty-two percent of the state is Hispanic. Nine percent of residents are Native Americans. Three percent of New Mexico natives are African-Americans while one percent of the populace is Asian. So then he said, "We're looking for someone with a lot of energy." And I said "Ok, that I have."

So that is what took me, with a lot of trepidation, to Montana. Montana is a state that has an incredible history of extraordinary and courageous women. Many of them, who at the turn of the last century after the congressional bill of 1862 that established the Homestead Act, decided to jump in a train that would take them west to a new life. A new reality, to take care of a piece of land, was on the horizon. Finally, Montana is also the state that gave us the first woman to be elected to congress, Jeanette Rankin. Congresswoman Rankin did not come from a progressive state. She came from Montana and in 1916 she warned, "I may be the first woman member of Congress, but I won't be the last."

A pioneer in many fronts, Rankin exhibited powerful convictions when as a Republican Congresswoman she casted a vote against entering World War I. She was defeated in this vote and in reelection but eventually was reelected in 1940 just in time to cast a vote against the declaration of war to Japan. I think of Janet Rankin when I read Maya Angelou's quote, "Woman should be tough, tender, laugh as much as possible and live long lives. The struggle for equality continues unabated and the woman warrior who is armed with wit and courage will be among the first to celebrate victory." After all these years it is interesting that the advent of women and underrepresented groups in positions of responsibility is still fairly new and limited.

For those of us in this group, I would like to say that our trajectory through the looking glass of leadership in academia can be so dazzling at times we may feel like Alice in Wonderland. As promised, I want to tell a story about Puerto Rican Alice. Once upon a time, Alice was a frail, untenured faculty member in an institution which shall remain nameless. Less than three years into her ten-year track appointment, she was called to serve in academic administration as an Assistant Dean for Academic Affairs. This Puerto Rican Alice looking for adventure and without a mentor by her side to provide wise counsel as for why not to do it, decided to accept an invitation. She opened the door and fell into a rabbit hole inside a world of awe and wonder. Puerto Rican Alice merely wanted to create order in an unruly world. Now, she was lost.

"Oh dear, oh dear I shall be too late," Alice worried. One of the peculiarities that she noticed in her new role was that during student registration times only the untenured faculty members were asked to work during the advising period. "But why," Alice thought. Little did Alice know that by sending her email, she unknowingly stumbled into one of the mysterious boxes of privilege that belonged to the mad tea party inside of the Academy. What would Alice do? Trying to find a solution she prepared a seamlessly innocuous template with time slots for every department. Since Alice believed in honesty and transparency, the template forms were democratically sent to every faculty member who, in consultation with the department head, would select a time slot therefore contributing to a more equitable distribution of the advising responsibility. In her state of innocence, Alice had no idea that she was defying the hierarchical system when she was expecting everybody irrespective of rank or status to serve. It was as if her email unknowingly altered traditional bureaucracy. To some, her message demanded, "Yes, for one hour would you please come back from your labs or leave that sentence in mid-thought of your next to be released paper? Please accept my cordial invitation to share the joy and blessing of guiding students."

People seemed to have viewed this new task with different degrees of amusement and resignation except for one faculty member: a full professor. In Alice's home department, incidentally she had noticed that this same professor had a tendency to be a little bit patronizing. In fact, it was known that he frequently raised the tone of his voice while dissertating about the right way of doing things. To match his tyrant monologues, this professor would also wave his index finger in mid-air to punctuate remarks. He had been known for this type of behavior for ages but no one in the department wanted to address his manners as an issue of concern. Of course Alice was too young and inexperienced to think about an alternative. So, it was the day of the advising email that this full professor taught Alice about academic politics. As soon as he recovered his voice, which thumbed of angered cynicism, reverberated against the wall of the office was, "Ha! Her mother will come to do advising!" When the distant echoes of this terribly disrespectful remark reached her desk, Alice was shocked as well. You know how trying to make sense of uncivil behavior can paralyze you? Alice sat frozen in time. Never had she witnessed something like this in the Academy. What would Alice do? She picked up the phone and cordially talked to enraged department head.

"Make sure that he and the faculty members understand that this was meant to be a participatory process and that I am grateful for their collaboration," Alice said to herself. Alice thought this moment was a teachable moment. When the sun came up on registration day, guess who was there ready and eager to advise? Yes! Dr. Full Professor. So what did Alice do? She listened carefully. She approached him very cordial and collegial. Alice proceeded to greet him in these terms, "Good morning doctor, I am very glad to see you!" Alice exclaimed. She continued, "I called Hector to confirm that you had an opportunity to choose a convenient time because you know, my mom will not be able to join us for registration, too." Needless to say he immediately understood. The full professor apologized. And a good conversation was had about the importance of respect in human relations in general and in the Academy in particular. But wait, there is more.

That is not the end of the story, and yes, Alice was subsequently tenured and promoted. Years after this event, the full professor was appointed to an administrative position and he asked Alice to be his associate. Later on when she occupied the leadership position at that institution, he served as her advisor. And, they lived happily ever after. Alice had been full circle and now she moved forward. My dear colleagues, I am Puerto Rican Alice. I own every experience I have grown through. I am here, I am resilient, and I am a success on my own terms. I am here to say that in the Academy, and in life, it is not enough to survive. *We need to learn to thrive.* That is one of the takeaways I bring forth.

Now having shared my biography and having told a story, here are some questions. I will preface them by saying that as of late I have discovered that I have less and less patience. I have less tolerance for euphemisms and it is becoming increasingly difficult for me to understand self-centeredness. So I would like to ask my first set of questions. Please tell me how are we going to effectuate change in the Academy? What is our strategy in order to open more doors of opportunity? And how do we protect ourselves against what I call "elitism in disguise"? Perhaps we need to take a peek at a page in our history. As I mentioned at the beginning of my remarks, the concept of a system of colleges and universities built in the people's interest was actually a project that was initiated by Jonathan Baldwin Turner. Turner was an educator from Illinois. He was a graduate of the New Haven Institute, or what is now known as Yale University. Jonathan Turner devoted his entire life to advocate for a reality different than the one he witnessed, in which only two percent of the American population had access to a college education.

It was Turner who came up with the basic concept of the land grant bill. It was Turner who sent his concept papers to Congressman Morrill as a representative of one of the oldest states in the Union. And, it was Turner who approached his friend, President Abraham Lincoln, whom he had helped learn grammar when the future president was only a harvest ham. "Why is this relevant to us today as we ask these questions?" The answer is simple: it is a great example of what big ideas and bold leadership can accomplish. The notion of establishing a university in each state and every territory of the union … think about that! That is why Puerto Rico was included. And up until that moment, what were everyone's chances of attending college? People would have to choose a university either on the East Coast or West Coast; and good luck paying tuition in a private institution. Think about this concept that was so ahead of its time.

It was proposed that there should be one public university in each state and territory of the Union. Not in those states that were better populated or more sophisticated or more mature, but one in every state. Of course, for us today it looks fantastic but at the time it was a very egregious, radical, populist movement. The reality that Congress approved it right in the middle of the Civil War, to me, is immensely inspirational. What a powerful lesson for all of us. Rather than be constrained by the circumstances of the time, Congressmen could have said, "No. Not now. Let us wait until the war is over." Those Congressmen decided that they were going to make a choice. They chose to envision a better and brighter future by educating the sons and daughters of the working families of America. America has never been the same.

If I can digress a little bit more, 1862 also gave us the Homestead Act and the Pacific Rail Road Act. The way I explain this to myself is that while the Pacific Railroad Act and the Homestead Act gave us geographical and horizontal stability, it was the Land Grant Act that gave us the social and vertical mobility. We strengthened the middle class and in doing that we strengthened American democracy forever. So I need to ask, "Are we still responsive to the model of a university that is committed to access and success? In our quest for excellence and for national rankings, which are prepared by the same media that sometimes derides a college education, can we please answer: Who are we leaving behind?" The founding of a system of public universities in 1862 was not limited to regions where the educational system was established and mature, or where students would be better prepared for a college education. Let us be honest here.

How many homesteaders were college ready? Yet, as a nation we were still undeterred. The fundamental principle of higher education, particularly in its much battered public expression, should not be to exclude the individuals who perhaps might fail but rather, to challenge everyone to succeed. However, I still hear it all the time that, "College is not for everyone." Many people remember the way and manner in which as a timid entering class we were welcomed by a university President. Do I need to specify male? Who in his opening remarks welcomed us with something like, "Look to your left, look to your right: Only one of you three will graduate."

How many have heard that before? It was pervasive. It was always the poor souls who were to your left and to your right that were not going to make it. This should be a particularly burning issue for us as women of color in the Academy because now that the demographics of our country are being subverted, now that the constitution of the student bodies reflect an increasing number of women and underrepresented minorities, it is interesting to observe how the public discourse emphasizes the magnitude of difficulty rather than the potential that this new order represents.

I am actually amused when I attend national conferences and almost every speaker on those panels focuses on the word "challenge" instead of the word "opportunity" when describing the education of our current and future students. Much has changed. What is different? The change overtime is what I call "elitism in disguise." No one wants to say that these are "Brown students." They look different. I still remember my days as Dean of the College of Arts and Sciences at New Mexico State University. I remember some of my Ivy League professors would come and complain about the students at the university. The professors would say, "They are ... the students are ... ummm ... uh ... different." And, I would lean forward and ask, "Different how?"

Please do not misunderstand me. It is crucially important to recruit outstanding students because they enrich our classroom in more ways than just intellectually. But if we subscribe to an exclusive model in which we only recruit the best and brightest of students, we reduce the promises of our institutions. I believe in the model of a university as a proposal to add value in both the classroom and also the broader construct of society. We must skillfully work to draw out the best talents of our students. Just as it was in the archetypical myth of the hero's journey, I believe it is true that the person that emerges triumphant is not the same person that accepted the ordeal. Challenges conquered make stronger and more resilient men and women, especially as presidents.

My final set of questions is simply: So, what are you waiting for? What do we need to do for women of color faculty to gladly accept the responsibility for the past, present, and future that you represent? I attend many meetings with women who want to have everything perfectly planned before they launch their career. Almost invariably, after finishing inspirational presentations, in a note of exultation and victory, I ironically wait for the ubiquitous question during the Question and Answer segment. "How do we balance it all?" Gloria Steinem had a great answer when she said, "I have yet to be in a campus and hear a man ask how to combine marriage and a career." Or perhaps we need to quote former First Lady Michelle Obama, "You can't make decisions based on fear and the possibility of what might happen."

It is good to plan ahead but we cannot condone or allow structures and strictures to intrude in such a manner that it paralyzes our momentum and suffocates our spirit. Sometimes when wanting to have absolute certainty and control about our future, we forget how fortunate we are and how much has been accomplished on our behalf and for our sake. I am not talking about historical accomplishments that have benefited women's rights. Nor am I evoking extraordinary women leaders of our past. I could do both things. I am talking about immediacy here. I am remembering our very own families. Specifically, I am thinking about our own mothers and grandmothers who were not afforded half of the opportunities we have but still had all the intelligence and even the ambition that we sometimes lack. I had never thought too much about this before until my mother was diagnosed with a terminal illness. See, my mother is a cancer survivor ... twice over. I remember when it first happened. Every night over the phone, in a long distance call, I would try to reassure my mother and I would say things like, "One day at a time mom. Let's take it one day at a time." Until one day she retorted, "How easy for you to say."

To my surprise, she did not respond in that way because I was healthy. Mom continued, "You can say that because you have studied." Huh? I was perplexed. What does she mean? Was she not proud of me anymore? Then, it was all clear. My mother thought that my years of study and the accumulation of academic degrees had inoculated me against despair. Shielding me from the powerlessness that she was feeling, by arming me with the knowledge to name things and phenomena, in my mother's eyes I had a definitive advantage over her. I was able to find and convey meaning to events that in her case eluded comprehension.

Years later while reading "The Road from Coorain" by Jill Ker Conway (1990), the first woman president of Smith College, I learned that she had lived a similar situation with her own mother. Conway (1990, p. 115) summarized it in the following manner: "Her lack of education was a real handicap because she had no historical or philosophical perspective from which to analyze her own experience of grief and loss." This, for me, illuminates a new dimension where we must affirm once again that knowledge is power. We have a great responsibility, sisters. This is evident. Sheryl Sandberg (2013) also bemoaned that our lack of participation and our reluctance to sit at the table when decisions are being made prevents us from "leaning in."

Sandberg (2013) explained, in her book "Lean In," that,

> In addition to the external barriers elected by society, women are hindered by barriers that exist within ourselves. We hold ourselves back in ways both big and small, by lacking in self-confidence, by not raising our hand, by leaning back when we should be leaning in. (p. 8)

Remember the five-foot-tall Latina who speaks with an accent? Sometimes when discussing diversity, particularly gender participation, there is a subtle tendency to concentrate on the negative aspect of our experiences. However, it is through setting aside negative episodes and fears and focusing on lessons learned that we start moving ahead.

Once again the words of another woman president, the wonderful Johnnetta B. Cole (1991) provides us with encouragement as she said, "We are for difference: for respecting difference for allowing difference, for encouraging difference, until difference no longer makes a difference." It is through this attitude of generosity of spirit that we discover the power of transformational leadership. At the end of the day it is about accepting the challenge to become a servant leader. Change occurs because the person who inspires a shared vision enables others to accomplish extraordinary things. In essence, my message is plain and simple: We need you. Our families need you. Our society, our disciplines needs you. Our young men and women of color desperately need you. Do not second guess yourself anymore. Accept the leadership challenge that can make a difference in the world.

Let me conclude with one of my favorite passages from author Clarissa Pinkola Estés (1996), writer of "Women Who Run with the Wolves." Estés reminds us of the important transition from survival to thriving; culminating in a big celebration like we are joined in today. According to Estés (1996),

> Instead of making survivorship the center of one's life; it is better to use it as one of many badges, but not the only one. It is not good to base the soul identity solely on defeats and losses and victories of the bad times otherwise, nothing else can grow. I liken it to a tough little plant that managed—without water, sunlight, nutrients—to send out a brave and ornery little leaf anyway, in spite of it all. (p. 195)

Thriving to me now means that the bad times are behind. Thriving is when we defy adversity while aiming higher, accomplishing our goals, and mentoring one another. It is better when we challenge ourselves to grow. That is thriving. That is what was meant for us. Our purpose is to thrive. If you have ever been called defiant, incorrigible, forward, cunning, insurgent, unruly, assertive, rebellious ... you are on the right track. If you have never been called these things, there is yet time.

References

Cole, J. (1991). *American Association for Higher Education conference remarks.*

Conway, J. (1990). *The road from Coorain.* New York, NY: Vintage Books.

Estés, C. (1996). *Women who run with the wolves: Stories of the wild woman archetype.* New York, NY: Random House Publishing.

Sandberg, S. (2013). *Lean in.* New York, NY: Knopf Doubleday.

13. Reflections about Latina/Chicana Leadership in the Academy

Johanna B. Maes

Introduction

The narratives of women leaders in the academy are heavily discussed in academic research. Whether it be the mention of their rise from faculty to administrative ranks (Madsen, Longman, & Daniels, 2012), or documenting the shortage of women in leadership positions in higher education (Madsen, 2012), or noting how the processes of mentoring and decision making impact women leaders in the academy (White, 2012), these issues are readily apparent in mainstream research. However, one has to search extensively to learn how these experiences impact Latina leaders within the academy because their narratives and experiences are rarely discussed in academic research (Maes, 2012; Mendez-Morse, 2004).

This chapter discusses the experiences of Latina/Chicana leaders in higher education, while paying particular attention to those experiences of current and former university presidents Drs. Rusty Barceló and Waded Cruzado. Drawing from dissertation research (Maes, 2012) and other scholarship on Latina women and Latina leadership, this chapter explores how these women along with members of this underrepresented subpopulation of women lead differently within their respective institutions. The literature review section examines the key factors that influence Latina leaders and Latina leadership. These factors include educational experiences, work experiences, family background, and spirituality. The experiences of Waded and Rusty are then analyzed through an intersectional lens revealing the ways in which their journeys were influenced by multiple factors. Their leadership journeys are critical for understanding how to increase the representation of Latina presidents, especially as the Latino/a student population continues to increase. Their narratives also explore how they view and practice leadership through a Chicana/Latina lens, which focuses on traits such as character, competence, compassion, and being a servant within their respective communities. The intention of this research is to not only highlight how these nontraditional university leaders lead differently but also to share their narratives which are often absent from mainstream academic research.

Literature Review

Latinas in Education

According to Maes (2012) and McGlynn (1998), Latinas can often be termed as possessing a triple minority status: they are women, they are members of a racial and ethnic minority group, and many are born into and some remain in a low socio-economic status group. Latinas also comprise nearly half of the total Latino population in the United States and their numbers are expected to reach over 51 million in 2050 (Gilroy, 2006). Latinas possess socio-economic and cultural factors that are not necessarily present in the lives of women in the majority in society. For example, in a socio-economical context, as indicated by Segura (2003) and Gonzalez (1996), Latinas traditionally are positioned in a working class, blue collar environment where many tend to live in poor, racially-segregated neighborhoods. Their school systems are substandard, resources are limited, and there is little attention paid to them and other students of color (Gonzalez, 1996; Segura, 2003). These school systems do not necessarily prepare them for higher education (Maes, 2012, p. 10). They are often viewed through a deficit lens rather than an asset-based lens. Young girls of color, especially Latinas, are often invisible within their K–12 school systems. This results in their lack of placement in advanced or gifted and talented programs which are the natural pathway to college. This time in their academic career is when educators speculate that Latinas can be casualties of their own "broken educational pipeline" (Maes, 2012, p. 10).

Latinas, along with other students from underrepresented backgrounds, particularly African American students, have different types of cultural capital that may not be always regarded within their school systems. In fact, Rodriguez, Guido-DiBrito, Torres, and Talbot (2000) describe this type of cultural capital as one that "encompasses implicit and internalized beliefs and values, including attitudes and perceptions toward education" (p. 516). Many of these Latinas possess other forms of cultural capital which continue to be disregarded by their educators. These include aspirational, familial, social, and navigational capital (Sandoval-Lucero, Maes, & Klingsmith, 2014). It can be concluded that although many young Latina students equally compete in their school systems and possess the intellectual capital and capacity to be successful, many of their school systems devalue their unique forms of cultural capital which "reinforces and perpetuates social inequality for them within their school systems. Thus becomes the apparent break in their educational pipeline" (Rodriguez et al., 2000, p. 516).

It is important to note that not all Latinas are casualties of a broken pipeline in their K–12 environments. Many of those who are among the 31% who graduate from high school (Jackson, 2013, p. 2) often find themselves tracked into a curriculum path that only prepares them for trade schools or community colleges where there may not be enough support for their matriculation to a four-year institution (Sandoval-Lucero et al., 2014, p. 523). If a break in their educational pipeline does not occur in their K–12 education, it can occur at this time. Yet there are those Latinas who manage to advance onto a four-year institution and are often subjected to a racist, classist, gender-biased, and hierarchal educational environment that does not always encourage them to advance on to graduate school (Segura, 2003). This creates yet another break in their educational pipeline. Then one must question how can the academy groom aspiring Latinas to become university presidents when this population is nearly absent from graduate programs in general?

Latinas and Family Connections

The Latino family structure significantly influences progression or regression of many Latina females as leaders (Maes, 2012, p. 12). Often times, Latinas can struggle with maintaining their family obligations, duties, and gender role expectations while they aspire to compete and ultimately advance in the United States educational system (Maes, 2012; Rodriguez et al., 2000). Many of their parents question their choice of higher education while noting that only "rich kids" attend college or that they should place more emphasis on getting married and having children (Rodriguez et al., 2000). These dilemmas add additional stress to those Latinas who are already venturing outside of their comfort zone to either acculturate or assimilate into their educational system.

However, Maes (2012) and Rodriguez et al. (2000) note that high achieving Latinas tend to have different expectations placed upon them by their family. "At times in these households the Latino parents tend to be non-authoritarian while breaking their stereotypical patriarchal, and authoritarian role. These parents also place great emphasis on their children being self-reliant and highly educated" (Maes, 2012, p. 13). Additionally, high-achieving Latinas who attend middle-class schools are "academically competitive with their classmates and their teachers tend to place higher expectations on them, which ultimately raise Latinas' overall confidence in academics" (Rodriguez et al., 2000, p. 520). Often times, these high-achieving Latinas steer away from traditional gender-role expectations and behaviors and when they become adults, they find that being single and without children is not only acceptable but is positively associated with achieving in higher education (Rodriguez et al., 2000).

Although Latinas often live in patriarchal families, some family members champion their efforts to achieve socio-economic and educational advancement despite cultural expectations (Maes, 2012). Mendez-Morse (2004) states that many Latina leaders indicate their parents are their strong advocates who stress "a strong work ethic, the importance of education, and concrete support of academic efforts" (p. 581). Latina parents often emphasize to their daughters that education is key to not work as farm laborers, and work "out in the sun," as they, themselves, had to do (Mendez-Morse, 2004, p. 577).

Some Latina leaders state that it was their parents who provided the most encouragement, "even when they, themselves, had minimal education levels" (Avery, 1982, p. 590; Maes, 2012). These unskilled laborers or service workers often stressed to their Latina daughters to achieve what they were unable to given their limited educational and professional opportunities (Avery, 1982, p. 590).

According to Mendez-Morse (2004), many Latina leaders consider their mothers to be their first mentors and advocates. These mothers would often "take an active role in the educational successes of their daughters, despite that they, themselves, lacked educational credentials" (Mendez-Morse, 2004, p. 578). Many Latina mothers are the first to stress to their daughters the importance of completing homework prior to engaging in extra-curricular activities. Mothers also model female competence and often say to their daughters that "women can do anything" and "never use being a woman as an excuse for doing certain things" (Mendez-Morse, 2004, p. 578).

In addition to mothers, Latina leaders typically had distant female relatives, often an aunt or a cousin, who encouraged them to become college educated (Maes, 2012; Mendez-Morse, 2004). These individuals were often enrolled in college themselves or had completed a degree, and in turn, provided academic, personal, and financial guidance to these emerging Latina leaders. Most importantly, these relatives validated the importance of earning a college degree while dismissing the conflicting expectations that were sometimes given by other members of their families (Mendez-Morse, 2004, p. 579). This process can be considered providing another generation with aspirational goals (Sandoval-Lucero et al., 2014, p. 530).

Latinas and Spirituality

The strong connection to religious and spiritual practices remains constant with many Latina leaders (Maes, 2012). When considering the notion of spirituality, Latina leaders tend to be different from women leaders of other races and ethnicities (Rodriguez, 1999). Traditionally, many Latinas are reared in Roman Catholicism where many of its practices tend to be the foundation of many Latino family traditions. Because Latinas are raised in this patriarchal church environment, as adults Latinas often retrieve and integrate their traditional Catholic beliefs with their newly-founded spirituality by "reclaiming the Spanish language, strengthening and reinterpreting key religious symbols such as Our Lady of Guadalupe, providing and introducing ancient rituals, and transferring communal/inclusive ritual practices into their organizational leadership" (Rodriguez, 1999, p. 5).

If a Latina chooses to leave Catholicism or any other organized religion, she may encounter personal conflict and struggle. Her religion may have been a strong source of connection between her and the Latino family (Maes, 2012, p. 16; Rubio & Lugo-Lugo, 2005). Catholicism tends to be a "cultural identifier" for Latinos and when they decide to venture from this organized religion, they are often viewed as disrespecting their families along with not being "good Catholics" (Maes, 2012, p. 16).

Latinas can possess many identities such as being a feminist, lesbian, mother, or activist (Guzman, 2003; Maes, 2012). These identities can also influence their shift away from organized religion. Many Latinas note that the teachings of the Catholic church tend to "feel oppressive" and as they grow older and become more integrated into the White culture, they choose to view organized religion more critically (Guzman, 2003, p. 132). Yet the rituals of Catholicism, such as the sacraments, holidays, and certain prayers remain a rich part of their history given that they are closely associated as a Latino "cultural identifier" (Rubio & Lugo-Lugo, 2005, p. 109).

What remains paramount for Latinas is being spiritual while finding a source of personal strength and growth, whether this process is within organized religion or not (Maes, 2012). According to Rodriguez (1999), "Latinas bridge leadership with inner spirituality while recognizing the importance of human dignity, shared solidarity, respect, inclusion, and interrelated values learned in their formatted leadership style" (p. 4). Also, Latina leadership and spirituality is one of inclusiveness, of enabling others, of being "a part of" instead of separate. This process is accomplished with "the body, the heart, the hands, and the head" (Rodriguez, 1999, p. 3). Additionally, Latinas are often grounded in "formal knowledge" (which requires one to extract information from historical text books and other typical sources) and "informal knowledge" (which comes from myths, proverbs, songs, and spoken narrative experiences); informal knowledge is spiritually a part of the rich Latina culture (Rodriguez, 1999, p. 1).

Latinas as Professionals

The barriers Latina professionals face in the workforce are different from other women in our society: "many often face obstacles regarding equitable wages, while many find it difficult to fit in to their work environments, while some find that language acquisition and usage are barriers within their work environments" (Maes, 2012, p. 17). In a socio-cultural context, as noted in Maes (2012) and Gonzales-Figueroa and Young (2005), the theories associated with assimilation, acculturation, and ethnic identity at times correlate when analyzing the experiences of Latinas, particularly within educational and professional settings. For example, assimilation occurs when one experiences a loss of ethnic identity, undergoing changes or transformations until she is accepted into the majority culture as "blending in" (Gonzales-Figueroa & Young, 2005, p. 215).

Acculturation occurs when individuals of diverse cultural backgrounds spend an extended amount of time with one another and cultural patterns are altered. Whereas acculturation can weaken one's ethnic identity, assimilation often results in the loss of one's ethnic identity (Gonzales-Figueroa & Young, 2005, p. 216). One example that highlights the difference between assimilation and acculturation for Latinos is that

> even though Latinos and Latinas tend to experience assimilation and acculturation in various phases and stages in their lives, those who are bilingual (Spanish/English) tend to retain and utilize their Spanish language skills as a means of demonstrating their solid ethnic identity. (Gonzalez-Figueroa & Young, 2005, p. 215)

Latinas who break their stereotypical mold do so while compromising familial, cultural, and traditional beliefs that are passed along from generations past (Gil & Vazquez, 1996, p. 7; Maes, 2012). This "going against the grain" process can be very painful given that the women may have to acculturate or assimilate into the mainstream White American culture, which may entail sacrificing many cultural and familial beliefs and practices (Gonzales-Figueroa & Young, 2005). One must ask if the acculturation or assimilation process, which can involve giving up one's native language and constantly monitoring one's communication methods or ways of dress, are indeed worth the personal and emotional sacrifices these women make. The question is whether there is a way to remain connected to cultural beliefs, traditions, and values while merging her thoughts, attitudes and actions into the mainstream, White American culture.

Latina leaders often spend excessive amounts of time "fitting in" their work environments, which can "impede their professional success" or prevent them from advancing in their respective career (Catalyst, 2003, p. 23). Many Latina leaders face the undesirable option of "whether they should stand out or blend in to their work environments" (Maes, 2012, p. 17). Particularly, Latina professionals who are bilingual or speak with an accent are more likely to report that they are less respected and accepted within their work environments (Maes, 2012, p. 17). Additionally, "some Latina professionals feel as if they have to dress conservatively where they steer away from wearing bright colors while maintaining conservative hairstyles and make-up because that is what is expected of them more so than of their White counterparts" (Maes, 2012, p. 18).

Additionally, Latina professional leaders are often forced to modify their behavior (Catalyst, 2003). Modifications may include toning down their direct communication style, appearing to be less feminine for the fear of being perceived as flirtatious, or altering their Spanish accent to succeed in corporate environments (Catalyst, 2003, pp. 16, 24). Many Latina leaders often negotiate their ethnic identity within the workplace, which leads to stress for them. For example, they struggle when deciding if they should reveal their ethnicity to their colleagues for fear that negative stereotypes of a specific ethnic group will be projected upon them (Catalyst, 2003, p. 25). Latina college and university presidents often function in two socio-cultural environments, which include dualism or negotiation (Hansen, 1997; Maes, 2012). In dualism, the Latina president must draw on her identity while upholding the institutional values of her university. In negotiation, she must draw on her identity while also socially transforming her university (Hansen, 1997, p. 5).

Latinas in Academia

Latinas have extraordinary challenges to endure while on their leadership journey through academia (Maes, 2012). For example, the American Association of Community Colleges (2010) reports that Latinas and Latinos make up only 6% of all executive/administrative and managerial positions in higher education. Additionally, in 2003, there were more Latina full-time administrators than Latino administrators in higher education institutions, yet there were more Latino males as presidents or chancellors (de los Santos & Vega, 2008, p. 157). In that same year, there were 42 Latino presidents or chancellors of four-year colleges and universities and only 9 were female (de los Santos & Vega, p. 158; Maes, 2012).

For those few Latinas who are in leadership positions in academia, they have similar "standing out or blending in" experiences as Latinas in other professions (Maes, 2012, p. 19). Most Latinas in higher education leadership positions are concentrated in student services, such as counseling, student life, and academic support programs (Deitz, 1992). The unfortunate aspect of this is that Latinas often remain in these positions throughout their career in higher education, which is often called a "Hispanic box" (Martinez, 1999). Student service positions may not provide room for advancement or lucrative financial compensation given that there are not many opportunities for research, publishing, or professional exposure. This can also result in the lack of support by their higher education supervisor. Spending time in these student support areas is typical for Latinas because they often place themselves in mentoring positions where they feel obligated to work with and build the skills of Latino students (Deitz, 1992, p. 12).

The lack of Latina/Latino professionals in higher education institutions, which includes community colleges and universities, was described in a 2013 National Center for Education Statistics (NCES) report. In fall 2013, the report notes that of all full-time faculty in degree-granting postsecondary institutions, 2% were Latinas. Among full-time professors, 1% were Latinas, while Latinas made up 2% of associate professors and 2% of assistant professors. Finally, Latinas made up 4% of instructors and 3% of lecturers in the academy, respectively. Race, class, and gender also play a significant role in the stages of advancement for Latinas in academia, or lack thereof. NCES (2013) also reports that of all the faculty positions in higher education, 35% were White women.

There are other notable issues that face Latinas in academia (Maes, 2012; Segura, 2003). First,

> many are associated with developing interdisciplinary studies such as Chicana/o studies, ethnic studies, or women's studies that may not be seen as credible disciplines in mainstream academia; these programs are also in jeopardy of being eliminated. Latinas in these areas often find themselves repeatedly validating the importance of these disciplines with senior faculty who are unfamiliar with their research interests, methodologies, and non-traditional approaches. (Maes, 2012, p. 20)

Additionally, "those Latina academicians who have become affiliated with a traditional academic department often find themselves quite isolated in these traditional White male settings" (Maes, 2012, p. 20). More so than White academics, Latinas must negotiate the "publish or perish" mentality of academia while trying to stay true to their traditional expectations of

Latina motherhood, which often dictates having children should not only happen early in life but should also be a priority (Maes, 2012, p. 20). Finally, because of the paucity of Latina academicians, they are often asked to be involved in a variety of formal and informal projects (Maes, 2012, p. 20). They often are not rewarded for these activities; receive little recognition from the department chairs and deans, and are often penalized for their roles (Maes, 2012, p. 20).

Latina academicians who are presidents have unique challenges (Maes, 2012; Viernes Turner, 2007). Latina college and university presidents attribute their success and survival in their respective positions to the following experiences: (a) the importance of early educational and career success, (b) the importance of interpersonal connections, (c) their nontraditional leadership style focused on community-building, (d) their immediate responses to their challenges in their role as president, (e) their courage to accomplish way beyond what was expected of them, (f) acknowledging that they are indeed trailblazers in their respective areas, and (g) acknowledging that their individual selves clearly matched their institutional setting (Viernes Turner, 2007, p. 15).

Martinez Ramos (2008) discusses the structures, institutionalized filters, and other social selection factors that affect the trajectory of Latina university officials toward their presidential positions (Maes, 2012). Martinez Ramos (2008, p. 12) also notes mechanisms that can be put into place to increase the number of Latinas in presidential positions such as recognizing bias in higher education, and noting the importance of providing mentors, champions, and strategic measures to assist in the promotion and retention of this subpopulation in higher education.

Most research regarding the experiences of Latinas in presidential positions has been about those in community colleges (Knowlton, 1993; Rodriguez, 2006). Knowlton (1993) studied one Latina chief executive officer of a California community college and compared her socio-cultural experiences to eight other Latina community college presidents. Knowlton (1993, p. 284) noted how family ties, cultural identities, family's educational expectations, and gender-related experiences affected all of their presidential experiences. Knowlton (1993) also discussed the collaborative leadership style possessed by the featured Latina chief executive officer and how that style was exhibited by the other Latina presidents who were interviewed.

Rodriguez (2006) examined four California community college chief executive officers' experiences from their working-class, immigrant families to their trajectory to their presidencies. The themes developed from this narrative inquiry included: (a) the powerful influence of family; (b) a sense of struggle, overcoming obstacles, and resilience; (c) positive connections to schools and learning; (d) benefits from quality mentoring experiences; (e) growth from participation in leadership programs; (f) an unusual commitment and dedication to public service; and (g) an impact of race, gender, and culture on their presidency (Rodriguez, 2006, p. 163). These works illustrate the role of family, gender, race, and culture for Latina professionals. These are also important factors in Latina leadership styles.

Latina Leadership

Latina leadership is different from mainstream leadership traits and values (Ramirez, 2006). The National Community for Latino Leadership, Inc. (NCLL) conducted a study where more than 3,000 Latinos of all backgrounds were asked to identify their visions, values, and expectations of Latino leaders and leadership (Ramirez, 2006). Through their responses, NCLL identified the Four C's of Latino leadership that reflect the traits that Latinos expect their leaders to possess (Ramirez, 2006). They include character, competence, compassion, and community servanthood (Ramirez, 2006, p. 86). Additionally, NCLL found that Latino leaders are often known to be more "communal, collectivist, and people-centered" (Ramirez, 2006, p. 86) while also demonstrating leadership traits that are "interpersonal, participatory and collaborative" (Ramirez, 2006, p. 87).

Latina leaders also encompass the notion of "exercising one's power, knowledge, and access to change those aspects of society that are inequitable" (Bordas, 2007, p. 98). Latina leaders are also advocates for social justice and equal opportunity; they are consensus builders and community organizers (Bordas, 2007). They are often noted as "weaving social and political unity from diverse Latino subgroups" which motivate people to address the many critical issues that affect the lives of the overall Latino community for future generations (Bordas, 2007, pp. 103, 105, 129).

Latina leaders tend to place emphasis on improving their communities through their leadership practices (Mendez-Morse, 2000). Their leadership is influenced by the strong role modeling they received from other Latinas in their lives, who are usually mothers or aunts (Mendez-Morse, 2000, p. 591). Latina immigrant mothers are often the most influential in developing leadership skills in their daughters (Practical Wisdom: Where Leadership Is Really Learned, 2005). They are the first to introduce the concepts of stewardship, community engagement, and interdependence that are carried throughout their daughters' adulthood leadership positions (Practical Wisdom: Where Leadership Is Really Learned, 2005).

Additionally, Latina mothers also teach their daughters that power and resilience come from within and leadership or followership "requires vision, courage and wisdom to know which one is needed and when" (Practical Wisdom: Where Leadership Is Really Learned, 2005, p. 57). Finally, the author describes this type of leadership development as a "delicate dance," which requires "an agile, giving spirit, unity, trust and cooperation that seeks the overall good" (Practical Wisdom: Where Leadership Is Really Learned, 2005, p. 57). Based on the research, many Latina leaders gain strength from leaders who have come before them, who also happen to be role models who are within their family structure.

This literature review has demonstrated how emerging Latina leaders have personal and educational challenges while in K–12 and higher education which are not typical in the lives of White, majority students. As adult leaders, Latinas tend to draw on the strength they receive from their family as well as from their own spiritual beliefs which can help rectify their recurring negative experiences they have as professionals inside and outside of academia. Finally, Latina leaders lead differently as they merge social justice themes along with practices that embrace service and inclusivity which inevitably create diverse working environments for them and their colleagues.

The Trailblazers: Rusty Barceló and Waded Cruzado

When I decided to focus my doctoral dissertation on Latinas who are presidents of four-year institutions I had a list of less than a dozen women who occupied these positions at that time. I literally called each of them, one by one, and asked if they would be interested in telling me their stories for my research. A few of them could not participate because of competing demands, one outright said no, and three were eager and humbled to be a part of this very important project. Two of those three amazing women were Waded Cruzado, a Latina from Puerto Rico and Rusty Barceló, a Chicana from the southwestern region of the United States (Barceló, 2016; Cruzado, 2016).

I had the fortune of being introduced to Rusty by one of my academic mentors and personal friends, Dr. Elisa Facio, who had a long friendship with Rusty. When Rusty heard that I was a *compañera* of Elisa, she immediately invited us both to stay with her at her luxurious adobe presidential quarters in the middle of the New Mexico desert. It was then when I was to be engulfed in Rusty's passion for education, social justice, and her unique sense of Chicana *feminismo* which was something I had never seen in a woman in higher education, even in a college president.

When we first arrived at Rusty's house, she greeted us outside in the desert moonlight. I remember Rusty saying aloud to us, while extending open arms, "Welcome, mujeres. Can you believe how ridiculous this is?" She was referring to her presidential quarters which were glamorous and way too over-the-top for this modest Chicana. I learned she was raised as a military child who not only moved around the country due to her father's military orders but did so with basic bare necessities. What I quickly realized during that first meeting is that Rusty Barceló is real. She didn't need lavish presidential quarters to exhibit her positional power. In fact, that made her uncomfortable. She would have been perfectly content occupying a humble cottage somewhere near her college. From that weekend visit, I recognized that Rusty was humble, authentic, and different, and like many who are fortunate to be within her space, I was quickly captivated by her spirit.

My introduction to Waded happened serendipitously. While interviewing Dr. Elsa Nuñez, another Latina university president for my dissertation research, I mentioned to her that I was in need of another president for my study. She remembered Waded from a previous interaction, immediately contacted her on my behalf, and days later I received an email from Waded who graciously accepted my invitation to be interviewed by me. Although I was not able to meet with Waded in person, she and I arranged a series of conversations via Skype which proved to be just as powerful and meaningful as they would have been had we been together in person. Waded was just as warm and welcoming as Rusty and treated me like an old friend whom she had not seen in years. She was compassionate and sensitive and I was immediately drawn to her power.

Research on Latina/Chicana scholars are what Perez Huber and Cueva (2012) consider *testimonios*. As an educational research method, reveal the systemic and biased subordination in the academy. Through this *testimonio* process, Latina/Chicana scholars uncover "resistance, resilience in hopes that their research challenges and transforms subordination to move toward a vision of social justice" (Perez Huber & Cueva, 2012, p. 392). One of the more important processes of *testimonios*, which is in essence a self-reflective movement, is to draw importance to passing along narratives, knowledge, and experiences from one generation to another. This enables the next generation of Latina/Chicana scholars to learn from the experiences of their elders to change the fabric of the homogenous and often biased academy.

The time I spent with Rusty and Waded were powerful reminders of how they and other Chicana and Latina leaders share themselves with others through the power of *testimonios*. Whether we were engaged in a formal interview session or if Rusty and I were just sitting down for dinner at an area Espanola, New Mexico restaurant, both Rusty and Waded spoke in stories, in *dichos*, that often took me back to the original site of their experiences.

It is important to note that even though Rusty's and Waded's cultural identities could be placed under the umbrella of what could be called "Hispanic," they still come from two very different socio-cultural and geographical backgrounds. However, what was most ironic when conducting this research originally in 2010 and reviewing it again in 2016 is that Rusty and Waded are more alike than anticipated. The below sections will analyze the educational, familial, spiritual, professional, and academic similarities of Rusty and Waded while framing it all through intersectionality and the Latina leadership lens.

Intersectionality

When reflecting on the narratives and presidential experiences of Rusty and Waded the theory of intersectionality must be brought forth. Knudsen (2007) states that intersectionality is

> the classical models of oppression within society, such as those based on race/ethnicity, gender, religion, nationality, sexual orientation, class, species or disability do not act independently of one another; instead, these interrelate creating a system of oppression that reflects the "intersection" of multiple forms of discrimination. (pp. 61–76)

The idea of intersectionality has been brought forth by Critical Race theorists and LatCrit theorists in a way that "one's identity is not based on the social construction of race but rather is multidimensional and intersects with various experiences" (Delgado Bernal, 2002, p. 118; Maes, 2012, p. 4). Race, class, and gender are critical identities in the experiences of Rusty and Waded; and sexual orientation is an important identity for Rusty.

Rusty and Waded experienced racial, gender, and social class biases when they were young women (Maes, 2012). Yet these experiences provided them with a foundation of who they would become as successful Latina professionals. When Rusty was a young girl, her family moved from France to San Antonio, Texas. This was a period of heightened racial tensions both nationally and internationally where she was exposed first hand of how members of the White culture viewed Mexican Americans. She was startled when she saw signs stating "No Mexicans or dogs allowed here" (Maes, 2012, p. 77). It was also during this time when Rusty's racial and cultural identity continued to be challenged during this time as she found herself in a physical altercation with a childhood bully named Aurora. The two girls acted out their own internalized oppression. Rusty indicated that this was her first experience with identity transformation and awareness given that she mustered enough courage to confront Aurora. Rusty considered herself to be an acculturated Mexican-American who had to physically fight the non-assimilated Mexican-American (Aurora). Rusty said that her rage, or internalized oppression, existed because generations of Mexicanas were told that they should not "act White" in society and they needed to be true to their culture (Maes, 2012, p. 78).

In Waded's case, even though she did not personally experience cultural or racial bias as a child, she learned how her grandmother and other Puerto Rican students experienced these biases while in school (Maes, 2012). Waded learned how their school systems would require the Puerto Rican students to speak in English, which was a foreign language to them. Their schools would also use racially and culturally biased standardized tests, which resulted in inaccurate evaluation and labels for Puerto Ricans as underachievers or less intelligent. From these stories Waded gained a better appreciation of the struggles her grandmother and other family members faced. But she was quick to point out that her immediate family did not adhere to the racially biased practices that were demanded by their school systems given that they still considered Spanish to be their first and only language (Maes, 2012, p. 110).

Both women grew up in lower social class, blue-collar environments where their families had minimal financial resources. Both Rusty and Waded were first generation college students which, according to Rusty, meant that "there were no road maps to higher education" (Barceló, 2016). As aspiring college students both lacked navigational capital (Sandoval-Lucero et al., 2014, p. 531) and had to acquire the skills to move through their higher educational institutions in order to be successful and prosperous students. Rusty and Waded had to figure out these processes for themselves without the help of their parents because they had not experienced any college educational processes themselves. But as Waded stated, her parents supported her emotionally because they believed that "getting a college education also fulfilled the concept of social mobility and enhancing the opportunities through me to future generations" (Maes, 2012, p. 114). With their own form of cultural capital, Waded believed that her parents went against the stereotype that stated "Hispanics don't appreciate education" (Maes, 2012, p. 115).

It is also important to note that both Rusty and Waded remained "the only ones" in their academic settings throughout undergraduate and graduate schools which often created a sense of self-doubt and internalized oppression because of feeling like they did not belong within their academic settings (Maes, 2012, p. 113). As a result, Rusty took this "only one" label and used it to be the champion in helping her institution recruit more students of color (Maes, 2012, p. 79). As Rusty climbed her own academic ladder, she always reflects upon her "only one" status. She stated,

> When people say that I'm the first, I know they say it with a great deal of excitement. But it really makes me sad. We're well into the 21st century and this should not be the case. There shouldn't be any more "firsts." This work should be about continuing a legacy. (Maes, 2012, p. 80)

When analyzing how Latina professionals present themselves within their respective employment settings, the issues of "standing out" or "fitting in" play an important part in their advancement or lack thereof (Maes, 2012, p. 17). Early on in their academic careers both Rusty and Waded felt as if they did not belong. She felt as if she did not fit because she was a Chicana and a lesbian. Rusty discussed how when she was a child, her grandmother recognized that men would never be important to her while her parents also knew that she was "different." In her words, her family knew that she was lesbian before she did. Now, as an "out and proud," Spanish-speaking, Chicana lesbian in academia, Rusty believes she is very much an anomaly. But she also believes that if her many identities were an issue to her presidential search committee, then she would not have pursued the position. Rusty said that her multiple identities have "now become a whole" within her and she carries them with pride. She also wanted to be in an institution where her multiple identities would be valued and not challenged (Maes, 2012, p. 185).

Waded felt as if she did not fit because she was short in stature and spoke with a strong accent. Like many women from underrepresented backgrounds, particularly in higher education, because they do not necessarily fit into the typical White male culture of the academy, many tend to internalize their oppression and it can manifest in self-doubt (Maes, 2012, p. 17). As Waded stated, "I am Puerto Rican, five feet tall, I majored in comparative literature, I speak with an accent, all minuses, minuses, minuses" (Maes, 2012, p. 122). But her university was aggressive in recruiting her for the presidential position and saw something in her that she, herself, did not see. Her university appreciated her immense humility and liked that she one who "rolled up her sleeves and would take her university to the next level of excellence" (Maes, 2012, p. 122).

As Rusty stated:

> No one was more shocked than I was when they offered me the position. First of all, I never aspired to be a president. I never aspired to be a vice president. I was never on a trajectory, but things just happened. You have to know when to step in when you see a need, and women of color know how to do that. Women of color often feel a sense of responsibility in looking out for everybody. (Maes, 2012, p. 87)

Rusty concluded by stating that because her many identities do not necessarily fit into the academy, she is often "tokenized." But she takes uses this token role to take a seat in the many boardrooms within the academy where she sometimes provides the only voice for change and inclusion for underrepresented populations in higher education (Barceló, 2016).

For Rusty, as she progressed through her career in higher education, she witnessed racial and cultural bias in recruiting and retaining Chicanas in graduate schools. She believes this contributes to the lack of Latina presidents in our nation's colleges and universities. One way she combats this problem is by advising her faculty to refrain from telling their Latina students that the tenure process is a difficult one because their words are dissuading them from pursuing the professoriate. She notes that the tenure process can be racially and culturally biased, but she believes that Latinas must persevere through it in order to increase the numbers of Latina higher education executives, particularly presidents (Maes, 2012).

A faculty member at Montana State indicated that Waded has an interesting way of combating racial and cultural bias. She said that Waded goes about her everyday life as president assuming that people do not have prejudices against her as a Latina. But when she discovers that they do, Waded redirects the bias to be their problem and not hers while completely removing herself from the situation. It is unclear if this method is completely effective for Waded, but this faculty member stated that Waded practices it with grace and conviction (Maes, 2012, p. 146).

In another instance, a staff member at Montana State took a very different view in regards to the racial and cultural diversity that Waded brings to their institution. He noted that individuals at their institution do not necessarily see her as "Hispanic," rather, they just see Waded as their leader. It is questionable if this notion can be viewed positively or can be viewed as a color-blind and racially biased indicator that Waded's racial and cultural diversity is not respected and acknowledged but rather ignored (Maes, 2012).

Indeed, their family background and cultural background have played a significant role in their identities. Both Rusty and Waded discuss how the *mujeres* in their lives (mothers, grandmothers, aunts) provided the personal and academic foundation for them to be who they are today (Maes, 2012). Waded's *mujeres* schooled her on the importance of education and how Puerto Rican children were just as smart as other children so she should not pay attention to the stereotypes that were being placed on them (Maes, 2012, p. 110). While Rusty's mother and grandmother taught her the traditions and customs of her Mexican American culture which later on helped her recognize and battle the racist, classist, and sexist inequities that members of her culture and other underrepresented cultures experience (Maes, 2012, pp. 161–162). It is important to note that these lessons were taught to Rusty and Waded through *testimonios* and *dichos* (Perez Huber & Cueva, 2012) and how they, themselves, continue this very important tradition of storytelling to generations that come after them. In fact, one of the more important lessons that Rusty's mother taught her was how to channel her own strength and wisdom. Rusty honors her mother's legacy by wearing a long braid down her back. Her mother taught her that when life becomes difficult she should hold on to her braid and she will regain her own power (Maes, 2012).

Rusty's deep connection to the power that surrounds her, as discussed by the above-mentioned symbolic practice she has with her braided hair, expands to her professional workplace and her home. She doesn't necessarily consider herself a practicing Catholic but like many Chicanas, she displays many religious icons and images, particularly of the Virgin of Guadalupe, which she believes guide her and provide her with strength (Maes, 2012, p. 72).

Waded, too, believes that there is a higher being that guides her through her life, especially when she was considering her job as president. She discussed how a spiritual sign came to her and told her that this would be a perfect job for her. She said:

> When I was waiting for the committee to make a choice, every day I would try to learn a little bit more about Montana. Well, one night I received an email from an extension agent at my last university and she said, "I read this story and I thought about you." I opened the attachment and this was a story of a group of women who liked to read books. On this special occasion they read from the scriptures a passage from Malachi, Chapter 3, verse 3, it says, "He seeks as a polisher and refiner of silver" and they said, "well, that's very confusing, what does that mean?" So, they decided to go as a group and visit a silversmith. They walked into his shop and the first thing they saw was what the scripture stated, the silversmith sitting in front of the flames. They approached him and started talking to him. They asked him, "so what are you doing?" He said, "well, I'm polishing this piece of silver." Then they asked him, "why are you sitting down?" He said, "well, I want to be very balanced because no matter how hot the flames get, I will never allow this piece of silver to fall into the fire." Then they looked at him and said, "how do you know when it's done?" He lifted up his eyes and said, "oh, it's easy. When I see my image reflected on it." So that night, I Googled information about the seal of Montana and the picture came up. It is a round seal that has mountains, rivers, and then it has this line at the bottom that says, and this is not a translation … it says, "oro y plata" (gold and silver). Then I said, "ok, I get it!" It was this beautiful message telling me that I belonged here." (Maes, 2012, p. 125)

Like many Latinas and Chicanas, Rusty and Waded ground themselves in a unique spirituality which does not necessarily mean being heavily involved in an organized religion. Their own form of spirituality, as Rodriguez (1999, p. 4) discusses, is an informal process which embraces "being a part of" instead of being separate, while also recognizing and valuing such things as human dignity, shared solidarity, respect, and inclusion. The role of race, gender, class, culture, language, and spirituality, are part of the intersectional lens that informs their experiences.

Servant and Transformational Leadership

When analyzing the thoughts, themes, and practices of Rusty and Waded through a leadership lens, it can be concluded that they demonstrate traits of both servant and transformational leaders. Servant leadership is evident when someone serves others as a steward of sorts and focuses on their and their organization's primary needs and thus transforms herself into a leader in the process (Komives, Lucas, & McMahon, 2007). This servant leader does not serve others for the sheer notoriety and recognition but rather does so to make a difference within a community or organization, for example (Komives et al., 2007). Whereas transformational leadership is "a process where leaders and followers raise one another to higher levels of morality and motivation" (Komives et al., 2007, p. 54). Transformational leaders possess "higher ideals and moral values such as liberty, justice, equality, peace, and humanitarianism, not to lesser emotions such as fear, greed, jealousy or hatred" (Komives et al., 2007, p. 54).

Waded is a servant leader who views her presidential processes as not only student-centered but community centered. These are the values, lessons, and traditions she learned as a child living in a house filled with *mujeres*, who taught her how to build community from within (Maes, 2012). One of her greatest community-building accomplishments to date was when she was challenged to raise $10 million for her university's football stadium and she did so, with the help of her university community where together they accomplished this feat in 90 days (Maes, 2012). To this day, when speaking to Waded about this football stadium expansion she refuses to take credit for this tremendous accomplishment but rather refocuses the glory and recognition to the others involved in this process—consistent with servant leadership.

Rusty, on the other hand, does not consider herself a "leader" per se, but rather a community servant. However, when reflecting on Rusty's journey through her presidency, her actions could be considered those of a servant leader. She is humble and modest with her positional power and with all the notoriety that her presidency gave her. Yet she still serves as a role model to those in higher education who feel marginalized like she did. She realizes the importance of grooming and mentoring other Latinas/Chicanas, especially as they are in graduate school, so that they can advance on to positions of leadership in higher education. She said:

> I'm not afraid to bring in people who are smarter or more talented than I am. I depend on them, and I give them my trust. But I also want to make sure that they share the values that I have. There are other presidents who don't embrace that concept. (Maes, 2012, p. 91)

Additionally, as a "community servant" or servant leader, Rusty believes that women of color who are pioneers of experiential learning have the responsibility to mentor younger women in the academy. The heavy lifting that women of color often do within the academy simply cannot be done without collaboration (Barceló, 2016).

Rusty, Waded, and many and other Latina leaders in academia from the 70s and present day have created a movement of activism through their transformational leadership. They have transformed their own careers in higher education with the hope of transforming the lives of other Latinas and women of color in the academy. With their transformative mission and passion, Rusty and Waded, who were considered "outsider voices on the inside," took the leap from faculty to administration and did so because they realized that their power would be better utilized within the walls of administration to transform higher education entirely.

Yet the notion of being "outsiders" within the academy remains an issue of concern for Chicanas/Latinas who are in administrative and presidential positions. These often painful accusations often force these women to "go back to the margins" which is reminiscent of the notion that many people of color are told by members of the majority population during battles of bias. The statements of "go back to where you came from" is often the internal oppression revisited by women of color in the academy. Ironically, Rusty often commented how as a Mexican American growing up in a highly marginalized and racialized United States in the 1950s she would often hear those very words "go back to Mexico" when she and her family were indeed United States citizens (Maes, 2012, p. 188). The words reflected the failure to recognize that Mexico was annexed during the Mexican/American War and the very land that Rusty and her family stood on was Mexico at one time. This is another example of how people of color are often ridiculed and placed in a negative light because of the misinterpreted history lessons that were taught to others.

Rusty often used the terms *reclamation, affirmation*, and *transformation* within her discussion (Barceló, 2016). For example, she believes that women of color in the academy are not being taken seriously therefore they need to *reclaim* their rightful spaces, both literally and metaphorically, which will give them legitimacy (Barceló, 2016). She also believes that these women need to reclaim their activism they had in the civil rights movement in order to institute change within the academy.

Women of color in the academy also *affirm* that they indeed straddle the "borderlands": they live in one world which embraces their racial and cultural beliefs and work in another, which is the academy that does not honor or acknowledge these racial and cultural beliefs and practices but rather stifles them (Barceló, 2016). Finally, Rusty talks of how women of color in the academy need to "embrace the struggle" that many experience in their predominately White, male environments. She believes when they embrace their struggle, *transformation* occurs (Barceló, 2016).

It is also important to note that Waded's sheer presence as a Latina president of Montana State University, a land-locked institution where just 3% of her student body is considered "Hispanic" is transformational (Montana State University Quick Facts, 2015–2016). Staff members of her institution indicated that Waded's presence as a university president dispels stereotypes that many may have about Latina women not being intelligent, articulate and transformational leaders (Maes, 2012). These staff described Waded as "charismatic," "visionary," and "participatory" while they believe that she, a graduate of a land grant university herself, is the right spokesperson for her own land grant university where she serves as president (Maes, 2012, p. 174).

As leaders, Rusty and Waded

> value their role as community members within their respective cities where they often blend in as "normal" citizens and are often known to converse with the community members in Spanish. These practices not only honor their blue-collar upbringings, but also keep them grounded in their mission of serving the needs of their community members. (Maes, 2012, p. 184)

Rusty and Waded also spoke of having to carry themselves differently as Latinas or Chicanas in environments comprised of mainly White men. They talked of how they often have to bridge their academic personas with that of a Latina or Chicana who speaks Spanish and comes from a working class background. For Waded specifically, she states how she has to have one foot in her academic world and one foot in their Puerto Rican world, which creates juxtaposition for her own identity development. Now, while living in an upper-class university presidential lifestyle, Waded still prides herself in holding true to her lower socio-economic class values and traditions that she learned as a Puerto Rican.

The stories of both presidents reflect what many Latina leaders face which is the idea that they live in two different lands; that they have to merge two different lifestyles divided by one border (Moraga & Anzaldua, 1983). These women strive to be respected on both sides of the border, which can cause them distress (Moraga & Anzaldua, 1983). Many Latina college and university presidents survive in their presidential positions while experiencing dualism and negotiation (Hansen, 1997; Maes, 2012). In each of their cases dualism is present as they merge their Puerto Rican or Chicana cultural beliefs and values with their practices as a university president. These women also negotiate their socio-cultural and leadership experiences with their role as president, where their goal is to transform their institutions to become more inclusive and progressive than they have been in the past.

Conclusion and Counterstorytelling

To conclude this reflection, the concept of counterstorytelling is used. Counterstorytelling is "… a method based on the narratives, *testimonios*, or life stories of people of color, a story can be told from a nonmajoritarian perspective—a story that White educators usually do not hear or tell" (Delgado, 1989, p. 2411). These stories are important because:

> (1) they can build community among those at the margins of society by putting a human and familiar face to educational theory and practice; (2) they can challenge the perceived wisdom of those at society's center by providing a context to understand and transform established belief systems; (3) they can open new windows into the reality of those at the margins of society by showing the possibilities beyond the ones they live and demonstrate that they are not alone in their position; and (4) they can teach others that by combining elements from both the story and the current reality, one can construct another world that is richer than either the story or the reality alone. (Delgado, 1989, p. 2411; Lawson, 1995, p. 354)

Counterstories show us that "oppressed groups have known instinctively that stories are an essential tool to their own survival and liberation" (Delgado, 1989, p. 2436; Maes, 2012). In essence, counterstories are positioned to go against those of the grand narratives; they challenge the majoritarian way of thinking and operating.

There cannot be a counterstory told about these Latina presidents unless the grand narrative is first understood. Grand narratives are described as "theories of the world that could be applied universally, regardless of particular circumstances" and the "careful study and accumulation of facts from which laws are determined" (Clandinin, 2007, p. 22). In this case, the grand narrative is that according to the 2011 Chronicle of Higher Education's *Almanac of Higher Education* report, 74% of our nation's colleges and university presidents are White males (Feinberg, 2011, p. 8).

Most of these men have traveled the ranks to their presidencies because their White male privilege provided them with social, cultural, and/or economic capital: "Cultural capital involves having access to a quality education and language, while social capital is having access to social networks and connections. Finally, economic capital is having access to money and other material possessions" (Yosso, 2005, p. 76). It is assumed that many of these

White male presidents possessed the abovementioned capital, while also having White privilege, which McIntosh (1989) defined as having "an invisible, weightless knapsack of special provisions and codebooks" (p. 10).

These men were able to vertically travel the academic ladder where they were "groomed" for their presidency. Many of these White male presidents' experiences could also be reflected in the "Great Man" theory of leadership, which states that not only were they born leaders but they were "gifted" with traits such as self-confidence and intelligence that enhanced their leadership (Daft, 1999; Northouse, 2007). Many White male presidents are also benefactors of their college and university search committees and boards that claim to be ethnically and culturally inclusive when searching for their new school leaders, but still chose a White male to lead their institution. Finally, "many White male presidents' experiences and narratives are often known in public form, particularly in academic research, where their stories become part of the dominant ideology in academia" (Maes, 2012, p. 187).

The stories of Rusty and Waded counter the typical White male president narrative given that they have encountered vastly different educational, economic, and socio-cultural experiences, yet they still advanced to presidential positions. According to Delgado (1989, 1993), Rusty's and Waded's narratives are from a nonmajoritarian perspective where their experiences may not reflect those of an Anglo, male, university president or even an Anglo, female university president.

Rusty and Waded come from lower socio-economic backgrounds where they had limited educational opportunities or social mobility. Their educational experiences may not always reflect those of White men or White women presidents because their counterstories originate in their primary school settings. These settings failed to promote and acknowledge their racial and ethnic diversity, but rather stifled it, which negatively affected their overall educational experiences. After they successfully completed primary school and were ready to advance on to higher education, as first-generation college students, they had to maneuver these processes alone because no other family members had gone through these same experiences. Waded, for instance, commented that she would have made a different choice for her graduate program had she been better versed in the importance of college rankings. But "being a first-generation student who knew little about the importance of rankings, she chose a school that did not offer her the quality of education that she could have had" (Maes, 2012, p. 116).

Rusty's entire professional career could be considered a counterstory to the traditional White male president. She uses the politically-charged term "Chicana" to describe herself while also being an "out" lesbian in her personal and professional circles. She recognizes that she took a fairly traditional route to her presidency; she transitioned from the faculty ranks to administrative ranks where she served mainly in positions that focused on diversity and multiculturalism. Then she advanced to her presidency. Yet she realizes that many White men who become presidents have not traveled the traditional academic route to their presidency and have advanced by utilizing networks that are a result of White privilege and higher social class status. Rusty believes that "Chicanas lack this privilege and capital which has resulted in their lack of advancement into presidential positions" (Maes, 2012, p. 188).

Waded's trajectory to the presidency was traditional as well; she quickly advanced from a faculty position to numerous executive positions in higher education. Yet when she was approached to apply for the presidential position, she knew that everything about her would counter the other White male finalists. She was small in stature; a Latina; she had majored in comparative literature; and she spoke with an accent. But she felt that her board of regents acknowledged her diversity along with her expansive list of professional accomplishments and decided that she was the right person for the presidency when they could have easily chosen one of the White male candidates (Maes, 2012).

Rusty's and Waded's presidential narratives are unique and distinct as Latinas/Chicanas are in general. They lead their institutions with compassion and *cariño*. Unlike many "traditional" presidents, Rusty and Waded ask to be called by their first names by their constituents rather than be called "President" or "Doctor." They are visible and accessible to all within their institutions where they lead with the Four C's of character, competence, compassion, and community servanthood (Mendez-Morse, 2000; Ramirez, 2006). They do not travel around their campuses or their states surrounded by security detail but rather they feel most comfortable when they are near and connected to their constituents. They value such things as a friendly hug or conversing in their native Spanish language. Finally, what makes Rusty and Waded and other Latina university presidents unique is that they realize that they are part of something bigger than themselves. They use their position as role models and trailblazers as a way to build legacy and tradition within the Latino/Chicano communities. They will not be completely content until there are others who look like them, who come from similar backgrounds as them, and who will walk in their presidential paths one day.

References

American Association of Community Colleges. *Staff Employment Distribution: Full time staff employment distribution for executive/administrative and managerial.* Retrieved

May 20, 2010 from http://www.aacc.nche.edu/AboutCC/Trends/Pages/staffem-ploymentdistribution.aspx

Avery, D. M. (1982). *Critical events shaping the Hispanic woman's identity.* Chicago: Chicago State University, Center for Woman's Identity Studies.

Barceló, R. (2016). Journeys into leadership: A view from the president's chair. In M. Pratt-Clarke & J. B. Maes (Eds.), *Journeys of social justice: Women of color presidents in the Academy.* New York, NY: Peter Lang.

Bordas, J. (2007). *Salsa, soul, and spirit: Leadership for a multicultural age.* San Francisco, CA: Berrett-Koehler.

Catalyst. (2003). *Advancing Latinas in the workplace: What managers need to know.* Retrieved February 15, 2007 from http://www.catalystwomen.org

Clandinin, D. J. (2007). *Handbook of narrative inquiry: Mapping a methodology.* Thousand Oaks, CA: Sage Publications.

Cruzado, W. (2016). Thriving as administrators at America's land grant universities. In M. Pratt-Clarke & J. Maes (Eds.), *Journeys of social justice: Women of color presidents in the academy.* New York, NY: Peter Lang Publishing.

Daft, R. L. (1999). *Leadership theory and practice.* Fort Worth, TX: The Dryden Press.

Deitz, R. (1992). Mentoring and early encouragement as key to getting more Hispanic women into higher education. *The Hispanic Outlook in Higher Education, 2,* 12–14.

de los Santos, A. G., & Vega, I. I. (2008). Hispanic presidents and chancellors of institutions of higher education in the United States in 2001 and 2006. *Journal of Hispanic Higher Education.* Retrieved September 13, 2009 from http://jhh.sagepub.com/cgi/content/abstract/7/2/156

Delgado, R. (1989). Storytelling for oppositionists and others: A plea for narrative. *Michigan Law Review, 87,* 2411–2441.

Delgado, R. (1993). On telling stories in school: A reply to Farber and Sherry. *Vanderbilt Law Review, 46,* 665–676.

Delgado Bernal, D. (2002). Critical race theory, Latino critical theory, and critical raced-gendered epistemologies: Recognizing students of color as holders and creators of knowledge. *Qualitative Inquiry, 8*(1), 105–126.

Feinberg, S. (2011). Hail to the chiefs/The 21st century president … not just a president anymore. *The Hispanic Outlook in Higher Education, 21,* 8–10.

Gil, R. M., & Vazquez, C. I. (1996). *The Maria paradox: How Latinas can merge old world traditions with new world self-esteem.* New York, NY: The Berkeley Publishing Group.

Gilroy, M. (2006). Hispanic women exerting economic influence. *The Hispanic Outlook in Higher Education, 16,* 37–39.

Gonzalez, G. G. (1996). A brief review of Chicano educational history in California: A legacy of inequality. In A. Hurtado, R. Figueroa, & E. E. Garcia (Eds.), *Strategic interventions in education: Expanding the Latina/Latino pipeline* (pp. 28–47). Santa Cruz: University of California.

Gonzales-Figueroa, E., & Young, A. (2005). Ethnic identity and mentoring among Latinas in professional roles. *Cultural Diversity & Ethnic Minority Psychology, 11,* 3.

Guzman, S. (2003). *The Latina's Bible*. New York, NY: Three Rivers Press.

Hansen, V. L. (1997). Voices of Latina administrators in higher education: Salient factors in achieving success and implications for a model of leadership development for Latinas. *Dissertation Abstracts International, 58*, 08A.

Jackson, M. (2013, November 7). *Fact sheet: The state of Latinas in the United States*. Center for American Progress. Retrieved on July 16, 2016 from https://www.americanprogress.org/issues/race/report/2013/11/07/79167/fact-sheet-the-state-of-latinas-in-the-united-states/

Knowlton, L. M. (1993). Leadership in a different voice: An ethnographic study of a Latina chief executive officer in a California community college. *Dissertation Abstracts International, 53*(10), 3431.

Knudsen, S. (2007). Intersectionality—A theoretical inspiration in the analysis of minority cultures and identities in textbooks. *Caught in the web or lost in the textbook*. Retrieved October 1, 2009 from http://www.caen.iufm.fr/colloque_iartem/pdf/knudsen.pdf

Komives, S. R., Lucas, N., & McMahon, T. R. (2007). *Exploring leadership: For college students who want to make a difference*. San Francisco, CA: Jossey-Bass.

Lawson, R. (1995). Critical race theory as praxis: A view from outside to the outside. *Howard Law Journal, 38*, 353–370.

Madsen, S. (2012, February). Women and leadership in higher education: Learning and advancement in leadership programs. *Advances in Developing Human Resources, 14*, 3–10.

Madsen, S., Longman, K., & Daniels, J. (2012, February). Women's leadership development in higher education: Conclusion and implications for HRD. *Advances in Developing Human Resources, 14*, 113–128.

Maes, J. B. (2012). *The socio-cultural and leadership experiences of Latina four-year college and university presidents: A través de sus voces (through their voices)* (Doctoral dissertation). Retrieved from Proquest Dissertations and Theses database (UMI No. 3509591).

Martinez, R. (1999). *Hispanic leadership in American higher education*. Hispanic Association of Colleges and Universities. San Antonio, TX. Retrieved May 20, 2010 from http://www.hacu.net/sponsors/NICHE/pdf/Martinez/pdf

Martinez Ramos, S. (2008). *Latina presidents of four-year institutions. Penetrating the adobe ceiling: A critical view*. (Doctoral dissertation, Graduate College, the University of Arizona, 2008). *Dissertation Abstracts International, 01*, 70A.

McGlynn, A. (1998). Hispanic women, academia, and retention. *The Hispanic Outlook in Higher Education, 8*, 12–14.

McIntosh, P. (1989). White privilege: unpacking the invisible knapsack. *Peace and Freedom, July/August*, 10–12.

Mendez-Morse, S. (2000). Claiming forgotten leadership. *Urban Education, 35*, 584–596.

Mendez-Morse, S. (2004). Constructing mentors: Latina educational leaders' role models and mentors. *Educational Administration Quarterly, 40*, 561–590.

Montana State University. (2016). *Quick facts: 2015–2016*. Retrieved October 7, 2016 from http://www.montana.edu/opa/facts/quick.html#Demo

Moraga, C., & Anzaldua, G. (Eds.). (1983). *This bridge called my back: Writings by radical women of color.* New York, NY: Kitchen Table.

National Center for Education Statistics. Digest of Education Statistics. (2013). *Race and ethnicity of college faculty.* Retrieved August 7, 2016 from http://nces.ed.gov/fast-facts/display.asp?id=61

Northouse, P. G. (2007). *Leadership theory and practice.* Thousand Oaks, CA: Sage Publications.

Perez Huber, L., & Cueva, B. (2012). Chicana/Latina testimonios on effects and responses to microaggressions. *Equity & Excellence in Education, 45*(3), 392–410.

Practical wisdom: Where leadership is really learned. (2005). *Leader to Leader, 35,* 56–58.

Ramirez, A. (2006). Hispanic leadership development and its policy impact. *Harvard Journal of Hispanic Policy, 18,* 85–89.

Rodriguez, A. L., Guido-DiBrito, F., Torres, V., & Talbot, D. (2000, Spring). Latina college students: Issues and challenges for the 21st century. *NASPA Journal, 37,* 511–527.

Rodriguez, F. C. (2006). Immigrant lives and presidential dreams: Exploring the experiences of Latino community college presidents. (Doctoral dissertation, Oregon State University, 2006). *Dissertation Abstracts International, 02,* 67A.

Rodriguez, J. (1999). Toward an understanding of spirituality in U.S. Latina leadership. *Frontiers: A Journal of Women Studies, 20,* 137–146. Retrieved February 15, 2007 from http://www.findarticles.com/p/articles/mi_qa3687/is_199901/ai_n8834944/print

Rubio, L., & Lugo-Lugo, C. (2005). The cultural Catholic who may not be Catholic: Latinas, education, and attitudes toward religion. *McNair Journal.* Washington State University Graduate School, *Fall,* 104–113.

Sandoval-Lucero, E., Maes, J. B., & Klingsmith, L. (2014). Latino and African American community college students: Counterstories, social capital, and student success. *College Student Journal, 48*(3), 522–533.

Segura, D. (2003). Navigating between two worlds: The labyrinth of Chicana intellectual production in the academy. *Journal of Black Studies, 34,* 28–51.

Viernes Turner, C. S. (2007). Pathways to the presidency: Biographical sketches of women of color firsts. *Harvard Educational Review, 77,* 1–38.

White, J., (2012). *HERS institutes: Curriculum for advancing women leaders in higher education. Advances in Developing Human Resources,* I, 11–27.

Yosso, T. J. (2005). Whose culture has capital? A critical race theory discussion of community cultural wealth. *Race, Ethnicity, and Education, 8,* 69–91.

14. *Closing Reflections*

MENAH PRATT-CLARKE AND JOHANNA B. MAES

Menah Pratt-Clarke

What are the lessons we can learn from the experiences of women of color leaders in the academy? Women of color are qualified. These are all exceptional women; they have outstanding histories of achievement, academic excellence, and visionary leadership. They are women who have an incredible work ethic and commitment to excellence. These are women who care about social justice, who care about access and equality, and who have a deep appreciation for issues of gender, race, and class. These are women who understand the mission of public higher education institutions.

We know that the academy is still struggling to accept women leaders. The academy was not designed for women, for people of color, or for women of color. Women of color have had to fight for their rightful place in leadership roles, despite being as qualified (if not more) than men. Though the social justice work for women of color presidents in the academy is difficult, we must encourage more women to be light bearers, to take up the torch, and to lead new generation of our society forward.

Leadership programs will continue to play an important role in helping women advance through the pipeline to presidencies. They provide important resources, including networking and professional contacts, tools, and knowledge about the complexities of higher education administration. We must continue to encourage women and women of color to take advantage of programs like the American Council on Education Women's Network and the HERS Leadership Academy. While these are important leadership programs, it is important to acknowledge that they are designed for women broadly, not women of color, specifically.

Women of color face unique challenges. Racism, sexism, and class dynamics are real factors in their academic journeys. Not only must women of color navigate the typical and every day political and economic challenges of higher education administration, they must be able to navigate the oppression, and still perform at a high level. Leadership programs need to recognize the very real role of intersectionality and the unique challenges that women of color experience in the academy.

Women of color, however, must not be expected to shoulder the entire weight and responsibility for transforming the academy. Men, especially older white men who dominate the academy, must begin to shift their understanding. They need to be able to think differently about the value of diversity, about the value of different leadership styles, about the value of different cultural backgrounds, and about the value of race and gender diversity in the academy. The landscape of American higher education can no longer be a bastion for those who are wealthy and white. In addition, we cannot also solely rely on international students to diversify the academy. While they provide an important perspective, presence, and voice, they cannot replace the academy's accountability and responsibility, particularly, for large public land-grant institutions, or public urban institutions to educate the citizens of the state.

The growing mandate related to access for historically marginalized racial and ethnic groups in the United States, as well as the rapidly changing racial profile in the United States, will require higher education institutions to make faster adjustments and shifts to respond to a new environment. These institutions must begin to be intentional about the creation of spaces and seats for these populations at all levels of the institution—undergraduate students, graduate students, professional students, assistant professors, associate professors, full professors, deans, provosts, and presidents. The academy must commit to actualizing the potential of all its members, including women of color. The academy and higher education can only be as great as the diversity of its leadership and women of color have extraordinary capacity for leadership. The glass ceiling, the adobe ceiling, the bamboo ceilings, and plantation roof must be opened up to ensure that women, and women of color, can ascend to the highest peak of their potential.

Johanna B. Maes

We are in an interesting time in higher education. We are interacting with students of color who have a completely different world view than those who were college students some twenty years ago. Many of these students are living and practicing inclusivity; they know the theories behind sexism, racism, classism, and ableism. They know that our society is struggling with people who are seen as "different" while they, themselves, see that "difference" is indeed an asset. These students are a part of an interesting paradigm shift where they are thinking more critically as they are asking difficult questions to those "adults" around them. One of those questions I am always asked by today's undergraduates is "where are the women of color leaders in academia?"

It should be noted that both the majority student population and students of color are asking this question. But somehow it is heard more frequently from the students of color who are the first in their families to walk the halls of higher education. They are searching for those women who are much like their *mamas*, *tías*, and *nanas*, who are compassionate and communal and sincerely care that they are recruited, retained, and graduate from their respective universities. But these women are few and far between within the Academy, especially within presidential positions.

When I share my research on Latina presidents to my undergraduate students at the University of Colorado Boulder, I first ask if they know the name of our own president at CU. Usually more than half of my students state that they do not. Then I ask if they would ever call our president by his first name. Almost all of my students say, "No," Then I ask if they would ever imagine our president meeting with them personally the day after they were arrested after a wild night of partying. Most always giggle; they eventually say, "No, of course not." Then I introduce three Latina university presidents from my research (two of them are featured in this book). I tell them that these highly respected presidents are not only well-known within their institutions but they also want to be addressed as Rusty or Waded versus President Cruzado or Dr. Barceló. My students think I'm telling them a lie.

Then I introduce another university president I featured in my research, Dr. Elsa Nuñez. I share that she, too, only wants to be called Elsa. I also state that once, not long ago, Elsa personally met with students from her university after they were arrested because of excessive partying. Elsa proceeded to scold these students for their behavior only like a mother would. After I tell this story my students then look at me as if I've completely lost my mind.

What is surprising to my students is not only that these three Latinas are (or once were) prominent university presidents, but how "different" they believe a university president should be. These are the same students who view the concept of "difference" or "diversity" as an asset versus a deficit. When my students are introduced to other women of color who also hold university presidential positions, I tell them that they, too, share similar leadership traits as Rusty, Waded, and Elsa. They want to know more about them.

Now, through this book, they, along with countless others in academia, will be able to do so.

What we have seen through the material presented in this book is that women of color university presidents at times use a combination of a maternal-like instincts coupled with grace, compassion, and tough accountability to carry out their jobs during this interesting time in higher education. This also rings true for many women of color who are in faculty, chair, dean, and provost positions. Because they are often "the Only Ones" in these respective positions, they walk a fine line of being that female figure who spends hours counseling students of color about fitting in to their university environments, as well as spending even more hours writing culturally relevant curriculum or crafting that departmental policy that is promised to be inclusive for all students. Women of color in higher education, especially presidents, not only wear many hats in their respective positions, they also run their institutions much like family business where they value open communication and a unique shared form of governance. These women are unlike the traditional White, male university president. Yes, the "differences" that these women of color presidents possess are cutting-edge and truly extraordinary.

We in academia should continue embracing the concepts of social justice within our universities. We should continue relaying to our students that women of color presidents are rewriting the script and are living their counterstories within their presidential positions. By doing this, together we are shifting the paradigm of what academia as a whole should be—diverse and inclusive.

Contributor's Biographies

Paula Allen-Meares is Chancellor Emerita and the John Corbally Presidential Professor, Professor of Medicine, and Executive Director of the Office of Health Literacy, Prevention, and Community Engagement at the University of Illinois at Chicago (UIC). She earned her bachelor's degree at the State University of New York at Buffalo and master's and PhD degrees from the University of Illinois Urbana-Champaign.

Nancy "Rusty" Barceló served as President of Northern New Mexico College from July 2010 to December 2015. Dr. Barceló is also a full professor in Northern's College of Education. Dr. Barceló received her bachelor's degree in social work from Chico State College and her master's degree and her PhD from the University of Iowa.

Victoria Chou is Interim Dean for the School of Education at Dominican University and serves as Dean Emerita for the College of Education at the University of Illinois at Chicago (UIC). Dr. Chou earned her master's and PhD degrees from the University of Wisconsin-Madison.

Waded Cruzado is the twelfth President of Montana State University (MSU). She enrolled at the University of Puerto Rico at Mayagüez and graduated magna cum laude with a bachelor's degree in comparative literature. She earned her master's degree in Spanish language and literature and her PhD in the humanities at the University of Texas at Arlington.

Gabriella Gutiérrez y Muhs received her PhD in Spanish from Stanford University, and is a full professor in the Departments of Modern Languages and Women & Gender Studies at Seattle University. She is also Director for the Center for the Study of Justice in Society.

Melissa Leal earned her PhD in Native American studies from the University of California, Davis in 2012. She teaches at Sierra College and is currently the Executive Director of Education for the Wilton Rancheria Tribe of Miwok Indians.

Valerie Lee retired in 2015 from holding three administrative appointments at The Ohio State University. She served as Vice Provost for Diversity and Inclusion, Vice President for Outreach and Engagement, and Chief Diversity Officer. Dr. Lee earned a PhD in English from The Ohio State University.

Johanna B. Maes is a faculty member at the University of Colorado Boulder's Leadership Residential Academic Program/Ethnic Living and Learning Community. Dr. Maes received her bachelor's degree from the University of Colorado Boulder; her master's degree in multicultural education from Regis University; and her PhD in education leadership and human resource studies from Colorado State University.

Cassandra Manuelito-Kerkvliet is President Emerita of Antioch University Seattle. She received a bachelor's degree in social work; a master's degree in counselor education; and a PhD in educational policy and management, with a specialization in higher education administration, from the University of Oregon.

Irma McClaurin is Chief Diversity Officer at Teach for America. Dr. McClaurin received a bachelor's in American studies from Grinnell College; a MFA in English with a specialty in poetry; and a PhD in anthropology, both from the University of Massachusetts, Amherst.

Jasmine D. Parker is affiliated with Texas Tech University and the owner and founder of Parker Educational Consulting, LLC. She obtained her bachelor's in history with a minor in sociology at Prairie View A&M University, and her master's and PhD in education policy, organization and leadership from the University of Illinois at Urbana-Champaign.

Menah Pratt-Clarke is the Vice President for Strategic Affairs and Vice Provost for Inclusion and Diversity at Virginia Polytechnic Institute and State University (Virginia Tech). She is also Professor of Education in the School of Education in the College of Liberal Arts and Human Sciences, with affiliations in Africana Studies, Women's and Gender Studies, and the Department of Sociology. She received her bachelor's and master's degrees from the University of Iowa and her JD, master's, and PhD in sociology from Vanderbilt.

Tanaya Winder is a poet, writer, artist and educator who was raised on the Southern Ute reservation in Ignacio, Colorado. She has a bachelor's in English from Stanford University and an MFA in creative writing from the University of New Mexico.

Phyllis Wise is CEO of Colorado Longitudinal Study and previously served as Chancellor and Professor of Molecular and Integrative Physiology, Animal Sciences, and Obstetrics and Gynecology in the School of Molecular and Cell Biology at the University of Illinois at Urbana-Champaign. She holds a bachelor's degree from Swarthmore College in biology and a PhD in zoology from the University of Michigan.

ROCHELLE BROCK & CYNTHIA DILLARD
Executive Editors

Black Studies and Critical Thinking is an interdisciplinary series which examines the intellectual traditions of and cultural contributions made by people of African descent throughout the world. Whether it is in literature, art, music, science, or academics, these contributions are vast and far-reaching. As we work to stretch the boundaries of knowledge and understanding of issues critical to the Black experience, this series offers a unique opportunity to study the social, economic, and political forces that have shaped the historic experience of Black America, and that continue to determine our future. Black Studies and Critical Thinking is positioned at the forefront of research on the Black experience, and is the source for dynamic, innovative, and creative exploration of the most vital issues facing African Americans. The series invites contributions from all disciplines but is specially suited for cultural studies, anthropology, history, sociology, literature, art, and music.

Subjects of interest include (but are not limited to):

- EDUCATION
- SOCIOLOGY
- HISTORY
- MEDIA/COMMUNICATION
- RELIGION/THEOLOGY
- WOMEN'S STUDIES

- POLICY STUDIES
- ADVERTISING
- AFRICAN AMERICAN STUDIES
- POLITICAL SCIENCE
- LGBT STUDIES

For additional information about this series or for the submission of manuscripts, please contact Dr. Brock (University of North Carolina at Greensboro) at r_brock@uncg.edu or Dr. Dillard (University of Georgia) at cdillard@uga.com.

To order other books in this series, please contact our Customer Service Department:

(800) 770-LANG (within the U.S.)
(212) 647-7706 (outside the U.S.)
(212) 647-7707 FAX

Or browse online by series at www.peterlang.com.